D0872335

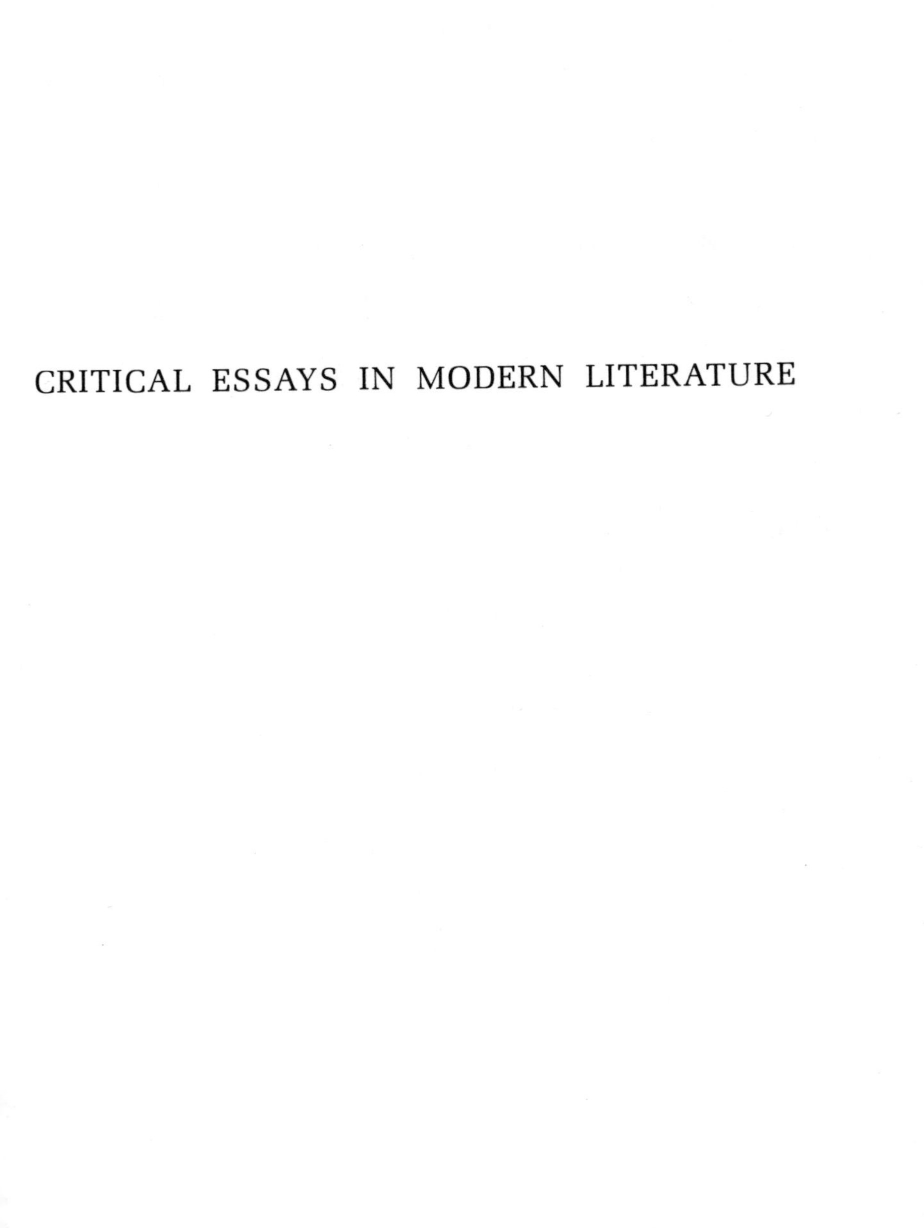

CRITICAL ESSAYS IN MODERN LITERATURE

CRITICAL ESSAYS IN MODERN LITERATURE

The Fiction and Criticism of Katherine Anne Porter (revised)
Harry J. Mooney, Jr.

Entrances to Dylan Thomas' Poetry
Ralph Maud

The Fiction of J. D. Salinger (revised)
Frederick L. Gwynn and Joseph L. Blotner

Chronicles of Conscience: A Study of George Orwell and Arthur Koestler
Jenni Calder

Richard Wright: An Introduction to the Man and His Work
Russell Carl Brignano

The Hole in the Fabric: Science, Contemporary Literature, and Henry James
Strother B. Purdy

Tragic Realism and Modern Society: Studies in the Sociology of the Modern Novel
John Orr

Reading the Thirties: Texts and Contexts
Bernard Bergonzi

The Romantic Genesis of the Modern Novel
Charles Schug

The Great Succession: Henry James and the Legacy of Hawthorne
Robert Emmet Long

The Plays and Novels of Peter Handke
June Schlueter

Yeats, Eliot, Pound and the Politics of Poetry: Richest to Richest
Cairns Craig

After Innocence: Visions of the Fall in Modern Literature
Terry Otten

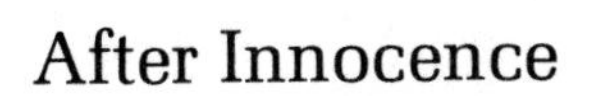
After Innocence

After Innocence: Visions of the Fall in Modern Literature

Terry Otten

CRITICAL ESSAYS IN MODERN LITERATURE

"The oldest dream of all—the oldest and most dreamlike," says James Dickey, is the dream of falling. The fear of falling, the awareness of lost innocence, lost illusions, lost hopes and intentions, of civilization in decline—these are the themes which link imaginative literature to theology, both concerned with the shape of human destiny. Professor Otten discusses the continuing viability of the myth of the Fall in our times. *After Innocence* treats a wide variety of romantic and modern works centering on the theme and relates them to fundamental issues in modern Christian existentialism.

The biblical myth tells us that perfection, innocence, and stasis are incompatible with the human condition, that only by escaping such sterility can mankind approach self-knowledge and freedom—including the freedom to commit evil. The fall from childhood innocence links James's *The Turn of the Screw* and Golding's *Lord of the Flies*, while Conrad's *Heart of Darkness* and Hesse's *Demian* extend the myth to Western culture in decline. *La Chute* by Albert Camus and *After the Fall* by Arthur Miller both focus on the protagonist's recognition of personal guilt and coming to self-knowledge. The Alice stories by Lewis Carroll and *2001: A Space Odyssey* by Stanley Kubrick and Arthur C. Clarke present the myth in fantasy literature. Edward Albee's *Who's Afraid of Virginia Woolf?* and James Dickey's *Deliverance* dramatize the welcome disruption of a false order—the sterility of the academic and commercial worlds—as a fortunate fall.

"*After Innocence* will have something new to teach everyone."—Donald H. Reiman.

Terry Otten is Chairman of the English Department at Wittenberg University.

UNIVERSITY OF PITTSBURGH PRESS

Pittsburgh, Pa. 15260

ISBN 0-8229-3453-1

After Innocence: Visions of the Fall in Modern Literature

Terry Otten

UNIVERSITY OF PITTSBURGH PRESS

Published by the University of Pittsburgh Press, Pittsburgh, Pa. 15260
Copyright © 1982, University of Pittsburgh Press
All rights reserved
Feffer and Simons, Inc., London
Manufactured in the United States of America

Library of Congress Cataloging in Publications Data

Otten, Terry.
After innocence.

(Critical essays in modern literature)
Includes bibliographical references and index.
1. Fall of man in literature. 2. Literature, Modern—19th century—History and criticism. 3. Literature, Modern—20th century—History and criticism. I. Title. II. Series.
PN56.F2908 809′.93353 81–11538
ISBN 0–8229–3453–1 AACR2

.933
8a

To Jane—of Eves, most precious

196840

Contents

Acknowledgments

For encouragement, insights, and suggestions, I thank many faculty colleagues at Wittenberg—especially Cynthia Behrman and Albert Hayden of the Department of History, and Roy King, Imogene Bolls, Allen Koppenhaver and Richard Veler of the Department of English. I owe a debt of gratitude to the staff at Wittenberg's Thomas Library and its director, Bob Lee Mowery. Without the special assistance of Rita Harnish and Al LaRose, my research simply could not have been completed. I express my thanks to Nancy Miller and Rosemarie Burley for their long-suffering patience in typing the manuscript for submission. My gratitude extends as well to the Wittenberg University Research Fund Board for granting me the financial assistance needed to research a difficult and far-ranging topic. For the discerning eye of Jane Flanders of the University of Pittsburgh Press I am most grateful. As always, my wife, Jane, and children, Keith and Julie, have lent their support and encouragement. Above all, I thank those students from various disciplines and interests who have shared in my class "The Fall and After." Their enthusiasm has reminded me anew just how personal and timeless the Fall really is—their ideas and discoveries have provided the inspiration and, in truth, some of the substance of this book. I gladly acknowledge their contributions, both direct and indirect. Though grateful to all those who have made this study possible, I alone must assume responsibility for its faults. Having run the risk myself, I cannot do otherwise.

Portions of the discussion of "Christabel" and *The Cenci* first appeared in "Christabel, Beatrice and the Encounter with Evil," *Bucknell Review*, 17 (1969). The discussion of "The Secret Sharer" first appeared in slightly different form in "The Fall and After in Conrad's 'The Secret Sharer,' " *Southern Humanities Review*, 13

(1978). A part of the discussion of *Who's Afraid of Virginia Woolf?* is taken from "Ibsen and Albee's Spurious Children," *Comparative Drama*, 2 (1968). The discussion of *2001: A Space Odyssey* appeared in slightly different form in "Other Worlds: Fantasy and Science Fiction since 1939," a special issue of *Mosaic: A Journal for the Interdisciplinary Study of Literature*, 13, nos. 3–4 (1980), published by the University of Manitoba, to whom acknowledgment is herewith made. The discussion of *Alice in Wonderland* and *Through the Looking-Glass* first appeared in *Lewis Carroll: A Celebration*, ed. Edward Guiliano, Potter/Crown Publishers, Inc., 1982.

Grateful acknowledgement is made to the following publishers for permission to quote material in this book: Atheneum Publishers and William Morris Agency, Inc., for excerpts from *Who's Afraid of Virginia Woolf?*, copyright © 1962 by Edward Albee. Alfred A. Knopf, Inc., and Editions Gallimard, for excerpts from *La Chute* by Albert Camus, trans. Justin O'Brien, copyright © 1956. Doubleday & Co., Inc., and Trustees of the Joseph Conrad Estate for excerpts from "Heart of Darkness" from *Youth* and "The Secret Sharer" from *Twixt Land and Sea* by Joseph Conrad, copyright 1910 by Harper Brothers. Harper and Row, Inc., and Georges Borchardt, Inc., for an excerpt from *The Phenomenon of Man* by Teilhard de Chardin, trans. Bernard Wall, copyright 1959 by William Collins Sons Ltd. and Harper Brothers. Houghton Mifflin Co. and Raines & Raines for excerpts from *Deliverance* by James Dickey, copyright © 1970 by James Dickey. Harcourt Brace Jovanovich, Inc., and Faber and Faber Ltd. for an excerpt from *The Cocktail Party* from *Complete Poems and Plays 1909–1950* by T. S. Eliot. G. P. Putnam's Sons and Faber and Faber Ltd. for excerpts from *Lord of the Flies* by William Golding, copyright 1954 by William Golding. Harper and Row, Inc., and Peter Owen Ltd. for excerpts from *Demian* by Hermann Hesse, trans. Michael Roloff and Michael Lebeck, copyright 1925 by S. Fischer Verlag, copyright © 1965 by Harper & Row Publishers, Inc. Vintage Books, a division of Random House, Inc., for an excerpt from "Original Sin" from *Selected Poems* by Robinson Jeffers, copyright 1948 by Robinson Jeffers. Atlantic-Little, Brown, Co., for an excerpt from *The Undiscovered Self* by C. G. Jung, trans. R. F. C. Hull. Macmillan Publishing Co. and The Bodley Head Ltd. for an excerpt from *Out of the Silent Planet* by C. S. Lewis, published in 1943 by Macmillan Publishing Co. Viking Penguin Inc. and International Creative Management, Inc., for excerpts from *After the Fall* by Arthur Miller, copyright © 1964 by

Arthur Miller. Alfred A. Knopf, Inc., for an excerpt from *Tar Baby* by Toni Morrison, copyright 1981 by Toni Morrison and Alfred A. Knopf, Inc. Viking Press, Inc., and William Heinemann Ltd. for an excerpt from *East of Eden* by John Steinbeck, copyright 1962 by John Steinbeck.

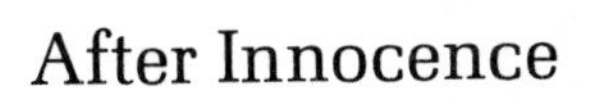
After Innocence

‡ 1 ‡

Introduction

The story of Eden is a greater allegory than man has ever guessed. For it was truly man who, walking memoryless through bars of sunlight and shade in the morning of the world, sat down and passed a wondering hand across his heavy forehead. Time and darkness, knowledge of good and evil, have walked with him ever since. —Loren Eiseley, *The Immense Journey*

It is of course the oldest myth of all. No culture, no individual, can long claim innocence. On the jailhouse walls, Faulkner has said, are written the true histories of man "in unbroken . . . continuity." Symbol indeed, the jail remains "one towering frantic edifice poised like a cardhouse over the abyss of the mortgaged generation."[1] We know that all generations are mortgaged. If someone claims to be innocent, Camus once quipped, ask him whether or not he has been born. Somehow, it seems, we must account for this basic truth: man is fallen, is estranged from whatever cosmic order may exist—be it god or fate or nature or whatever. No one, finally, can escape his fallen condition. "But what is the most innocent place in any country?" asks Arthur Miller. "Is it not the insane asylum? There people drift through life truly innocent, unable to see into themselves at all."[2] It matters little whether the Fall occurs by choice or by act of destiny, whether it comes at adolescence or birth or even old age, whether it takes place quietly within the self or dramatically and in public view. Everywhere testimony of the Fall surrounds us. However, whenever, wherever—it is.

Like all enduring myths, the Fall offers truth but not dogma; it defines for us the nature of human experience, but it offers little to satisfy the rational mind in search of certainty. Whether we look back to the multiple sources of the myth in Western thought or venture into the mazes of contemporary theology, we can expect to find contradiction and ambiguity. Irreducible in its richness, the story of the Fall demands formulation while it defies it. The amalgamation of sources which underlie the biblical version of the legend and the variations of the myth in Greek, Roman, Egyptian, Sumero-Babylonian and Persian versions, not to mention the conflicting biblical accounts, make any literalistic or definitive historical interpretation presumptuous if not foolhardy.[3]

Given what Matthew Arnold would call the "multitudinousness" of our own age, it is all the more futile to speak of an accepted version of the Fall, even though we may trace the development of a somewhat orthodox view in Christian dogma. If the biblical account of the myth owed much to diverse, often contradictory sources, modern theological interpretations of the Fall have had somehow to assimilate new modes of learning to maintain the myth as religious statement. Within the camp of orthodoxy itself, theologians have necessarily turned to humanistic psychology to aid in explaining the Fall. Since the Enlightenment, they have attempted to resolve the apparently conflicting views of psychology and religion, scientific humanism and theology, in order to rediscover the religious significance of the story.[4] For since the end of the eighteenth century, the Fall has been viewed more essentially in broadly humanistic or even secular terms, less as religious dogma than as an expression of the human condition outside the framework of organized religion. To some the myth has become utterly secularized; but one might claim with equal conviction that the pervasiveness of the myth has brought us once more to sense the religious, that it has revealed, even in its more apparently secular terms, that "the sacred" underlies human destiny. To speak of the Fall is to speak universally of the human predicament; to speak of the human predicament is somehow to define humanity's engagement with what Mircea Eliade simply calls the "wholly other."

To be sure, every age consciously or unconsciously constructs in its literature and art its own paradigms of the Fall. For Elizabethan England, tragedy provided a ready means whereby to glimpse the myth. Tragic heroes either violated the garden (usually England itself) and so earned the wages of sin, like Macbeth or Lear, or tried to restore it and paid the price of redemption, like Hamlet. Translating the myth into an encompassing communal ritual, *de casibus* tragedy defined a garden shattered by those who sought "to gain a deity," created death and destruction (most often symbolized by the fracturing of the community), achieved self-knowledge, and ultimately suffered the consequences—death, suffering, or expulsion. In more modern times, the paradigm has become less communal, more personal and subjective.

There was a time no doubt when the Fall was a common referent. Like all great myths, in its simple narrative form the Genesis story presents an elemental explanation of human experience free of the doctrinal complexities which encumbered it the moment theologians began to translate myth into dogma. Arguments and differences which began to surface even in later biblical accounts of the myth soon emerged, culminating in the debate of Pelagius's claim that man innately possesses grace enough to live in perfection and that Adam's offense could not blemish future generations. Against this assumed heresy Augustine defended the idea of original sin and, to accommodate the belief in a loving god, spoke of a *felix culpa* or happy fall. But as a result of the tension created by the growing humanism of the early Renaissance and different factions of the Reformation, the myth began again to assume new and varied meanings. We see the seeds of such change in the imaginative portrayal of *Paradise Lost*, a transformation caused by the shift from a public to a private myth. By the romantic period, literalistic interpretations of the Fall had been seriously challenged, along with all religious orthodoxy, by a humanism more than ever influenced by secular and specifically non-Christian traditions. It was left to the romantics to redefine and in some way recover the Fall as a religious and mythic statement, even given the strength of that vein of romanticism which believed in the inherent goodness of man. Of course the romantics' definition of religious experience differed substantially from earlier conventions, and they began to develop strikingly new concepts. It is hardly surprising that William Blake, like Shelley after him, could find in Milton's classic statement a powerful expression of the myth and yet, ironically, could invert it. The truth was there, Blake contended, but Milton simply misunderstood it: "He was a true poet and of the Devil's party without even knowing it."

Despite the protean quality of their art, the English romantics found the myth a valid explanation of their essentially subjective concept of reality. For them, the Fall conveyed psychological rather than historical or primarily theological themes; it provided a means of articulating personal experience, of defining their rebellious nature, of charting the movement from self-ignorance to awareness, innocence to experience. The features of the myth depicted for them an internal drama, the quest for the self. The garden came to represent the system of constraints and repression, whether seen in the guise of organized religion or the state or the dominant superego. The serpent, with whom they most fully identified, symbolized the spirit of freedom, the irrepressible will of the unconscious manifested in revolution against the established order of things. Expulsion carried with it a humanistic or existential version of the fortunate fall: it did not reveal God's grace so much as man's triumphant destiny, not divine judgment so much as courageous self-assertion.

The evolution of the myth in modern literature further reflects the pluralism of the age, the existential conditions recognized by the romantics. Contemporary versions of the Fall, not antiromantic but an extension of the romantic temperament, reveal an ever-increasing secular humanism, the myth itself often being expressed in complex levels of irony—romantic self-knowledge at times succumbing to self-deceit, personal quest to unresolved ambiguity, and self-affirmation to staggering incapacity. Nonetheless, the paradigmatic elements still supply a suitable analogue to the human experience. In its extraordinary adaptability, the motif provides both a common historical and a cultural referent, however anachronistic, and a concept of structure and dramatic movement. Its primordial, encompassing vision lends substance and allows for critical discrimination. If the attempt to redefine myth is symptomatic of an alienated age in search of meaning in the universe, then the Fall reflects the state of our time as few other fables can.

In our age secular humanism has seemingly laid claim to the myth. Some tend to assume that such use of the myth leads to a general "demythologizing" of its religious significance. But this is simply not the case. It is characteristic of modern culture that religion has accommodated secular humanism even as secular thought has embraced religious traditions. In a way, no true religious myth can finally be secularized. Despite the fragmentation of our age, the university of the Fall myth remains. However altered by psychology and behaviorist thought, by technology and scientific determinism, it still offers an appropriate metaphor for what it means to be human. And the very pattern of the Fall—the movement from a garden state to temptation to self-knowledge to consequences—remains an apt description of the human drama. In adopting the greatest biblical fable, twentieth-century writers have more often than not expanded rather than diminished the insights of modern theology.

Beginning with a brief discussion of the concept of the Fall as it emerged in the post-Enlightenment period, I wish to examine how several modern, primarily twentieth-century, works treat the myth. I say post-Enlightenment because I share the commonly held view that the development of romanticism marks the beginning of the modern temperament. In William Blake we first see a major change in the interpretation of the Fall, a shift from what Eric Smith calls a "developed story" to a "personal myth."[5] Using Blake, with references to works by Coleridge, Shelley, and Byron, I shall identify some of the major questions raised by modern adaptations of the Fall and outline the shaping ideas that underlie many modern versions of it. I conclude my introduction by exploring Joseph Conrad's "The Secret Sharer" to illustrate a fortunate fall. In subsequent chapters I examine variations on the theme by analyzing paired works under five topic headings: Childhood's End (*The Turn of the Screw* and *Lord of the Flies*), Civilization and Its Discontents (*Heart of Darkness* and *Demian*), The Fall and After (*La Chute* and *After the Fall*), The Fall in Fantasy (*Alice in Wonderland, Through the Looking-Glass* and *2001: A Space Odyssey*), and Running the Risk (*Who's Afraid of Virginia Woolf?* and *Deliverance*).

I intend to show the persistence and variety of this most elemental of myths, what James Dickey calls "the oldest dream of all, the oldest and most dreamlike." Though I wish to avoid at all costs what Kafka refers to as "religion . . . reduced to aesthetics," I nonetheless hope to locate the universal pattern of the myth as it is woven into the texture of the particular literature I shall discuss. Following the direction charted by Paul Tillich and others, I intend to correlate the existential and theological questions inherent in modern literature as they relate to the myth. To reduce the magnitude of the topic to a functional methodology, in each chapter I limit the focus to the two representative works treating the given subtheme rather than attempt any kind of comprehensive analysis of the Fall in modern literature or any extended commentary on a particular interpretation, work, author, genre, or culture. I trust that each of my studies of individual works will have some value in its own right as well as forming part of a larger, synthesizing view.

‡ 2 ‡

A Romantic Enlightenment

"Two stories have haunted us and followed us from the beginning, the story of original sin and the story of Cain and Abel. And I don't understand either of them." —Samuel Hamilton in John Steinbeck's *East of Eden*

In *The Tradition of English Morality*, Mark Roberts contends that romanticism may be approached more as a "moral" than a "literary or artistic phenomenon." He concludes that although the "literary impetus of the Romantic . . . has long since spent itself . . . the moral influence endures."[1] Though some may doubt it, most cultural historians would agree that we live in the elongated shadow of the romantics. Our age has not exceeded so much as extended romanticism. For good or ill, we have inherited both its hope and despair.

Northrop Frye has said that romanticism marked "the beginning of the first major change in the pattern of mythology" that conveyed the thought and philosophy of Western Europe for centuries.[2] At the heart of the cultural inheritance is the primal myth defining human destiny, that of creation and fall. In the essentially theocentric view of medieval theology, which undergirds preromantic thought, the fall is interpreted as follows:

> God intended that man live in paradise; man sinned; he was expelled; he suffers in consequence of his sin; but God promised to restore him; and God sent his Son to earth to make that restoration possible, at least for a few, or, according to more sanguine interpreters, for everyone.[3]

Such a "theological" reading, Morse Peckham goes on to say, runs counter to another view:

> Man is the victim of a cosmic joke the point of which he can never see—and consequently he can respond only to its cruelty but never to its humor.[4]

The seeds for such an iconoclastic reading were surely sown in the humanism of the Renaissance—at least the romantics seemed to think so. We sense already a violation of the orthodox view of the myth in the emergence of the Renaissance hero. Even amid the medieval themes of Elizabethan tragedy, we find strong sympathy for the rebel against God. For all its apparent allegiance, at least in plot, to the doctrine that "the wages of sin is death," Marlowe's *Doctor Faustus* surely garners as much admiration as condemnation for its protagonist. The line between Marlowe's overreacher and Goethe's hero is very short indeed. And, as I have noted, it is understandable that Blake, Byron, and Shelley would make Satan the true hero of *Paradise Lost*, even if Milton did not intend such a reading. With the emergence of a new humanism evolved a different conception of the Fall, though it was to be delayed by the scientific and empirical rationalism of the Enlightenment. It found its full expression in the romantic version of the fortunate fall—*felix culpa*. If humanistic thought tended to make man the center of reality, romantic thought placed reality in the center of man. The Fall entered the psyche.

To invert myth is to reaffirm its meaning, to prove its "stubborn logic," in Rosamund Tuve's phrase. Though it would be a mistake to claim originality for the romantic version of the fortunate fall, the generally accepted reading of the myth in the age certainly followed the long-established biblical tradition, even if it was somewhat modified and significantly diminished in impact by eighteenth-century deism. The romantic versions, as first developed by William Blake, inverted its meaning and reclaimed its validity not as abstract, depersonalized allegory, but as a profound and universal myth.

At the heart of the "new" conception is the belief that the Fall refers neither to a historical time nor place but rather to a state of mind, that it takes place within the self. Though the romantics employ the narrative pattern of the story, they tend to describe the action as a psychodrama, a revelation of "the development of a soul." God, paradise, the serpent, the tree of good and evil, all the elements of the Fall, exist within; and the action from temptation to expulsion is played out in the psyche. To understand the myth, then, is to account for the emergence of the self and, ultimately, to marry psychology and religion. The narrative depicts an existential rather than allegorical drama, a psychological rather than historical record. In large measure, the romantics anticipate Paul Tillich's attempt to describe the Fall as a "transition from essence to existence."[5] For them, as for many modern theologians, the Fall does not so much record man's disobedience as his awakening of consciousness.

The "transformation of the objective fact God" into a "figment of man's imagination"[6] demanded a complete rerendering of the culturally inherited story of creation and fall. The nature and motivation of the creator-god becomes highly suspect in such a reversal. More often than not, the deistic god of eighteenth-century empiricism is seen as the oppressive creator of a flawed universe. Whether in the guise of Urizen—Blake's mythological name for the "Nobodaddy" god of reason—or in the guise of Jupiter—the tyrant god in Shelley's *Prometheus Unbound*—or in the guise of the distant cruel god in Byron's *Cain*, the deity becomes a censorious dictator. Those who pay homage to his reign are generally seen as inferior beings in the romantic reading of the myth. It is the rebellious figure who assumes the role of hero and achieves a "higher morality." Such a character, in Robert Langbaum's phrase, becomes "an agent of experience."[7] Before the Fall, Adam existed in self-ignorance; fallen, Peter Conrad notes, "he acquires an intelligence and a character."[8]

Consequently, the agent of Adam's fall, the serpent, becomes an essentially sympathetic character, though, as we shall note, one to be feared as well. To put the matter too simply, as a kind of internal drama, the Fall posits the serpent as a projection of the id in direct conflict with God, the superego. Under any circumstances, the devil is necessary to one's salvation because he provides the needed pole in the internal dialectic. As Rilke once commented when he withdrew from psychotherapy, "If my devils are to leave me, I am afraid my angels will take flight as well."[9] Even if he poses a dangerous threat to man's freedom by seeking to dominate man, the satanic figure, like Goethe's Mephistopheles, galvanizes the protagonist into action. Indeed, Gerhard von Rad has suggested that the serpent is cleverer than the other creatures because he is in effect an image or projection of man's developing consciousness.[10]

Duality also exists in the definition of sin. Lucien Goldmann traces the emergence of dialectical thought in the West to Pascal; "Pascal's work marks the great turning-point in Western thought, the moment at which it began to abandon the atomistic approach of rationalism and empiricism, and to move towards dialectical reasoning."[11] As writers on the frontier of the new age, influenced to varying degrees by Hegel and various English writers in the "dialectical tradition" cited by Goldmann, the romantics tended to see the Fall as establishing a dynamic process against a deistic universe reduced to a mechanistic, closed system of laws. To the romantics, good demands evil; and good ever becomes evil as evil ever becomes good. Blake could therefore exchange good and evil, showing in *The Marriage of Heaven and Hell* how Jesus broke the commandments to achieve a higher morality. The greatest sin is against the self, not the abstract God of a deistic cosmos, the romantics seemed to say. Paradoxically, one sins to a higher morality, on the one hand struggling against an established and repressive system and, on the other hand, struggling to find a new morality and wholeness. The Fall, in other words, redeems man from the greatest of ills—stasis.

At base, the Fall is fortunate, because, as M. H. Abrams writes, it is "an indispensable first step along the way toward a higher unity which will justify the sufferings undergone enroute. The dynamic of the process is the tension toward closure of division, contraries, or 'contradictions' themselves."[12] It initiates consciousness, "knowing," and so makes man morally responsible for his actions. We should add that the idea of the fortunate fall probably gives undue emphasis to the positive features of the experience. In fact, as we shall note in several works, although the Fall seems in all cases a first step toward self-actualization and a necessary means of salvation in the existential sense of that word, it involves enormous risk. For those who are not redeemed by *and from* the Fall, death by violence via the Fall seems every bit as frightening as death by stasis via the garden. As Rollo May puts it, "It is dangerous to know," even though "it is more dangerous not to know."[13]

We cannot speak of a romantic concept of the fortunate fall without realizing, first, that the idea itself can be found in various forms in earlier periods and, second, that there is no single romantic version. Together the writers reshaped the dominant myth passed from earlier generations, but each presented it in his own way and emphasized different aspects and themes. Nor did their conclusions necessarily correspond. For some, like Coleridge, there was a strong reluctance to accept, certainly to embrace consciously, the theological implications of the new myth. Others like Byron, far less rooted in theology, readily abandoned the tradition, at least as they understood it. For people like Shelley, the idea of the fortunate fall came to offer as corollary a deeply disturbing view of man's capacity for evil as well as for good—if man rather than God or the system is the agent of good, is he not therefore the agent of evil as well? While drawing parallels among the writers, I wish to examine briefly how, in selected works, each of them consciously, or perhaps unconsciously, depicts the myth of the Fall. Realizing that Blake wrote at least three distinct versions of the Fall and that Byron, Coleridge, and Shelley all treated the myth in varying degrees and ways in several works, I reiterate that my intent is not to trace the idea in any one writer but rather to show the varieties of religious experience in representative works. Having done so, I want to conclude this chapter by using "The Secret Sharer" as an exemplum of the fortunate fall in more modern literature.

Blake's Bible of Hell

William Blake looked for "the God out there" in a landscape of metaphysical terror. He found instead the obscure and rapidly fading image of a distant God born of the deism of Locke and Newton. If God exists, Blake surmised, he must exist in me. Blake would have understood perfectly Ray Bradbury's definition of God—"man awakening"—and Alan Watt's claim that "we are each the Lord in hiding."[14] And he most certainly would have embraced Kierkegaard's conclusion that "the only salvation is subjectivity . . . God as infinite compelling subjectivity."[15] Indeed, Blake created the first great mythology to describe God and man in the modern age, a mythology that has become a classic definition of the modern temperament. Blake's mythology, like all myth, attempts to relate "a sacred history, that is a primordial event that took place at the beginning of time *ab initio*."[16] What is more, it treats creation, fall, and redemption as elemental stages of human life. Blake's mythic construct reflects the profound relationship and cooperation between the conscious and the unconscious. Sensing the paucity of the established version of the creation-fall myth, Blake sought "new" definitions in gnostic, Manichean, and various other sources he could appropriate in his own conception. The mythology he constructed is at once electic and new, universal and intensely personal.

Because Blake so modified and expanded his mythology, emphasizing one aspect in one work, another in a different one, it is difficult and sometimes impossible to account for all its shifts and seeming contradictions. Nonetheless, we can safely trace its essential outline—and at the very center of Blake's mythology is the idea of creation and fall. As Thomas Merton has observed, without the Fall, "Blake . . . becomes incomprehensible."[17] I agree with J. G. Davies that Blake uses his mythology principally "as a framework around which to build his interpretation of man's psychology."[18] I shall therefore concern myself more with Blake's shaping overview of man than with any particular poems or aspects of his myth.

To begin with, Blake conceives of the Fall in completely anthropomorphic terms; that is, man is the progenitor and repository of all truth. Hence, God and Satan, good and evil, Eden and the Tree of Knowledge, all form part of his composite whole. Blake's Albion, his universal man, is God in his total unity, and he existed *before* creation. The primal fall occurred before the creation of the world or Adam and Eve within the psyche of the eternal man. We might comprehend Blake's idea if we think of the Fall as a vast psychological drama. To Blake, the psyche consists of four functions which he calls "The Four Zoas" or "Mighty Ones":

> Four Mighty Ones are in very Man;
> a Perfect unity
> Cannot Exist but from the Universal
> Brotherhood of Eden,
> The Universal Man, To Whom be
> Glory Evermore, Amen.[19]

Like Jung, Blake identifies the four faces of man as reason (which he calls Urizen or "your reason"), feeling or emotion (which he calls Luvah), the senses or the body (which he calls Tharmas), and spirit or imagination (which he calls Urthona or, in the fallen world, Los). The material universe was created by Urizen, the fallen part of man, who egocentrically sought to circumscribe and control a world. And so, as Northrop Frye notes, for Blake "the fall of man and the creation of the physical world were the same event."[20] Adam's fall, in consequence, reenacts in microcosm the primal fall of cosmic man. It results in a process of separation, "a progressive dissociation of the collective human psyche into alien and conflicting parts, each of which strives for domination."[21]

When man fell from harmony into imbalance, dissociation, and fragmentation, he imitated Urizen's original fall from the "universal brotherhood" described in Blake's vision of "eternity." As a result of the fall of eternal man, unity lay buried beneath the fragmented matter perceived by the senses. "The Atoms of Democritus / And Newton's Particles of Light" formed part of a mechanistic "mill with complicated wheels," and the universe was diminished to "the same dull round" of cyclic laws of nature. To Blake, the fallen universe therefore reflected the temporal and spatial world of eighteenth-century rationalistic thought. Urizen became the Elohim of the Old Testament, a pseudo-god of cruelty. The acknowledged biblical account of creation and fall in Genesis is therefore transformed into Blake's "Bible of Hell": Elohim/God/Urizen did not create the world from chaos but fell into chaos; the world was not the work of a beneficent deity but a fallen one; the material universe does not display the beauty of the divine but obscures the sacred in the phenomenological realm of the senses—hence Adam does not sin against God in disobedience to Him but rather takes a first step from enslavement to a false deity.

What is true for the universe at large is true for the individual. Every man moves from unity and harmony with the divine in Edenic childhood to experience, where he is dominated by Urizen. Reason seeks sole control and represses the psychic and sexual energies especially released at the onset of puberty. Hence man repeats the cosmic fall by establishing moral categories and restraints in his own spurious Eden. He weaves his own "veil of Moral Virtues, woven for Cruel Laws" (*Jerusalem*, p. 646). Such self-suppression continues until the individual sides with his own rebellious nature (Orc in Blake's myth, the libidinous serpent in the garden) and consciously breaks the law of reason by eating the apple of knowledge. In consequence he must pay the price for his fall—estrangement from the primal oneness enjoyed in childhood, a painful journey through "generation," and division of his androgynous whole into male and female (*anima* and *animus* in Jung's scheme). In short, when man falls prey to his reason, he falls into disarray, and his spiritual powers sleep. To be saved from "the Sleep of Ulro" (a state of "rational self-absorption"), he must be awakened by the rebellious powers of the unconscious. Finally, though, he must transcend the destructive nature of Orc and by an act of the "divine imagination" (identified with Los in the mythology, ultimately Christ) achieve reintegration of the self. The dialectical process is unending until the conflicting powers are united in creative tension, and Albion once more embraces his female nature (in Blake's vocabulary, his "emanation"), Jerusalem; and "Urizen & Luvah & Tharmas & Urthona" stand as one "fourfold among the Visions of God in Eternity" (*Jerusalem*, p. 744).

As Blake's mythology applies to the individual, it implies that man falls *within* himself, sins against his own divine nature, when he allows his reasoning faculty to tyrannize his will. In this sense he endures an *unfortunate* fall from childlike innocence. Paradoxically, though, he can recover from the Fall only by disobeying his own reason—that is, only by a *fortunate* fall. In fact, as we shall note later, in Blake's idea of states of being, the innocence of childhood is itself flawed simply because it is unconscious and therefore unearned. When Blake refers to the material world or to the social or political order, however, he emphasizes the idea of the fortunate fall.

If the natural world, or "the mundane shell" described by Newtonian physics, atomistic theory, and Lockean empiricism, conceals the sacred, then man must violate its illusory veil by seeing not with but "thro the Eye." To those who truly "see," the infinite cannot be totally obscured, and "everything that lives is Holy" ("Visions of the Daughters of Albion," p. 195). Again, Blake speaks in paradox. The phenomenological universe of time and space is at once a consequence of the Fall and a testimony of the divine. In a sense Blake is less an antimaterialist than an ultimate materialist. To those who see "into the life of things," he suggests, the physical world mirrors eternity. Blake's attractiveness to modern scientist-humanists like Jacob Bronowski is easily understandable, for he anticipates the collapse of Newtonian physics with its dependence on fixed time and space. And Blake not only offers a poetic vision of relativity, he also conceives of spiritual energy fields underlying the phenomenal world of matter, a sort of religious version of the quantum theory which can turn "the Atoms of Democritus / And Newton's Particles of light" into "sands upon the Red sea shore / Where Israel's tents do shine so bright." To Blake, the error of Urizenic science is more in what it does not say than in what it does, for in its empirical assumptions it cannot penetrate the illusory shell of matter. Yet, as Blake states in *The Book of Urizen* and elsewhere, the fallen physical world of creation is finally a blessing precisely because it establishes the extent of man's fall and, paradoxically, reveals eternity. In "Auguries of Innocence" he urges his reader

> To see a World in a Grain of sand
> And a heaven in a Wild Flower
> Hold infinity in the palm of your hand
> And Eternity in a hour. (P. 431)

The fortunate fall, therefore, does not imply disobedience of the true God, the divine in man, but disobedience of the god of science, the Urizen who circumscribes the universe with the five senses.

The fortunate fall refers to man's adversary relationship with political and social systems as well as to an oppressive intellectual and scientific system. In Blake's more polemical works, such as *America, a Prophecy* and *The French Revolution*, those who sin against the system are, as in all his works, harbingers of freedom. Against the French nobility stand the revolutionaries ready to shatter the false Eden guarded by priests, nobles, and the king. In *America, a Prophecy*, Orc appears as serpent-dragon, "Albion's wrathful Prince," calling men to just revolt. "Wreath'd round the accursed tree," Orc demands the overthrow of the Urizenic god George III (Louis XVI in *The French Revolution*). Blake's radical social and political views thus correspond to his elemental myth. Moving from innocence through knowledge to experience, man becomes aware of the Urizenic forces at work in society and struggles in opposition—Urizen's good becomes the divine evil.

As the title of *The Marriage of Heaven and Hell* implies, a fundamental doctrine of what might be called Blake's "Bible of Hell" is that good and evil coexist in creative tension. In most of his works he describes this basic dialectical pattern, even though he speaks of four-sided man. In *Jerusalem* he distinguishes between the moralistic definition of good and evil and what he means by the statement, "Without Contraries is no progression":

> They take the Two Contraries, which are called Qualities
>   with which
> Every Substance is clothed; they name them Good
>   & Evil.
> From them they make an Abstract, which is a Negation
> Not only of the Substance from which it is derived,
> A murderer of its own Body, but also a murderer
> Of every Divine Member; it is the Reasoning Power.
> This is the Spectre of Man, the Holy Reasoning Power,
> And in its Holiness is closed the Abomination of
>   Desolation. (*Jerusalem*, p. 639)

"Negations are not Contraries," he remarks later, for they cannot accommodate the opposite and so produce stasis, the sterile abstraction of moral codification. "Contraries mutually exist," however, and generate movement; they accommodate but do not repress opposites. If good and evil are relative terms subject to the circumstances of the moment rather than concrete absolutes frozen on tablets of law, then we have an ongoing dynamicism. "To be Good only is to be / A God or else a Pharisee," Blake writes sarcastically in *The Everlasting Gospel* (p. 754). Denying the established moral categories, he lays out his new gospel, identifying "good" with reason, passivity, and restraint; and "evil" with energy, exuberance, and freedom. "Active evil is better than Passive Good," Blake scribbled on the margin of Lavater's *Aphorisms on Man.* Offering the "Proverbs of Hell," he assaults the "one law" of reason. In surrealistic, bizarre visions he insists on the dialectical relationship between good and evil, the "prolific" and the "devouring"—"Whoever tries to reconcile them seeks to destroy existence." Trying to cleanse "the doors of perception," Blake saw the necessity for disobeying "good." The Fall triggers action; therefore, it can generate being. Not to fall means remaining motionless—and one should "expect poison from the standing water."

Blake's mythology, then, spans the cosmos, society, and the self. It offers a holistic view of man. For Blake, God is completely human; and man, created in his image, reflects the essential fact that the

creator Elohim of the Old Testament is a fallen god whose fall he is doomed to imitate. For modern man, he insists, has created out of the rational thought of Locke, Newton, and the empirical "scientific" tradition, a stagnant Eden devoid of the spiritual power and energizing forces that might free him from his self-imposed chains. With devastating power, Blake turned his mythological lens toward his age and witnessed a society enslaved by a mechanistic view of man and nature, a world ruled by abstraction and impoverished moral categories. Every where he saw the imagery of chaos—growing urban squalor and industrial blight, horrifying child labor, oppressive imperialism and political tyranny. Against what he conceived to be a secular, mechanical, deistic, dehumanized concept of man, he proclaimed his gospel—fallen prey to his own Urizenic principle, man has by an act of selfhood shattered the universal brotherhood. Redemption lay in rebellion against the reductive rationalism of the age—but not in that alone. To recover "the human form divine," man finally has to forgive his own Urizenic nature by taking on the mantle of the God of love. Jesus, the ultimate God-man and "human form divine," replaces Urizenic judgment with the law of love and forgiveness. In "I saw a chapel all of gold," Blake illustrates his belief that man must follow Christ to the stable, rejecting both the cold moral architecture of Urizenic religion and the destructive violence of the Orcean reprobate, represented here in bold sexual imagery:

> I saw a chapel all of gold
> That none did dare to enter in,
> And many weeping stood without,
> Weeping, mourning, worshipping.
>
> I saw a serpent rise between
> The white pillars of the door,
> And he forc'd and forc'd and forc'd,
> Down the golden hinges tore.
>
> And along the pavement sweet,
> Set with pearls and rubies bright,
> All his slimy length he drew,
> Till upon the altar white
>
> Vomiting his poison out
> On the bread and on the wine.
> So I turn'd into a sty
> And laid me down among the swine. (P. 163)

In sum, Blake gives us a record of human existence. Born in unconscious innocence, man, like the children in "Holy Thursday," lives in the radiance of eternity. Here sin does not exist, for the child has not yet tasted of the Tree of Knowledge. Entering "experience," which is most often associated with the conflicting forces of the conscious rational faculty and sexual desire, man becomes aware of good and evil. He sees the chaos of the created world, the cruelties in nature and society. Such "knowledge" is twofold. On one hand, the emerging self recognizes, like the chimney sweeper in the *Songs of Experience,* that "God & his Priest & King . . . make a heaven of our misery." On the other hand, such knowledge is ultimately self-knowledge. The evil assumes a human form. Man tends to protect his own innocence by holding to a code of moral imperatives. Like Theotomoron in "Visions of the Daughters of Albion," he denies his lustful, "evil" self and claims a hypocritical chastity. His good thereby becomes his evil, even as his evil drives him toward his good. In fear and tyranny he constructs a system of good and evil that reverses the truth. The man who refuses to exist in "contraries" and assimilate the relative claims of good and evil, falls in Ulro, where, like Urizen, he becomes "a shadowy hermaphrodite," an illusory image of the true self. Blake would answer Eve's question in *Paradise Lost*, "If Death / Bind us with after bands, what protects then / Our inward freedom?" by saying, "Just that—freedom." He knew, too, that innocence must ever give way to experience, and would say with Eve, "Experience, next to thee I owe, / Best guide: not following thee, I had remained / In ignorance." Those who journey through experience as though on the mythic night journey of the soul go on "till Generation is swallow'd up in Regeneration" (*Milton,* p. 533), and "Man walks forth from the midst of the fires" (*Vala*, p. 379). That final state Blake calls Eden, not the biblical Eden but the eternity which existed before creation. He refers to this highest state of being as "higher innocence," an "organized" innocence because man has chosen and existentially earned it. Here resides the Christ in man, the most fully realized manifestation of "the human form divine."

Blake presents the most fully developed version of the Fall in the romantic period, indeed the most fully stated commentary since *Paradise Lost*. His influence has magnified over the years, until he now seems not only a prophet of the radical theology of the mid-twentieth century but also a pivotal figure in the attempts by many thinkers to construct a holistic view of man. His name is as likely to appear in works by scientists, psychologists and futurists in general as in those by literary critics or theologians. No doubt we can overstate the case; and, as some scholars have reminded us, Blake owed much to earlier thought and to the cross-current of ideas in his own age.[22] Still, he must be considered a seminal figure in virtually any serious comprehensive study of the modern temperament. For the purposes of this study, he provides the basic vocabulary and concepts whereby to describe the Fall in romantic and postromantic literature. Though I shall refer to him throughout my study, I especially want to illustrate his ideas by looking at three other English romantic works which reflect the theological shift which occurred in the early nineteenth century.

Byron's *Cain*

For the romantics, Eric Smith concludes, Cain "is of more absorbing interest than are Adam and Eve." Not only is he "the direct heir to the Fall, an outcast with a sense of living within unreasonable limitations to his freedom,"[23] but also he is the prototype of the fully conscious rebel against the Nobodaddy God of Genesis. Adam and Eve, by comparison, act more out of ignorance than defiance in their fall. Helmut Thielicke remarks that Eve does not "sin bravely," but takes "one very harmless snatch of a tidbit." She merely gives notice "that she is quitting—not officially, not formally, and not by flinging an emotionally charged and defiant NO toward heaven like Prometheus."[24] The offense, in fact, can hardly be called a sin, if we imply by that word a wilful rebellion against God. As sinners, Adam and Eve seem vapid figures indeed, and not only in committing the act of disobedience but even in responding to the consequences. Adam lays the blame on Eve, Eve on the serpent. No wonder the romantics preferred Cain as more suited to their basic ideas of the Fall.[25] It is not without significance, as some biblical scholars have noted, that "sin" is actually first mentioned not in reference to Adam and Eve but to Cain (in Genesis 4:7). Here, at least, the romantics found a worthy revolutionary who possessed the energy, courage and conviction to "sin bravely."

A modified and mature representation of the Byronic hero, Cain in Byron's play reflects the primary attributes of the Blakean rebel. Not surprisingly, Blake admired Byron, finding him "of the Devil's party," and addressed his "The Ghost of Abel" "To LORD BYRON in the Wilderness."[26] The reasons for his affinity for Byron are easily discernible, and we can see Byron's play as an illustration and refinement of the same basic romantic myth espoused by Blake. Without the complexity and occasional obscurity of Blake's mythological construct and within the broad outlines of the biblical narrative, Byron depicts a fall both fortunate and unfortunate.

Beginning after the expulsion, Byron's drama provides an analysis of what transpired in Eden and dramatizes the inexorable movement to Cain's own fall. As David Eggenschwiler notes, in the first two acts Cain stands outside the myth and cynically evaluates it; in the last act he experiences it.[27] Making full use of the conflict recorded in the biblical text, Byron translates the old myth from a parable of long-accepted communal belief into a drama of the modern hero in search of self—but not without significant qualification. Ostensibly, the representatives of the moral code, Adam, Eve and Abel, are replaced by a villain-turned-hero, the biblical plot by a drama of expanded consciousness. But as he moves from intellectual analysis to direct involvement, Cain attests all the more to the validity of the Fall; for rather than excusing fallen man from guilt by making Cain a simplistic hero, the action finally places the guilt squarely on Cain's shoulders and demands that he act in awareness of it.

The first two acts explore the conditions of the Fall by setting the characters in dramatic conflict. Adam, Eve and Abel jointly represent conventional religion. Although he questions, "Why didst thou plant the tree of knowledge?"[28] Adam shrinks from defiant rebellion. Eve's favoring of Abel and her fraudulent, half-hearted expressions of concern for Cain foreshadow her brutal rejection of the murderer at the end of the play. Even more so, Abel appears the perfect opposite to Cain, a personification of the values most venerated by the super-ego—obedience, passivity and humility. Byron introduces another character, however, as the crucial pole in the internal dialectic, Adah, Cain's wife and sister. An *anima* figure like Blake's Emanation and Shelley's visionary ideal, she comes to be the true foil to Lucifer, the serpent-id in Cain's psychic conflict. At first, though, the conflict is external to character as Cain challenges the adherents of the judging god. In this respect, he is already fallen, because even before the action begins he has magnified Adam and Eve's disobedience. His personal fall occurs, however, when he kills his brother and violates his *own* morality.

The initial scene begins with the communal prayers of Adam, Eve, Abel, Zillah (Cain's sister and Abel's wife), and Adah and with Cain's subsequent refusal to participate. The apparent conflict centers on God's reasons for planting the Tree of Knowledge in Eden. When Cain insists on knowing why the fruit was forbidden, Eve insists that he be "cheerful and resigned" and Abel that he fear lest he "rouse / Th' Eternal anger." Cain's protest extends to his first soliloquy, which poses the timeless questions about human destiny, as he asks, "What had I done in this?" "Wherefore should I toil?" Why the Tree of Knowledge? How do we know that God is good? The dilemma Cain faces is both intellectual and ontological: how can he align the accepted view of the world with his own awareness? Cast from paradise as a result of someone else's offense, Cain plays Job in querying the justice of the Urizenic god. But having easily dismissed the feeble arguments of Eve and Abel, he lacks the impetus to act until the arrival of Lucifer—" 'Tis your immortal part / Which speaks with you."

The nature of Lucifer, like that of the serpent, remains paradoxical. On one hand he is the immortal rebel residing in the self, urging denial of the hangman god. In Blake's view, Urizen created a temporal and spatial world outside the eternal paradise, the true Edenic home of the eternals. Man was not cast out of paradise, therefore, but was already born into a fallen world. Byron's Cain inhabits the same world, simply because Adam and Eve have already fallen. In other words, Blake's Adam and Eve and Byron's Cain all live within the limits of mortality *before* the demonic figure appears, and the serpent in either case embodies their dissatisfaction. A manifestation of the unconscious self, the serpent assumes neither guilt nor innocence, but rather he plays a paradoxical role in the cosmic-psychic drama. In Byron's play he points Cain toward an inevitable fall, fortunate in its shattering of Urizenic oppression, unfortunate in its destruction of Cain's own moral principles. In the first case, Cain sins justly against tyrannical injustice; in the second case he sins against himself. In the final analysis, perhaps, the second fall is also fortunate in that it imposes upon Cain total responsibility for his existence and makes real the full extent of his potential for good or evil. In this sense the Cain myth advances the moral dimensions of the Fall. In acting against his own moral conscience, Cain gains a measure of existential freedom.

In the conventional reading of Genesis, Adam and Eve destroy their immortal state in disobedience to God; in Byron's play Cain ironically defines his mortality in disobedience to himself. In this action Lucifer functions like Goethe's Mephistopheles, driving Cain toward greater and greater self-realization, yet ever threatening to usurp control of the very self he frees. In the first two acts he energizes Cain's will. At once the symbol of Cain's Promethean spirit and a subtle danger to Cain's ability to live a genuine existence within the context of his humanity, Lucifer cynically outlines the boundaries of Cain's mortality just as the serpent gently mocked Adam's and Eve's diminished state before the Fall. Before Lucifer's arrival, Cain in Faustian fashion sought oblivion, willing never to have been born; yet by his very mockery Lucifer catalyzes Cain into action. Even more clever than the snake, Lucifer, in Byron's own words, tries "to depress [Cain] still further in his own estimation than he was before, by showing him infinite things and his own abasements."[29] From his first electric word, "Mortal!" he punctuates his conversations with derisive references to Cain as "poor clay!" Rather than tempting Cain to greatness, he first seeks to drive him to despair. In good romantic paradox, though, he inspires Cain even as he denigrates him. He reverses the role of the traditional Satan in the same way that Goethe's Mephistopheles inverts the medieval devil. Robert Langbaum suggests that the difference between Faust and Mephistopheles, as between Cain and Lucifer, "is the difference between rationalist rebellion which drives the soul and therefore Cain to moral destruction, and nineteenth-century romantic rebellion which affirms the soul and therefore leads to moral reconstruction."[30] In the inherited version of the myth a good man is done in by a Machiavellian Satan—and for the fallen protagonist "the wages of sin is death." In Goethe's adaptation, Mephistopheles's cynical nihilism activates Faust by establishing the needed pole in the dialectic. By articulating the hero's own intellectual cynicism, he both threatens him with "the sickness unto death" and frees his "immortal part." The conflict, finally, is not between good and evil but between affirmation and negation, between stasis and action.

Urging Cain to "look the omnipotent tyrant in / His everlasting face, and tell him that / His evil is not good," Lucifer praises "such who dare" defy "the omnipotent tyrant." Cain succumbs to Lucifer's rationale, for he has long seen the gate of paradise "guarded by fi'ry -sworded cherubim" and felt "the weight / Of daily toil and constant thought." Knowing he "never could / Reconcile what [he] saw with what [he] heard," Cain gives further evidence of his eagerness to accept Lucifer's pronouncements—his alienation:

> My father is
> Tamed down; my mother has forgot the mind
> Which made her thirst for knowledge at the risk
> Of an eternal curse. My brother is
> A watching shepherd boy, who offers up
> The firstlings of the flock to him who bids
> The earth yield nothing to us without sweat;
> My sister Zillah sings an earlier hymn
> Than the birds' matins; and my Adah, my
> Own and beloved, she too understands not
> The mind which overwhelms me. Never till
> Now met I aught to sympathize with me. (I.i.179–90)

Lucifer's concern for Cain remains ambiguous, however. Positively speaking, he calls Cain to his fullest potential. "Nothing can / Quench the mind, if the mind will be itself / The centre of surrounding things," he claims. He urges Cain to break anew "the narrow bounds / Of Paradise." When Cain seems to cower at the thought of death and wishes he "ne'er had been," Lucifer scowls at his cowardice: "That is a grov'ling wish, / Less than thy father's, for he wished to know." By his counteraction he thrusts Cain beyond self-pity. But he also endangers Cain. His skillful manipulation leads to his invitation, "Fall down and worship me." Offering to substitute one symbol of authority for another, he speaks in echo of the serpent of "the joy / And power of knowledge." In refusing to trade one parasitic existence for another, Cain agonizingly, if victoriously, discovers that "knowledge is sorrow."

Lucifer reasons that Cain must be his disciple because "He who bows not to him has bowed to me!" In fact no such either-or holds true. When Lucifer in the next few lines tempts Cain most fully to "be taught the mystery of being," Cain's only hesitation is his promise to Adah that he would present an offering with Abel. His involvement in the human community, not his allegiance to God, stands between him and Lucifer. Even though he creates sympathy for Lucifer as rebel against a tyrannical deity, Byron no more asks us to identify with him than Goethe asks us to identify with Mephistopheles. Lucifer's function is fundamentally structural; as "the spirit that always says no" he does not represent unqualified belief in rebellion so much as provide motivation for Cain, like the satanic figure in Byron's *The Deformed Transformed*. In Blake's language, neither Orc nor Urizen can save man. By mocking Cain's mortality Lucifer compels him to respond. The conflict between his negative rationality and Adah's simple human love constitutes Cain's dilemma and forces him to construct his own values.

On one side, Lucifer beckons Cain to transcend his clay and worship him; on the other, Adah asks a commitment of his flesh. Before Lucifer appeared, Cain could only strike out vainly against the sky; now he is empowered to act, to explore fully "the mystery of being." The conflict surfaces when Lucifer engages Adah in conversation and tries to undermine her simple faith. She does not, in fact cannot, counter his logic; but she makes a distinctly human appeal to Cain: "Walk not with this spirit, / Bear with what we have bourne, and love me. I / Love thee." She reiterates her fear of Lucifer—"He is not of ours." Her only defense against his piercing intellect is her simplistic faith—"Omnipotence / Must be all goodness." But though she accuses him of tempting "us with *our own* / Dissatisfied and curious thoughts" (emphasis added), she admits that she "cannot answer this immortal thing" nor "abhor him." Latent in Adah, just beneath the level of consciousness, is an awareness of the injustice Cain openly opposes, an unspoken dissatisfaction with life that underlies all versions of the Fall. Bound to the orthodoxy of belief, she is unable to initiate action, yet she holds desperately to Cain by virtue of her transcendent love.

Lucifer makes the choice intelligible to Cain:

> And if higher knowledge quenches love,
> What must he be you cannot love when known?
> Since the all-knowing cherubim love least,
> The seraphs' love can be but ignorance.
> That they are not compatible, the doom
> Of thy fond parents, for their daring, proves.
> Choose betwixt love and knowledge, since there is
> No other choice. (I.i.423–31)

So Cain seemingly faces an either-or choice. Adah cries out, "Oh Cain, choose love," and magnifies her claim by mentioning their child Enoch, the symbol of their human love. His name provokes Cain's horrible prophecy that here will be "unnumbered and innumerable / conceptions" to perpetuate human suffering. The dialogue conveys the tension between the impulse Lucifer articulates and the opposing imperative Cain feels. Although both characters reject the universal order, Cain, a wiser Adam, doubts Lucifer's claims and hesitates to commit himself to one whose "sorrow" is equal to his own. Moreover, his nostalgia for things human magnifies his impatience with Lucifer's partial demonstration of knowledge. As Lucifer takes him on the descent to Hades, he cries out, "The earth! Where is my earth / Let me look on it, / For I was made of it."

The action points directly toward Cain's experiential knowledge of the ultimate truth about man—mortality. In the second scene he descends into that final nothingness of "swimming shadows and enormous shapes." Despairing at Lucifer's degrading revelation of death, he demands, "Cursed be / He who invented life that leads to death!" But his humiliation is still incomplete. Lucifer informs him that the haunted specters of the earlier world which appear before them were once pre-Adamites:

> Living, high
> Intelligent, good, great, and glorious things,
> As much superior unto all thy sire,

> Adam, could e'er have been in Eden, as
> The sixty-thousandth generation shall be,
> In its dull damp degeneracy, to
> Thee and thy son;—and how weak they are, judge
> By thy own flesh. (II.ii.67–74)

These were "such noble creatures," Lucifer concludes, and all you share with them is "death: the rest / Of your poor attributes is such as suits / Reptiles engendered out of the subsiding / Slime of a mighty universe."

Confronted with a fall even before the Fall of his parents, Cain desires to escape self-consciousness, to "dwell in shadows" like Blake's sleeping man. But at the point of deepest despair, when Lucifer says, "*Their* earth is gone forever. . . . Oh, what a beautiful world it *was!*" Cain replies, "And is." Temporarily rejuvenated by recalling the beauty of the physical world, Cain resists Lucifer's profoundly nihilistic vision. Assuming the offensive, he complains that all still "seems dim and shadowy." The spirited debate continues until Lucifer draws from Cain the admission that he finds himself "most wicked and unhappy." Cain feels remorse, not because of guilt or crime, "but for the pain, / I have felt much." Finding himself sinful quite independent of guilt, he concludes, "My father's God did well / When he prohibited the fatal tree."

Unable to accept either his absurd world or himself, Cain stubbornly clings to his independence. He preserves himself from the "sickness unto death" by counteracting Lucifer's dominant pessimism with Adah's love. When Cain says, "The loveliest thing I know is loveliest nearest," Lucifer can only reply, "Then there must be delusion." Then he repeats the charged word with which he first greeted Cain, "Mortal, / My brotherhood's with those who have no children." Having to choose between superhuman and human kind, Cain echoes Adah's words, "Then thou canst have no fellowship with us." There remains that final separation between the two that Cain cannot bridge, and it is again the image of Adah which prevents him from surrendering to temptation. Despite all Lucifer's revelations, Cain will not sacrifice his humanity to exchange one kind of servitude for another.

Once Adah enters the discussion, the action takes a sharp turn. To this point we have watched Cain's exposure to the dreadful realities of the cosmic order and his cautious responses to Lucifer's vigorous cynicism. But the reference to Adah destroys the disinterested tone created by the dialogue with Lucifer. As Eggenschwiler notes, the action becomes more intense as we move ever closer to mythic

196840

reenactment of the story. Now Cain's humanity rebels against Lucifer's debasing vision. At first Cain asks to see Jehovah's paradise "or *thine*." "Thou hast shown me much," he confesses, "but not all." When Lucifer says that both he and God reign together in the universe, "but our dwellings are asunder," Cain asks why they came to separate. Lucifer throws the question back to Cain in full anticipation of his fall—"Art thou not Abel's brother?"

As Cain reaches for the ultimate truth, he speaks in rich dramatic irony: he will soon slay his brother and become a truly divided self. But now he dares "go on aspiring / To the great double myst'ries! the *two Principles!*" Reenacting the Fall in paradise, he tries to gain knowledge of good and evil; but Lucifer again confronts him with his humanity, ironically assuming God's role: "Dust! limit thy ambition, for to see / Either of these, would be for thee to perish." Cain seemingly exceeds Lucifer's limitations; and when Lucifer admits that death is merely the "prelude" to another state, Cain recants his earlier desire for oblivion—"Then I dread it less, / Now that I know that it leads to something definite."

At the end of the act, Cain gains a partial victory by refusing to bow to Lucifer's superiority. At this point, Byron almost seems to abandon his satanic figure and usurp his voice in order to envision Cain's end. Rather than trying to win Cain's allegiance, Lucifer tells him to "form an inner world":

> judge
> Not by words, though of spirits, but the fruits
> Of your existence, such as it must be.
> One good gift has the fatal apple giv'n—
> Your reason; let it not be over-swayed
> By tyrannous threats to force you into faith
> 'Gainst all external sense and inward feeling.
> Think and endure and form an inner world.
> In your own bosom, where the outward fails. (II.ii.456–64)

He urges Cain toward total independence, an independence so great as to destory his own authority. But genuine freedom can be achieved only through Cain's complete knowledge of human potential, a knowledge only accessible in the experience of a fall.

In revealing the spiritual void of the Urizenic universe, Lucifer places responsibility for constructing a moral order entirely on Cain himself. The last act completes this action. Edward Bostetter has contended that "the third act, with its return to the anthropomorphic myth of the first act, becomes dramatically anticlimactical and logically irrelevant." But, as Harold Bloom has noted, in it Cain "completes an act of knowledge."[31] Far from being "logically irrelevant," it is the natural culmination of Cain's self-actualization; that is, it completes the pattern of the Fall.

The first lines of the third act magnify the difference between the supernatural and human worlds: "Hush! tread softly, Cain. . . . Our little Enoch sleeps." Cain projects his despair into a description of the innocent boy asleep beneath a "gloomy" cypress. Paradise, " 'Tis but a dream," he insists. Adah prophetically asks, "Why wilt thou always mourn for Paradise? / Can we not make another?" But Cain is too deeply immersed in self-pity:

> I had beheld immemorial works
> Of endless beings, skirred extinguished worlds,
> And gazing on eternity methought
> I had borrowed more by a few drops of ages
> From its immensity; but now I feel
> My littleness again. Well said the spirit
> That I was nothing! (III.i.63–69)

Again Adah serves as foil, a benevolent *anima*. When Cain refuses to accept the "sin" of his parents—"*Let them* die!"—Adah returns, "Would I could die for them, so *they* might live!" With hollow rhetoric, Cain once more claims innocence and plays the adolescent Oedipus at odds with his father. When Adah charges him with impiety, Cain climactically replies, "Then leave me." Adah's devotion to him passes the final test—"Never / Though thy God left thee." Rejecting the cosmic order for human love, Adah argues for a higher innocence. Her love for humanity transcends her obligation to the Urizenic deity.

The encounter with Abel takes place against this highly charged conversation. The psychological moment ripens for Cain's fall. In anger motivated by his enlarged vision of the loss of paradise, his awareness of the universality of death, and his debate with Adah, Cain comes upon the prepared altars. He thinks sacrifice "a bribe / To the Creator." His sense of human suffering becomes so profound that he threatens to save his son by dashing him against the rocks. Adah's pleas to "touch not the child—my child—Thy child" reactivates the elemental conflict between negation and affirmation. She restates her right to his love—"Love us, then, my Cain! / *And love thyself* for our sakes, for we love thee." Her insistence that he bless the child foreshadows the redemption that may come. Cain's blessing, as Adah remarks, "may avert / A reptile's subtlety." Says Peter J. Manning,

"Cain's invocation of happiness for his son can indeed mitigate the consequences of the Fall, since it puts a stop to the oedipal struggle that *is* the 'Serpent's curse' in Byron's universe."[32] Yet Cain's very compassion for his son—his simple "Bless thee, boy!"—ironically motivates the tragic action that follows.

At this electric moment Abel arrives. Though he comes just when Adah seems to have restrained Cain, the psychological fact is that Cain has just reaffirmed his love for Adah and Enoch and so cannot bear the thought of sacrificing to the God who would destroy them in death. Ironically, the son and Adah partially motivate the murder. Abel is persistent in bowing "even to the dust" to the universal Nobodaddy. Cain stands unbowed, asking God to receive his offering, "If thou must be propitiated with prayers. . . . If thou must be induced with altars / And softened with sacrifice." Choose my brother's offering "if you love blood," or mine if God will accept "an altar without gore." Ironically, he adds,

> And for him who dresseth it,
> He is such as thou mad'st him and seeks nothing
> Which must be won by kneeling. If he's evil,
> Strike him. . . . If he be good
> Strike him or spare him as thou wilt, since all
> Rests upon thee; and good and evil seem
> To have no pow'r themselves, save in thy will. (III.i.268–75)

When Cain's sacrifice is scattered by the whirlwind, Abel warns him to offer another; but Cain refuses. Finally Cain strikes Abel with a brand. As he falls, Abel addresses Cain as "brother." Cain echoes, "Brother!" The simple contrast to Lucifer's sarcastic "Mortal!" marks Cain's inescapable humanity. Murder marks Cain's full knowledge of his mortality. Having entered the world of experience, he acts against his own values. The magnitude of the act is dramatized in physical identification:

> This is a vision, else I am become
> The native of another and worse world.
> The earth swims around me. What is this? 'Tis wet,
> *(Puts his hand to his brow, and then looks at it.)*
> And yet there are no dews. 'Tis blood—my blood—
> My brother's and my own and shed by me. (III.i.342–46)

All along, Cain's defensiveness, his extreme disgust at his human condition, and his unwillingness to accept its limitations or purposes keep him from dealing with his own divided nature. Ironically, he is humanized by the tragic enactment of his pride. Byron creates a sympathetic hero, but one nonetheless marred by guilt, by "sin" not against God so much as against the self. Struggling against injustice, Cain becomes "the progenitor of sin—rather than mere victim of it."[33] The ambiguity resides in the effect of that guilt. The criminal act is a saving act which frees the self from a false pride; and yet, paradoxically, it leaves the self as the only surviving source of value. Murder does not crush the self by demanding judgment before some cosmic court, some moral system existing outside the self. Rather, it transforms a fragmented and distorted image of self into something authentic by the catharsis of experience. It makes the self morally viable by demanding *self*-judgment. Consequently, the Fall is both fortunate and unfortunate.

The awareness of Cain's human commitment is the one act of knowledge Lucifer could not supply. Murder brings the knowledge of experience as opposed to reason, a knowledge that most fully defines the dimensions of Cain's humanity. After the murder occurs, Zillah, whom Abel has asked Cain to comfort, exclaims with harsh finality, "Death is in the world!" The word "death"—an ironic repetition of Lucifer's mocking "Mortal!"—awakens Cain to "the fearful desert of his consciousness." His crime, Leonard Michaels has declared, "is presented so as to make it the justification of an antecedent condition which is subjective and internal." In order to convert myth "to the personal psychology of his hero," Byron makes crime necessary in order for Cain "to identify or account for himself."[34] Murder, the nadir of Cain's experience, gives birth to remorse, the presence of which negates Lucifer's claim that good and evil are meaningless terms. Remorse verifies the moral values operative in the self. Even in opposing the conventional interpretation of the myth of the fall, Byron attests to its validity as surely as Blake does.

At the end of the drama, Eve pronounces a Urizenic curse on the first murderer. And although Adah tries to intervene on Cain's behalf, Adam finally disowns him as well. Cain stands alone, except for Adah; and he tries to force her to leave him. At this moment the angel of the Lord appears. By his harshness Urizen's agent earns our disrespect and polarizes our sympathy for Cain. In marking Cain's brow he guarantees prolonged suffering rather than mercy. In response Cain acknowledges a greater internal pain: "It burns / My brow, but naught to that which is within it. / Is there more? Let me meet it as I may." He is willing to suffer; and what is more, he is willing to trade his life for Abel's, thereby achieving the transcendent love of Adah and Blake's

Christ. As he stares at Abel's body, Cain remarks, "If you see'st what I am, / I think thou wilt forgive him, whom his God / Can ne'er forgive, nor his own soul." In causing Abel's death rather than his own, Byron's Cain presents a new kind of hero. In his continued existence, he is liberated from a traditional morality and becomes the maker rather than the agent of myth, an existential hero. He has learned that the only way to discover good or evil is to go beyond the external judgments of the "tyrant God." Ironically, Adam tells Cain early in the play that "evil only was the path / To good." In his prayer to God, Cain observes, "And good and evil seem / To have no pow'r themselves, save in thy will." In murder Cain fully realizes his own power of evil, and this recognition gives him autonomy. Crime leads to the only authentic moral judgment in a world devoid of moral vitality—the sentencing of self. Cain moves from rational analysis of the Fall and its consequences to participation. Once he experiences his human potential for evil by his own act, he transcends the stagnant values of the chastened Adam and Eve. Accepting self-judgment, he gains a moral superiority in his ironic freedom. Moreover, he renders Lucifer's subtle temptation void. No Adam and Eve restored to obedience by God's benevolence, Cain and Adah seek a new order—Milton's human archetypes will no longer serve.

In summary, Cain's detached intellectual rebellion undergoes the crisis of experience; he "sins" against himself. The guilt he feels is relative only to him; God's judgment and forgiveness are equally irrelevant. Unable to repent yet unable to escape from his fallen condition, Cain is an archetype of modern man, alienated from God, yet dissatisfied with self. Moving in a wasteland without value or meaning, bearing the almost unbearable weight of self-consciousness, Byron's protagonist is one early version of contemporary fallen man.

In his elaboration of the myth Byron parallels and alters Blake's portrayal of a fall. Certainly he does not share Blake's apocalyptic vision or his supreme faith in the final victory of "the human form divine." Nonetheless, insofar as they refer to the creator in the early chapters of Genesis, both Blake and Byron conceive of a fallen god. Similarly, they view the Fall as an internal action—Byron called his play "mental theatre"—occurring within the self, a reflection of the cosmic psyche. For both, the knowledge of good and evil must be acquired through experience rather than a prescribed moral code or rational discourse. Finally, despite their apparent belief in a fortunate fall, Blake and Byron fully acknowledged the necessity for suffering and alienation. Although *Cain* is neither "fullblown nihilism" nor simply an expression of masochism,[35] it in no way diminishes the terrifying consequences of the Fall. However much it fails to resolve the human predicament, though, Cain's tragic struggle redeems him from the certain spiritual death of stasis.

I have chosen to discuss Byron especially because of Blake's particular attraction to him and because of the obvious relationship between the Byronic hero and Blake's Orcean rebel. Coleridge's "Christabel" and Shelley's *The Cenci* are also related works, for both explore the psychological and religious implications of the Fall in seemingly innocent women. If anything, Coleridge and Shelley offer even fewer assurances of recovery from the Fall, however much they seem to point their heroines toward a "higher innocence."

Coleridge's "Christabel" and Shelley's *The Cenci*

On April 1, 1819, the following well-known anecdote appeared in the *New Monthly Magazine and Universal Register* concerning Lord Byron's reading Coleridge's "Christabel" aloud to Shelley, Mary Godwin, Claire Clairmont, and Dr. John Polidari in Geneva in mid-July 1816:

> The whole took so strong a hold of Mr. Shelley's mind, that he suddenly started up and ran out of the room. The physician and Lord Byron followed, and discovered him leaning against a mantelpiece with cold drops of perspiration trickling down his face.[36]

"Christabel" continued to fascinate Shelley; and a month later he read the whole poem aloud to Mary.[37] And when he wrote *The Cenci* some three years later, Shelley employed themes and devices strikingly similar to those in Coleridge's poem. Although it would be difficult to prove that "Christabel" directly influenced Shelley's writing of *The Cenci*, we do know that just two days before completing the play Shelley was reading Coleridge.[38] But even if we cannot be certain that Coleridge was a source for Shelley's drama, the affinities between Coleridge's narrative poem and Shelley's play at least suggest that the authors shared a common view of fallen humanity.

Some of the superficial likenesses between "Christabel" and *The Cenci* result from the authors' attempts to follow the Gothic tradition. A mysterious, morbid atmosphere hangs over both works. The heroines are both victimized by seemingly irresistible powers. They suffer perverse sexual violation: Cenci rapes his daughter, while Geraldine "lay down by the maiden's side!— / And in her arms the maid she took, / Ah wel-a-day!" (262–64).[39] Geraldine, like Count Cenci, is described as a dark parental figure, "as a mother with her child" (301). As in much of the later Gothic literature, these works function on both psychological and metaphysical principles. The psychological dreamlike quality of the plots is reinforced and extended by the serious treatment of evil. But although Shelley and Coleridge use Gothic accoutrements, they go beyond the limits of the popular Gothic literature and convey profound insights into the tortured workings of the human psyche. For both, the Fall initiates a process of self-realization by depicting a subtle dialectical tension between the protagonist and her illicit shadow figure, an erotic mother or an incestuous father.

The meaning of both works is conveyed essentially by the delineation of the heroines and the demonic beings who destroy them. At one pole is the innocence of the heroine, a character living in a dark and ominous world but apparently free from guilt; at the other pole is the seeming evil of her antagonist, more a symbol than a character, a demon bent on destruction. In the course of the conflict, the innocent and evil characters begin to mirror each other until we arrive at an enigmatic and insoluble mixture of seemingly antithetical forces. The relationship between the dialectical powers in each work has been frequently oversimplified or misunderstood by critics who are commonly misled into interpreting the works in line with contemporary Gothic masterpieces. But a comparison of the central characters in each will show that Coleridge and Shelley conceived of evil as an essential and paradoxical aspect of the human condition. In this regard, both supposedly evil characters are "twisted angels" in the most profound romantic fashion. Neither Geraldine nor Count Cenci is a character in the ordinary sense.

In each work the demonic character invades the heroine's psychic garden. Used in reference to a state of being, "garden" is a relative term. If it describes a condition of harmony and fecundity, it is obviously positive; if, instead, it refers to a parasitic existence or to a state of spiritual and psychological incapacity, it is as surely negative. In the dynamics of being, the garden is ever in a process of change: harmony moves inexorably toward stasis and apathy moves toward violation. On one hand it must be sought; on the other it must be shattered. In psychological terms, both Christabel and Beatrice Cenci dwell in debilitating gardens. Christabel's innocence rests in her ignorance. Confined in an idyllic Eden, dependent upon her overly protective father and the guardian spirit of her long-dead mother, she is in the language of situation ethics "a technical virgin." Although

Beatrice Cenci's external existence seems anything but a garden, her internal psychic world is precisely that. Though victimized by her father's unexplained cruelty, she maintains her innocence by holding resolutely to the Urizenic moral code which assures her purity. So long as she can place "sin" outside herself, she remains free of taint, though ironically trapped in her own "mind forg'd manacles" by an incapacitating self-ignorance. In the pattern of the Fall, Christabel and Beatrice live on the twilight edge of the unconscious; they unwittingly await "the other"—the shadowy satanic figure just beneath the surface of consciousness. For both, it is at least as crucial to be saved from innocence as to be saved from guilt.

Coleridge's Geraldine carries all the ambivalence of Melville's white whale or Webster's white devil. As several critics have noted, she embodies Christabel's illicit self and seems virtually "the incarnation of erotic life."[40] Significantly, she first appears at midnight beneath a tree as a virtual snake in a dream. Dressed in "silken robes of white, / That shadowy in the moonlight shone," she possesses the luminosity and sparkle of the watersnakes in "The Rime of the Ancient Mariner": "Wild glittered here and there / The gems entangled in her hair" (59–60, 64–65). Her mysterious appearance is heightened by obvious, conventional supernatural signs: the fainting at the gate, the dog's groan, the inflammation of the ashes, the effect of the angels engraved on the lamp. Like Count Cenci, she possesses the traditional evil eye and at first glance seems to take sadistic delight in her dismal task. Unconsciously if not consciously, Coleridge conceived of her as a villainous character, or rather not a character so much as the agent of some supernatural power. Indeed, she seems to have been appointed to inflict violence upon her given victim. At certain points, Geraldine appears to sympathize with her victim and to recoil from her evil mission. When Christabel laments, "O mother dear! that thou wert here!" Geraldine responds, "I would . . . she were!" (202–03), suggesting that she wishes for some force to restrain her. Coleridge depicts her in a moment of struggle when she stares "with unsettled eye." Finally she cries,

> "Off woman, off! this hour is mine—
> Though thou her guardian spirit be,
> Off, woman off! *'tis given to me.*"
>
> (211–13, emphasis added)

After a brief hesitation, she asserts the "divine" authority of her task and determines to carry it out.

But even when she is in control of the situation and all obstacles have been removed, Geraldine is incapable of simply committing the offense. She acts in a state of emotional uncertainty. Drawing a deep breath as she releases the cincture from beneath her breast, she stands naked before the fascinated Christabel:

> Yet Geraldine nor speaks nor stirs;
> Ah! what a stricken look was hers!
> Deep from within she *seems half-way*
> *To lift some weight with sick assay,*
> And eyes the maid *and seeks delay!*
> Then suddenly, as one defied,
> Collects herself in scorn and pride,
> And lay down by the maiden's side!
>
> (255–59, emphasis added)

Why does Geraldine halfway sympathize with Christabel? One answer may be that her sympathy is feigned. But why should she feign sympathy or hesitate to act when Christabel is already in her power? Surely Coleridge was not so much interested in creating a character in conflict with herself as in suggesting the ambivalence of her acts. She comes from another world, and is able to tell Christabel that "all they who live in the upper sky, / Do love you, holy Christabel!" (227–28). Functioning almost like the satanic emissary in the book of Job, she is the agent in a plot directed against the innocence of Christabel, a plot orchestrated by a mysterious, perhaps even divine, power.

Many critics have acknowledged the paradoxical nature of Geraldine,[41] but relatively few have discussed the equal ambivalence of Count Cenci. Beatrice's antagonist is frequently dismissed as "a typical Shelleyan villain," a symbol of tyranny. Earl R. Wasserman claims that "the identification of the Count's despotic fatherhood with God's" makes the drama "at least as much a theological as a human tragedy, or, rather, it becomes a human tragedy because of an acceptance of a theological model for moral behavior."[42] The Count's acts are not assignable to simple tyranny. He is less a character than a representation of the demonical, an opposing character to Beatrice's apparent goodness as Geraldine is to Christabel's. Whereas Geraldine temporarily sympathizes with her victim, Cenci is an unrelenting force, a self-confessed sadist. Like Geraldine, however, he claims divine authority: "Heaven has special care of me" (I.iii.65). He is confident that God will not take his life "till the lash / Be broken in its last and deepest wound; / Until its hate be all inflicted" (IV.i.66–68). "I do not feel as if I were a man," he confesses, "but like a fiend appointed to chastise / The offenses of some unremembered world"

(IV.i.161–63). In other words, Cenci is unconvincing as a character, but as a foil to Beatrice he serves a crucial function in the internal action of a fall. No simple villain, he like Geraldine is the embodiment of the forbidden self, a threat to Beatrice's absolute goodness as yet unsullied in the precarious Eden of her conscious self. What is more, he and Geraldine directly reflect the very characters they violate. The relationship between father and child, like the relationship between mother and child implied in Geraldine's being called "a mother with her child," cements the profound relationship between good and evil.

The protagonists in the two works may be more realistically drawn, but they are no less enigmatic. They are subtly conceived, and the incautious reader can readily believe them wholly innocent. Surely they are as innocent as human beings can be, but they are nonetheless inheritors of the Fall. Their innocence, paradoxically, is spiritually detrimental. Richard H. Fogle observes of Coleridge's heroine, "Christabel is lovely, holy and sheltered; the insidious Geraldine is the first evil thing in her experience."[43] Yet because she exists in a garden of absolute spiritual innocence, Christabel is incomplete as a human being. When confronted with the commanding presence of Geraldine, her human fascination for evil is manifested. At first glance, her motives for helping Geraldine seem entirely noble, her involvement with evil totally innocent. Her encounter with Geraldine "is ultimately contingent upon an act of goodness—her hospitable protection of a maiden in distress."[44] But psychologically, Christabel is clearly drawn to Geraldine. A dream figure from the dark unconscious world, Geraldine catalyzes Christabel into action. Drawn by her seductive charm and the magical aura of the moment, Christabel falls prey to Geraldine's erotic beauty. Ironically, she initiates her own fall by virtue of her unwitting acts of kindness. As Carl Woodring notes,

> She has come voluntarily to the oak. At request, she stretches forth her hand to Geraldine's. In a single invitation, she bestows her bed on Geraldine and begs a place in it, as she urges the stranger, in a hyperbole of courtesy, "this night, to share your couch with me." Arduously succumbing to mankind's hunger for ritual, she lifts her guest over the threshold of the gate. In what she supposes to be a consideration for her insomniac father, she assures a secret entry by making her feet as bare as Geraldine's. . . . Whether in direct or ironic analogy with the Eucharist or antithetically to it, Christabel next offers "a wine of virtuous powers" made by her mother, who died at Christabel's birth.[45]

Woodring's argument is much amplified by the more recent studies, which point to intensely psychosexual implications in all Christabel's actions (see n. 40). At the very least, we can conclude, Christabel's motives are highly ambiguous. In dealing with the attraction of evil, Coleridge exposed, knowingly or not, the uncertain workings of the human mind. As his *Notebooks* surely show, he possessed such psychological insights.

When Geraldine disrobes, for example, Christabel is transfixed by the sight. The psychosexual element in Gothic tales (particularly those of the "Monk" Lewis school which Coleridge attacked) is here given a new dimension. Christabel is caught in the web of her own human, if illicit, desires. Geraldine herself is dismayed by Christabel's stare and cries out in alarm, fearing perhaps that Christabel has seen her apparently shriveled breasts, the symbol of her depravity. (In the early version of the poem the description of Geraldine's deformity is overt; in the final version Christabel sees "a sight to dream of, not to tell!"—235.) Christabel, however, expresses no dismay. "Christabel is perhaps no more 'guilty' than the Mariner who killed the Albatross," Marshall Suther concludes, "but she is guilty nonetheless."[46] As Siegel observes, Geraldine's act of violation seems more "a seduction" than "the rape of good by evil."[47] In the presence of the evil being, who articulates her deepest and most forbidden desires, Christabel projects a latent attraction to evil.

Beatrice Cenci is most commonly thought the victim of Cenci's unrestrained cruelty. But *The Cenci*'s sensational plot tends to camouflage the moral judgment which Shelley presents in the preface that Beatrice is guilty of a crime. As a result, not a few critics have been understandably seduced—by her external sufferings, by the high praise given to her by Giacomo, Bernardo, and Lucretia, and by her own rationale—into expounding Beatrice's innocence. But although Beatrice endures enormous physical pain, she is essentially the victim of "her own loathing will" as surely as Christabel is destroyed by her own fascination for evil.[48] From the beginning, her innocence depends upon an externally earned righteousness, an almost fanatical devotion to an inauthentic morality, and not upon an existentially earned goodness. As a result of her absolute self-confidence, she is virtually dehumanized. Her "stubborn will" becomes little more than spiritual pride and transforms her into a brittle defender of her own virtue. She resents "that such a father" as Cenci "should be mine!" (I.ii.54). After she is raped by her father, however, her propensity for evil is fully realized; but even in the first part of the play it is obvious that Beatrice's innocence rests upon a blind obedience to a given Urizenic law. Unconsciously—perhaps unavoidably

—she becomes a willing martyr, perhaps a too willing one.[49] Her struggle against Cenci nourishes her spiritual pride. In the banquet scene in act 1, when Cenci announces his glee over the death of two of his sons, Beatrice temporarily lashes out at him. When she is ordered to retire to her chamber, she answers defensively, "Retire thou, impious man! Ay hide thyself / Where never eye can look upon thee more!" (I.iii.146–47). Her speech then becomes more subdued, and she ends by assuring her father that she will pray for him. We momentarily see the paradox of her character, the mixture of naked aggression and "the sweet look." Her potential for revenge and her underlying proclivity for violence surface in an unguarded instant, and we realize that innocence is not armor-plated.

A basic difference in Beatrice's engagement with evil is that she is actively involved in conflict with her antagonist, whereas Christabel is more or less a passive "victim." For Beatrice the outer garden has long since lain waste—she holds desperately to her own internal Eden. In each case, though, the heroine is the prey of her own fallen humanity. In a Blakean sense, neither character has achieved true innocence. Christabel has remained too long in the state of childlike innocence. She is spiritually stagnant, and only an "experience" with evil can raise her to higher innocence. Beatrice is caught up in the Ulro of rational self-absorption, and only an act of hideous proportion can free her from self-deceptive faith in the meaningless moral code of Nobodaddy's church. For both, the Fall involves loss and possible regeneration. Whether Christabel and Beatrice ultimately achieve spiritual wholeness or not, they both experience the shaking of foundations—their Edens cannot last.

Coleridge and Shelley were both fully aware of man's potential for good or evil. In *The Rime of the Ancient Mariner*—undoubtedly influenced by the fragment *The Wanderings of Cain*, which Coleridge was writing at the same time—the mariner, with no particular malice, kills the albatross. The other mariners are implicitly involved in the crime because they momentarily condone it: " 'Twas right, said they, such birds to slay, / That bring the fog and mist" (101–02). Coleridge says explicitly in the marginal notes that in justifying the shooting of the albatross the shipmates "thus make themselves accomplices in the crime." Christabel similarly allows herself, if unconsciously, to be enveloped by Geraldine's evil power. She is excited by the invader's demonic beauty. Because she is human, Christabel has something of the fallen Eve in her, and the evil in Geraldine strikes a familiar chord. She is seduced because she wants to be. The ambiguity of Geraldine mirrors the ambiguity of Christabel, and once Geraldine invades Christabel's world of supposed innocence, Christabel assumes the image of her enchantress.

Beatrice's susceptibility to evil is somewhat different. She too is trapped unwittingly by her own "mind forg'd manacles," but her blindness comes from her psychological need for self-justification. On one level her actions are totally understandable. After all, her predicament calls for extreme measures. She is locked in a struggle of wills, and Cenci's purpose is to break her spiritual pride—"the brow superior." He repeatedly says he does not seek her body, " 'Tis her stubborn will / Which, by its own consent, shall stoop as low / As that which drags it down" (IV.i.10–12). He wishes to force her into an overt sin, just as Geraldine intends to reveal Christabel's flawed humanity. Christabel is trapped by her susceptibility to the attraction of evil; Beatrice is driven to revenge by pride in her spiritual purity: "What she most abhors / Shall have a fascination to entrap / Her loathing will" (IV.i.85–87). Orsino identifies the chink in Beatrice's armor in a speech in act 2 which foreshadows Beatrice's rationalization of her deed:

> It fortunately serves my close designs
> That 'tis a trick of this same family
> *To analyze their own and other minds.*
> *Such self-anatomy shall teach the will*
> *Dangerous secrets:* for it tempts our powers,
> Knowing what must be thought, and may be done,
> Into the depth of darkest purpose.
>
> (II.ii.107–13, emphasis added)

In the hidden corners of Beatrice's mind there lurks an unconscious pride which demands expurgation of the blot she fears has marred her purity. Orsino "tempts her power . . . / Into the depth of darkest purpose." Prometheus may forgive his enemy and play God—Shelley was writing *Prometheus Unbound* at the same time he wrote *The Cenci*—but Beatrice will commit any violence to preserve her garden of innocence.

Significantly, Christabel and Beatrice think themselves contaminated by their assailants. Christabel feels an unexplained guilt: " 'Sure I have sinn'd!' said Christabel, / 'Now heaven be praised if all be well!" (381–82). In a state of psychic disorder, she suffers "such perplexity of mind / As dreams too lively leave behind" (385–86). The use of the dream reference is particularly apt, for the "wound" is clearly internal. The implied physical violation is a rich symbol for an assault on the soul. Initially, Beatrice too locates her "wound" within. After being raped by Cenci, she cries out in brilliant paradox: "Reach me that handkerchief!—My brain is hurt" (III.i.1). She insists that her body, not her soul, has been penetrated by evil, and she locates the evil in "putrefying limbs" that "shut round and sepulchre the panting soul!" (III.i.27). In fact, her father's incestuous act as much exposes as inflicts evil. Shelley remarks in the preface that no one's innocence can be destroyed by some one else's evil; but because Beatrice's innocence is itself dependent upon her allegiance to an externally defined morality, she must, like Othello, preserve her "perfect soul" by washing away the blemish on her honor.

Both characters are confident of God's grace. Christabel "knows in joys and woes, / That saints will aid if men will call: / For the blue sky bends over all!" (329–31). Though already thrust from the garden by virtue of experience, neither she nor Beatrice can acknowledge her own evil. Throughout the play, Beatrice assumes God's help. Even in the face of certain death, she tells Lucretia that God "seems, and but seems, to have abandoned us" (V.iii.115). Both heroines attempt to disengage themselves from any guilt. Christabel accuses Geraldine, just as Eve blames the serpent. Sir Leoline's opinion that Christabel is guilty of "woman's jealousy" is not to be dismissed lightly. Her motives are mixed. In part she is aware of Geraldine's evil, which she recognizes because she sees in Geraldine an aspect of herself, and also sees her as illicit rival for her father's love. In another respect, she attempts to protect her innocence by detaching herself from the evil she feels, as yet blinded to her own identity in Geraldine's demonic acts of will. Ironically, even as she accuses Geraldine, she herself assumes her snakelike features. She twice hisses like a snake (459, 591). When she looks into Geraldine's serpent eyes at the very moment she warns Sir Leoline of Geraldine's evil, she "passively did imitate / That look of dull and treacherous hate!" (605–06). If Coleridge wished merely to show the extremity of Christabel's mental state, he could have done so without drawing subtle parallels between her and the serpent-enchantress. But whether by design or not, he hints at an inherent relationship between the two females—the serpent has become the projection of the other self. As Lawrence S. Lockridge points out, "On a moral level Christabel retains her 'innocence' ";[50] but existentially speaking, she has exceeded moral categories and reached that state of awareness Kafka describes where one assumes "guilt" quite irrespective of "sin."

For her part, Beatrice will do anything within her power to be freed from "the thing that I have suffered" (III.i.88). Hence Orsino need only imply that God would want the "crime" punished in order to trap Beatrice in "her own will." In true Urizenic fashion, she reasons that murder is a justifiable solution. When Giacomo, her brother, hesitates to commit patricide, she tells him to harden his heart. She tells Savella, the pope's legate, that if he arrests her, he will be "the judge and executioner / Of that which is the life of life" (IV.iv. 141–42). She is so intent upon proving her innocence that she permits Marzio, one of the hired assassins, to be tortured to protect her purity. Just as Christabel reflects the evil of Geraldine, Beatrice reflects Cenci's evil. Cenci had hoped that Beatrice might bear a child so that "a hideous likeness of herself . . . a distorted mirror" might always be before her, "her image mixed with what she most abhors" (IV.i.148). Ironically, in guarding her innocence, Beatrice becomes Cenci's true child. Potentially freed by her father's act, she falls victim to it. She engineers his murder with the same delight with which he plotted the murder of his two sons. Cenci told Beatrice that he could sleep with no disturbance of conscience (Geraldine slumbers "still and mild"); and when Cenci is killed, Beatrice sleeps "fearless and calm." At the trial, she threatens Camillo, the impotent cardinal, just as Cenci had threatened him in the opening scene of the play. Also at the trial, she uses her eyes to subjugate Marzio, just as Cenci had "disordered" her with his stare at the banquet.

In sum, Christabel and Beatrice are not simply sullied by evil forces. Rather their experiences expose the "dark caverns" of the human mind, the latent tendency toward evil. In both works the encounter with evil, painful though it may be, is potentially ennobling. Both characters are to some degree spiritually depraved. The essential evil in *The Cenci* is not rape or murder but the tyranny of Beatrice's own will. Christabel's innocence is the whole of her frailty; and until Geraldine impinges upon it, Christabel is no more than a naive child subject to the dark, unseen forces in the human psyche. Both characters are deceived by their wills, and only the excessive actions of Cenci and Geraldine can bring them to a saving self-knowledge. The conclusion to part 2 of *Christabel* ends with the following suggestive lines:

> Perhaps 'tis pretty to force together
> Thoughts so all unlike each other;
> To mutter and mock a broken charm
> To dally with wrong that does no harm.
> Perhaps 'tis tender too and pretty
> At each wild word to feel within
> A sweet recoil of love and pity.
> And what, if in a world of sin

(Of sorrow and shame this would be true!)
Such giddiness of heart and brain
Comes seldom save from rage and pain,
So talks as it's most used to do. (666–78)

The poem *is* a collision of "thoughts so all unlike each other." The plot, like the action of *The Cenci*, concerns the inversion of apparent good and evil, a process "of sorrow and shame," "rage and pain." The flawed innocence of both Christabel and Beatrice (the names *Christ/Abel* and Beatrice ironically suggesting supreme innocence) is exposed by the juxtaposition of Geraldine and Cenci, the serpent intruders in their psychic gardens. There is no genuine good without evil, no spiritual vitality. So long as Christabel remains untouched by evil and so long as Beatrice can rest in her externally applied morality, neither is genuinely innocent. They need Geraldine and Cenci as much as Faust needs his Mephistopheles and Cain his Lucifer. The supposed evil complements good. Like the ambiguous water snakes in *The Rime of the Ancient Mariner,* Geraldine (the snake in Bracy's dream) and Cenci are both personifications of evil and the means to salvation, however uncertain that salvation may be.

Finally, both works end in uncertainty. Christabel is as innocent as her flawed humanity will permit her to be. If Coleridge's intended ending, as noted by Dr. Gillman and Derwent Coleridge, is accurate, then we can assume, in spite of the difference in the accounts, that Coleridge was going to vanquish Geraldine and reunite Christabel with her departed lover. Interestingly, in Gillman's account, Coleridge intended to show Geraldine's reappearance in the guise of Christabel's lover, which would indeed constitute an ironic parody of the virtuous maiden's innocent dream. But the fact is he did not—or could not—complete the poem. Many theories have been offered as to why, but perhaps the most sensible argument is that although Coleridge was convinced of the existence of evil in humanity and certainly in himself, he did not know how it could be expelled. Having Geraldine disappear into nothingness would hardly be convincing to the artist who described her presence with such skill. If Coleridge, like Blake, saw the Fall as "actually a gift of God's kindness, as a part of the divine plan for man,"[51] then he had profound difficulty in embodying such faith in the narrative. At any rate, the poem offers no solution—it remains a tantalizing fragment.

The Cenci, of course, is a completed work, but it ends indefinitely. Beatrice is stripped of her blind devotion to external authority: the law, the Church, perhaps even God. She acquires autonomy by means of her fall; her heart has been taught "through its sympathies and antipathies the knowledge of itself" (preface). In destroying Beatrice's outer shell of goodness, Cenci potentially transforms the goodness into something real. Perhaps in a twisted way Beatrice's final insistence upon her innocence is defensible, because she refuses to accept responsibility for her human limitation. Shelley himself calls Beatrice's revenge "a pernicious mistake," implying that although her act of revenge is wrong, she is no mere sinner in the orthodox sense. Once Beatrice has denied all outside assistance, she senses that the flaw is in the fabric of life itself. What "if all things then should be . . . my father's spirit," she asks (V.iv.60); "For was he not alone omnipotent / On Earth, and ever present?" (V.iv.68–69). Because she finds evil—the mark of Cain—an inevitable part of the human condition, she finds reason to assert her innocence again, claiming that "though wrapped in a strange cloud of crime and shame," she has "lived ever holy and unstained" (V.iv.148–49). Yet seldom in all of literature has so much innocence achieved so much evil. Whatever the interpretation, for Shelley, too, the Fall was an inevitable fact. C. S. Lewis writes, "It is simply not true to say that Shelley conceived the human Soul as a naturally innocent and divinely beautiful creature, interfered with by external tyrants; . . . no other heathen writer comes nearer to stating and driving home the doctrine of original sin."[52] Shelley undeniably understood the profound implications of the Fall and the fearful consequences of man's divided nature.

Of course, we might well treat other adaptations of the Fall in romantic literature; but, again, my purpose here is only to suggest the outlines of the newly shaping concepts of the myth. It hardly needs saying that nineteenth-century literature contains numerous related versions of the Fall, not only among English and European writers but especially among American writers, as R. W. B. Lewis notes in *The American Adam*.[53] My concern is more with recent literature, however; and I turn to "The Secret Sharer" both to illustrate the continued viability of romantic versions of the Fall and to exemplify the rich variations on the theme in early modern literature.

Conrad's "The Secret Sharer"

"Traditionally, he ought to see snakes, but he doesn't. Good old tradition's at a discount nowadays."
—Conrad, *Lord Jim*

In *A Study of English Romanticism* Northrop Frye suggests that man "cut off from nature by his consciousness is the romantic equivalent of post-Edenic Adam."[54] Yet, ironically, as I have suggested, only by an act of self-consciousness can man recover, however tenuously, from his fallen condition. The paradoxical nature of man's fall, at once the loss of innocence and the hope of what Blake called "higher innocence," seems to me to underlie many of Conrad's works. Furthermore, the frequent parallels to the essentially romantic concept of the fortunate fall often sustain and illuminate the ironies and ambiguities always associated with Conrad's writings. One must ask, is it better to know or not to know? Is the truth gained from the tree of knowledge redemptive or destructive? Is self-knowledge, the only knowledge that matters in a romantic sense, an act of self-affirmation? Or is it, to quote Conrad's Marlow, "too dark—too dark altogether"? Conrad consciously created artistic ambiguity; his protagonists exist in a state of incompletion in a world that appears neither certain nor whole. To conclude this chapter, I wish to examine the myth of the fortunate fall in "The Secret Sharer," a classic definition of the modern struggle to answer Stein's rephrasing of the ultimate question—"How to be! Ach! How to be."

In *Some Versions of the Fall*, Eric Smith differentiates between the Fall as "developed story" and as "personal myth." He suggests that *Paradise Lost* represents the divergence of the two concepts and that after Milton literary interpretations of the Fall tend to "change from the use of accepted myth . . . to a situation where the writer creates, indeed grows, his own myth, although aware of the accepted versions and parallelling and commenting on them."[55] William Blake reinterpreted the myth of the Fall by inverting it in ways that proved to have a special affinity for early modern writers. His attempt to marry "Heaven and Hell," his denial of Elohim, the Nobodaddy of orthodox religion, his admiration for the "devil," his idea of "contraries"—all echo in various ways and degrees in the works we have discussed and in much other postromantic literature. His psychological as well as moral revelations, though they may have blurred the "historical" myth of the Fall, have found expression in modern works essentially concerned with the "fallen" state of paralyzing self-consciousness. By whatever continuum, direct or indirect, Conrad inherited the tradition of the fortunate fall and gave it new and sometimes highly ironic meaning in many of his best stories.[56]

In "The Secret Sharer," Conrad describes the narrator's effort to explain what Blake would call a fall from innocence to experience and his subsequent "reintegration." The captain begins his story by depicting a sterile garden world in which he suddenly encounters a "snake" who brings to him self-knowledge, exposes the ambiguity of good and evil, and so reveals the narrator's nakedness and vulnerability. The captain-narrator then recounts his own risky attempt somehow to reconcile good and evil without ignoring the legitimate demands that both make upon him.

The captain is physically isolated as the story opens. The nature of his alienation requires comment. The narrator's initial description of the Edenic setting is couched in approximations ("resembling," "half-submerged," "as if," "suggesting," "looked solid," "as of," "as though"); and the opening paragraph concludes with the captain watching the one sign of humanity, "the tug steaming right into the land," disappear "as though the impassive earth had swallowed her up."[57] The fusion of earth, sea and land, the "monotonous sweep of the horizon," creates an eerie state of becoming, especially when observed in the "immense stillness" that so often underlies Conrad's descriptions of implacable nature. Though in a world of idyllic beauty, the newly appointed captain senses his estrangement from it. A spectator in an ironic paradise, he rests his hand on the ship's rail "as if on the shoulder of a trusted friend," but his communion with the ship is "gone for good" when he senses the indifferent "multitude of celestial bodies staring down." Locked in an indifferent garden, he suffers the most dreaded of romantic ills—stasis.

Having not yet eaten of the tree of self-knowledge, the captain lacks the ability to act freely or self-consciously. His momentary innocence is indeed spurious, depending as it does on an externally rather than existentially earned morality. Like Christabel, he is innocent only because he has not been tested, because, he confesses, "If all the truth must be told, I was somewhat a stranger to myself." His false captaincy impinges upon forces outside the self—a "consequence of certain events of no particular interest," an apparently admirable record at Conway, and, by implication, the assistance of influential people. In short, he bears the name "captain" but has not yet proved himself worthy of it. A stranger in paradise who has laid false claim to his title, he is, to use Martin Buber's phrase, "the matter to be transformed." Paradoxically, his salvation from stasis can come only by a fall, only by shattering the innocence that enslaves him and renders him spiritually impotent. An Abel embodying the values of the accepted social mores, the captain needs his Cain to free him and restore his spiritual powers. In Blake's terms, he must enter into experience, a new state of being, at the cost of his comfortable but arrested existence.

Enter Leggatt, who has been described as good and as evil, a *Doppelgänger*, a Jungian archetype, a Freudian symbol, a homosexual partner, a "legate" of the unconscious self. He has been condemned as guilty, praised as an existential hero, and excused as only marginally responsible for his crime. To understand him, however, we might see him in terms of the myth of the Fall, for he is the snake, the tempter, who brings the captain to knowledge. It should hardly be surprising to any reader of Conrad that snake imagery appears in the story. References to snakes or to temptation can be found throughout Conrad's works, and they serve a crucial function in novels like *Heart of Darkness* when Marlow begins his narrative by retelling how the "big river" on the map was the snake that had "charmed" him even as a boy. Nor does it do violence to most psychological readings of the story to suggest that Leggatt performs the function of the snake in the Fall myth, for surely Conrad integrates mythic elements with psychological revelations of character. In other words, he changes the "developed story to personal myth" in the captain's reenactment of the events. Leggatt's physical appearance first suggests a snake. The captain describes him in terms reminiscent of the water snakes in "The Rime of the Ancient Mariner":

> But I saw something elongated and pale floating very close to the ladder. Before I could form a guess a faint flash of phosphorescent light, which seemed to issue suddenly from the naked body of a man, flickered in the sleeping water with the elusive, silent play of summer lightning in a night sky. With a gasp I saw revealed to my stare a pair of feet, the long legs, a broad livid back immersed right up to the neck in a greenish cadaverous glow. . . . He was complete but for the head. A headless corpse! (P. 97)

He later speaks of Leggatt as "ghastly, silvery, fishlike." And as if to reinforce the snake image, and also to establish the close relationship between himself and Leggatt, the captain remembers dropping his cigar and hearing "a short hiss quite audible in the absolute stillness of all things under heaven." From the beginning this demonic force is not an intruder in the garden so much as a part of the captain.

The often-repeated idea that Leggatt is a mirror-image, the captain's double, is given new meaning when seen within the context of the romantic concept of the Fall; when the captain looks down into the water, Leggatt's face is in the captain's words, "upturned exactly under mine." The snake is the embodiment of the other self, the antithesis who catalyzes the captain into action. In Blake's language he is the "contrary," without whom there is "no progression." It may be said of him what Eugene O'Neill said of Mephistopheles in "Memoranda on Masks"—"is not the whole of Goethe's truth *for our time* that Mephistopheles and Faust are one and the same—*are* Faust?"

In *Conrad's Romanticism* David Thorburn relates the communion between Leggatt and the captain to the forms of unconscious communion established between characters in several of Wordsworth's poems ("Michael," "The Old Cumberland Beggar," "The Idiot Boy"), and places Leggatt in the tradition of the noble "outcast."[58] But another romantic heritage is more explicit in the text: the Cain figure. As we have noted, in romantic versions of the Fall, Cain assumes significance as "the direct heir to the Fall, an outcast with a sense of living within unreasonable limitations to his freedom."[59] Robert Langbaum further notes, "It is through their crimes that Faust and Cain come to understand the differences between themselves and the devil."[60] In "The Secret Sharer" it is through Leggatt's crime that the captain comes to understand the difference between "good" and "evil." Clearly, Leggatt represents the demonic potential in the captain, the "will to power" which will allow him truly to act as captain even at the risk of destruction. Although Leggatt is not "the ideal of selfhood which the captain must measure up to,"[61] he is nonetheless necessary to the captain's salvation. To understand Leggatt is to understand his potential for violence, but to understand also gives the captain the self-knowledge that allows him to act *consciously* as captain.

We should not overemphasize the idea of Cain as outcast and villain, since in the biblical account Cain also receives God's forgiveness. In idealizing Cain by granting him heroic stature and extending him admiration and pity, the romantic poets were challenging what they considered the conventional idea that Cain was the evil brother, ignoring that in the biblical account God had marked Cain's forehead partly as a sign of forgiveness. Porter Williams, Jr., quite correctly states that we often forget "that the traditional brand upon Cain's forehead was really a mark of God's compassion and not a stigma, except in the sense that a crime had made such a protective mark necessary."[62] The crucial point is that Leggatt is no simple villain. Surely it is wrong to argue either that "Leggatt is indeed a criminal" who fails to earn our respect, or that he is "clearly an exemplary sailor."[63] Furthermore, although we cannot make light of Conrad's letter to John Galsworthy expressing surprise ("I was simply knocked over") that some critic called Leggatt a "murderous ruffian,"[64] neither can we conclude that Conrad dismisses Leggatt's guilt. The narrative characterizes Leggatt as a morally viable creature who makes moral judgments, right or wrong, and who assumes responsibility for his choices and actions.

In many respects Leggatt abides by traditional moral values. His father, like Lord Jim's, is a parson, and he twice repeats "this important fact" in his very first conversation with the captain. His concern for his father and his expression of dismay that "a Conway boy" should have "to own up to" killing a man testify to his moral sensitivity, as does his hesitancy to escape the *Sephora* for fear that "somebody else might have got killed . . . and I did not want any more of that work." Furthermore, his attitude toward the captain and his willingness to go, in his words, only "as long as I know that you understand" make Leggatt an ambiguous criminal—but a criminal nonetheless. No explanation of why the murder took place can finally wash his hands clean. What, then, does his crime mean? To understand it, the captain must himself eat of the apple, must, in the biblical phrase, "know good and evil" and consciously choose between Leggatt's ambiguous "evil" and the equally ambiguous "good" of the moral code which condemns this Cain.

Leggatt not only bears the mark of Cain but also accepts the condition of his guilt. It is crucial here to differentiate between conscious and unconscious evil, for in a postromantic vision virtue and vice are sometimes "very much alike." On one hand, Leggatt shows little or no sympathy for his victim; on the other hand, he does show concern for his father, for the captain, and for the men who might have been injured or killed had he "bolted" from the *Sephora*. On one hand, he cannot imagine "coming back to explain such things to an old fellow in a wig and twelve respectable tradesmen"; on the other hand, he does *not* claim innocence and indeed accepts the judgment that he must "go off wandering on the face of the earth." He stops here, calling his sentence "price enough to pay for an Abel *of that sort*" (p. 107, emphasis added). That is, although he tries to explain the unconscious nature of his act and to measure it against his victim's unworthiness, he never really denies guilt. So also, when he objects to being judged in a court of law, he does *not* argue his innocence but rather contends that no jury can rightfully judge him—"What can they know whether I am guilty or not—or of *what* I am guilty, either? That's my affair." Like all romantic rebels, Leggatt lays claim to his own destiny. The only judge that matters is the self. To say this is neither to claim innocence nor to escape judgment. The Fall is at once an act of freedom and an act of self-judgment.

But perhaps too much emphasis has been put on Leggatt as romantic rebel, and too little critical commentary has been devoted to Captain Archbold. Only a few critics have defended Archbold, and they have overstated his case. J. D. O'Hara, for example, goes so far as to call Archbold "the moral center of the story,"[65] a reading which has the effect of totally exonerating Archbold and totally ignoring the dual demands placed upon the captain-narrator. In treating the dual morality of the story, J. L. Simmons defines two competing claims made upon the captain, a ship morality that offers "the clear-cut line of action" and a "land morality" represented by Captain Archbold. He defines Archbold as "a miserable failure" who cannot act "in the moment of crisis" because he is "too committed to the land," too enslaved by the passivity and obscurity of "the land morality."[66] By every definition Archbold's innocence impinges upon subservience to the external morality by which he is characterized. He stands as the total Apollonian symbol, the representative of the traditional, orthodox values embodied in the law, in the social-moral code and, given his wife's presence on board the *Sephora*, even in the family.

Translated into terms of the Fall, Archbold is "that sort" of Abel who cannot commit a saving sin and who, confronting the fact that he has been saved by Leggatt's crime, struggles to retain his innocence. He holds to his record of "virtuous command" as testimony of his righteousness. He exists in Blake's mythological Ulro. Nonetheless, he offers a choice to the captain. The climax of the action comes when the captain must decide either to preserve his specious innocence by acknowledging Archbold's legitimacy or to fall and lose his own innocence by consciously protecting Leggatt. To fall or not to fall becomes the equivalent of the ultimate question.

When he meets Archbold, the captain is no longer ignorant of the ambiguity of good and evil. Like Marlow in his encounter with Kurtz, the captain has already been "fascinated by the abominable." And just as Marlow must somehow judge Kurtz for himself, so must the captain accept Leggatt's "moral victory" and bear responsibility for him. To this point, however, he has tried to preserve his innocence while drawing sustenance from Leggatt's illicit spiritual powers. Now he must stand on his own. His encounter with Archbold is as much a psychological conflict as a moral one, for the captain competes more against himself than the captain of the *Sephora*. The Abel he confronts is as much a potential image of himself as is his Cain.

In large measure the antagonist in the Archbold episode is the frightening uncertainty that openly assaults the captain. The very fact that Archbold's moral position is absolute and readily discernible makes Leggatt's counterclaims all the more subjective and absurd. The captain must weigh an explicit moral obligation against a sort of dream-awareness, a subjective truth. His state of mind is best characterized by Marlow in *Heart of Darkness*—"impalpable grayness, with nothing underfoot . . . a sickly atmosphere of tepid scepticism, without much belief in your own right and even less in that of your adversary."[67] The captain can offer no rational explanation for harboring a fugitive; his protection of Leggatt runs counter to every logical claim made upon him by Archbold, his own crew, and the law. Though "dull" and "incomprehensible," Archbold threatens him spiritually with his moral absolutism as much as Koh-ring later endangers his life. He is a physical presence who ironically assumes the absurdity of a dream, whereas Leggatt becomes a subjective presence who surfaces as reality. In the midst of the conversation, the captain realizes that "it was the other [Leggatt]" he saw. As a result of his experience with "the stranger," the captain coexists in two worlds and with two selves. He dances on the edge of the abyss.

In the first part of the story, Leggatt the criminal becomes an increasingly moral force. In the Archbold scene the supposed moral figure becomes a criminal. The narrator sees Archbold's "guiltily conscientious manner" as that "of a criminal making a reluctant and doleful confession." Particularly as presented in the captain-narrator's sarcastic childlike paraphrases and cynical, clipped commentary, Archbold's morality becomes more comically absurd than meaningful. Yet, ironically, Archbold's very simplicity makes him a "tenacious beast." Furthermore, the captain's insistence that Archbold "had to look" in all the rooms and his acknowledgment that he could not "have met him by a direct lie . . . for psychological (not moral) reasons" indicate that he undergoes no simple test. And even more, the scene reflects the captain's unspoken, cowardly desire that Leggatt might be found and so free him from having to choose for himself whether or not to save his "secret sharer." Everywhere the Archbold passage exposes the nearly frenetic desperation of the captain, who comes perilously close to revealing the truth. He protects himself by feigning deafness and by bold, dangerous actions. But while he "plays the game" to put Archbold off guard and to enact a sort of revenge on him, he also half-invites discovery.

However slightly, he survives Archbold's threats; and because he does not expose Leggatt, he must assume full responsibility for him. When Leggatt later asks him if he "truly" understands, he must admit that he does, that he has already gained the knowledge of good and evil that Leggatt has brought him. Consequently, he must side with Leggatt, even though he fears that he himself might bear the taint of Leggatt's crime. When J. D. O'Hara suggests that it is Archbold, not the captain, who "has fully accepted his moral position as captain,"[68] he ignores the romantic vision of Conrad's work. The primary obligation is always to the self, and Archbold totally ignores self-knowledge by avoiding every suggestion of guilt or responsibility. On the other hand, the captain must accept his Cain-like brother, despite his violent act against him. For indeed Leggatt *has* killed the captain's fraudulent self. Although the captain is not a Cain but an Abel who necessarily represents the law, he must consciously choose his brotherhood with Cain. Symbolically, he must slay the spurious Appollonian self in the guise of his brother captain and thereby accept "the mark of Cain." In a sense he commits an act of self-annihilation and reenacts Leggatt's "suicide."

Albert Guerard calls the relationship between the captain and Leggatt "Jungian." He points out that "integration of personality cannot occur until the unconscious has been known, trafficked with, and in some sense liberated."[69] Such a reading mirrors the romantic version of the Fall—the tempter becomes the Jungian undiscovered self who releases the "will to power" in the protagonist by liberating the self from a stagnant garden existence and a false identify. The resolution of "The Secret Sharer" depicts the consequences of such a fortunate fall.

Quite simply, Leggatt defines the primary consequence—"It would never do for me to come to life again." Because he "truly" understands, the captain realizes that it would be "a sort of cowardice" to keep Leggatt on board his ship. Living in secret with Leggatt is "very much like being mad, only . . . worse because one [is] aware of it." So long as the fugitive remains, the captain not only endangers himself externally by risking discovery, but more importantly he endangers himself existentially by continuing a parasitic dependence on his double and by courting the madness that results from the total inversion of reality. The price of the Fall is always death, and when the captain "frees" Leggatt at Koh-ring, he not only physically confronts "the very gate of Erebus," but also symbolically kills off and buries his false, but safe, self. By the same token, as several critics have noted, the captain exorcises the criminal in himself. "It would never do" for the captain to kill someone in enacting the "will to power" that Leggatt has released in him.

But the end of the Fall also includes the paradox that, though doomed to mortality, man also now assumes the role of creator—he becomes in Coleridge's words the finite "I AM" who must now take charge of his own life and destiny. Significantly, the captain does become the active, Leggatt the passive, actor at the end of the story. He even mimics Leggatt's crime when, on the brink of disaster, he unconsciously fails to let go of his mate's hand and continues shaking it as he issues his orders to save the ship. He acts consciously, however, and by choice, when he charts the course for Koh-ring; he is willing to run the risk, to confront the fear of death and the fear of becoming the criminal. The often-discussed hat that he gives Leggatt to protect "his mere flesh" allows him to save his ship. Porter Williams, Jr., implies that Leggatt, in his role as Cain, intentionally leaves the hat to free the captain from all obligations to him—"This new Cain sacrifices a kind of 'saving mark' on his forehead in order to protect another from perils of 'ignorance' and 'strangeness.' "[70] If so, he plays a romantic rebel who saves the captain only after having first destroyed his innocence. For there is no salvation without a Fall—"Without Contraries is no progression."

Like Conrad's short story, many modern works embody the theme of the Fall as interpreted by William Blake and envisaged by Byron, Coleridge, Shelley, and various postromantic writers throughout the nineteenth century. In discussing the inheritance of ideas in modern literature, I am not arguing direct influence so much as affinity. For in very real ways, artists since the Enlightenment have continued to describe a common spiritual plight. Though emphasizing given aspects in various degrees and from different perspectives, they all portray certain basic elements of the pattern: a garden emblematic of a state of innocence, a serpent figure projecting unacknowledged "illicit" desire, an essential duality suggestive of the tree of good and evil, the nakedness of conscious awareness, and the ambiguous consequences of a completed action. By examining the inheritance of ideas under five subcategories of the Fall, the following essays exemplify this commonality of thought and pattern and yet illustrate something of the "varieties of religious experience" symptomatic of the modern age.

‡ 3 ‡

Childhood's End

Two conflicting attitudes toward children developed in the nineteenth century. In the essentially romantic conception, childhood is a blessed, if transitory, state. For Blake, as for Wordsworth, children rest secure in "Abraham's bosom" from what the adult world of fallen humanity may inflict upon them. Not until the rise of consciousness, most often associated with puberty, can this innocence be imperiled. The more fundamentalist evangelical tradition presents an opposing interpretation. It suggests that children left to their own feeble devices fall easy prey to Satan's wiles. Furthermore, in this view, children reflect the influence of original sin and must be protected and repressed lest they manifest their own diabolic powers. These contradictory viewpoints have given rise to any number of works about children and the Fall in modern literature, two of which are Henry James's *The Turn of the Screw* and William Golding's *Lord of the Flies*.

James's novel invites us to wonder if children are by nature protected from evil or if they can even choose not to fall when attacked by demonic beings struggling from within and without to possess their souls. *The Turn of the Screw* portrays the ambiguous state of childhood innocence as seen not only in the two children Miles and Flora but in their youthful governess as well. As the pastoral paradise of Bly changes to the dead of winter, we know beyond doubt that a fall has occurred, but we are left to ponder exactly whose fall it is. On the other hand, Golding's novel compels us to acknowledge unequivocally the potential for evil in the precarious Eden of childhood. His marooned schoolboys leave no doubt whatsoever that the inheritance of the Fall is the unavoidable consequence of human history. Whereas James makes us question the source of evil by exploring the deepest recesses of the psyche, Golding defines an elemental barbarity beneath the thin veneer of boyish innocence. The evil on the idyllic island comes from nowhere but the boys themselves. In both works we perceive unfortunate falls, unfortunate at least in the devastation of childhood innocence they seem ironically to portray.

The Turn of the Screw by Henry James

Goodness is not enough; goodness is never enough."
—Robert Heinlein, *Stranger in a Strange Land*

When a writer of such refined and conscious artistry as Henry James calls one of his own stories "a shameless potboiler," you can be certain that critics far and wide will rush to his defense.[1] They have. James's provocative short novel had by 1965 inspired 270 studies, the vast majority of which deny any acceptance whatever of James's claim to have produced "merely a piece of ingenuity pure and simple . . . an *amusette* to catch those not easily caught."[2] Since 1965, of course, the cascade of criticism has scarcely abated, fit tribute both to James's craftsmanship and, perhaps more, to his mythic sense of the ambiguous nature of good and evil. Simply put, this intriguing story of a lone governess's battle against evil beings that she is convinced are seeking to possess her two young charges raises the essential question of where the evil truly originates, in the supposed demonic spirits of Peter Quint and Miss Jessel or in the sexually repressed psyche of the governess herself. Whether one sides with those who accept the apparitions as real beings out to corrupt the children or with those who trace the evil to the governess's sexual frustration and neurosis, the fact remains that, whatever its source, evil exists. Someone has fallen—the children by demonic possession and/or the governess because of mental imbalance. In the final analysis, it scarcely matters which. Furthermore, in the light of numerous convincing studies on all sides of the critical debate,[3] it may be that the ambiguity not only cannot but should not be resolved. The loss of innocence occurs both for the children *and* the governess, it seems, and the action describes in both the ominous passage from Edenic ignorance to experiential knowledge.

The plot is deceptively simple. The twenty-year-old daughter of an "eccentric" rural pastor in Hampshire is engaged by a handsome and mysterious London bachelor to become governess to his nephew and niece, his wards in consequence of his brother's death. Commanding her "but never, never"[4] to bother him with events going on at Bly, the rural estate where he sends her to discharge her duties, he abruptly disappears from the tale. Arriving at Bly, the somewhat apprehensive governess meets Mrs. Grose, housekeeper of long standing, and the children, twelve-year-old Miles and eight-year-old Flora, who charm her despite her concern in learning that Miles, for some undisclosed reason, will not be permitted to return to his school. Alone late one June afternoon, she sees the ghost of Peter Quint, the master's former valet apparently killed when he fell drunk from a horse, standing atop one of the twin towers of the house. Soon after this, the governess sees him again, once at the dining-room window and once on the stairs in the house itself, and also confronts Miss Jessel, her infamous predecessor dead from unknown causes. Convinced that the "ghosts" seek possession of Miles and Flora, the governess struggles with the demonic spirits for the souls of the children. She turns to Mrs. Grose as confidante and tries desperately to convince her that the evil beings do exist, even in light of the children's supposed innocence and denial.

Finally, after a number of key conversations and stratagems, the harassed heroine finds Flora with Miss Jessel at the lake near the house. At first a disbeliever because she cannot see the apparition at the lake when the governess attempts to point it out, Mrs. Grose comes to accept the reality of the spirits and escapes from Bly with Flora in an effort to save her, while the governess remains to try one last time to dispossess Miles. In a masterfully constructed scene, the boy and the governess eat alone in the adult dining-room, carrying on a marvelously ambiguous dialogue. The scene rushes to a conclusion when the governess sees Quint at the window for the second time since her arrival. Pressing Miles against her, she cries, "No more, no more, no more!" In response, the boy asks, "Is she *here?*" an obvious reference to Miss Jessel. "It's not Miss Jessel!" his guardian replies, "But it's at the window—straight before me. It's *there*—the coward horror for the last time." When Miles asks, "It's *he?*" the governess demands total acknowledgment, a saving confession that she believes will redeem the boy—and her: "Whom do you mean by 'he'?" Miles cries out enigmatically, "Peter Quint—you devil!" Not quite satisfied by her seeming triumph, the governess drives him to face "the beast"—"for the demonstration of my work." The boy jerks around, utters "the cry of a creature hurled over an abyss," and dies.

Not often in literature does so much allegory and myth coexist with so much psychological detail. It is well-nigh impossible to avoid the Freudian implications in James's story, the sexual symbolism of corridors, chambers, the tower, the stairs, the lake, the window. Add to these such blatant occurrences as Flora's playing with "a small flat piece of wood which happened to have a little hole that evidently suggested to her the idea of sticking in another fragment" (p. 30), and we have a Freudian's delight. Sexual allusions underlie every key encounter, especially those between Miles and the governess; and perhaps more than a figurative climax takes place at the end just after the governess "whimsically" describes herself and Miles "as some young couple who, on their wedding-journey, at the inn, feel shy in the presence of the waiter" (p. 81). Trace the sexual innuendoes in the dialogue, and observe the governess's constant romanticizing and daydreaming, add her physical aggressiveness with Miles in particular, and the psychosexual interpretation seems incontestable.

One need not assume that James's novella is nothing more than an imaginative psychological portrayal, however. The so-called "apparitionist" critics note that James goes out of his way in the prologue to allow Douglas, who introduces the tale, and the outside narrator, the "I" of the prologue, to attest in some measure to the authority of the governess's point of view in the manuscript she provides. Though we cannot discount the governess's own candid admissions of naiveté and susceptibility during the time the events took place, she would seem to have had no reason for subterfuge or self-justification in writing her account. As for the narrative itself, we find numerous elements that Freudian interpretations apparently cannot accommodate. Critics have pointed out the extensive mythic features in the work. For some readers, Mrs. Grose's credulity gives even more convincing evidence that the ghosts exist.[5]

We can only resolve the issue by accepting both the psychological *and* the metaphysical dimensions of the story.[6] Both describe a fall. The governess's fall occurs quite apart from the children's, though it results from her very attempt to redeem them from their fall. Because hers is the central consciousness of the narrative, we need to speak first about both the governess's ability to "see" the evil creatures that seemingly haunt Bly and her inability to see the evil in herself. The truth, as it were, lies both within and outside the self. The evil, in good romantic fashion, is both what she "half-receives" and "half-creates."

Bly is Eden.[7] Viewed allegorically as the biblical paradise or psychologically as a stage of childlike self-ignorance, it represents a world of arrested becoming. We learn both from Douglas and from the governess herself that she is, like the captain in "The Secret Sharer," "somewhat a stranger to" herself when she arrives at her Eden. An uninitiated Eve, like Christabel, she unwittingly has assumed responsibility for the care and protection of the idyllic garden. As daughter to a rural preacher, she has been well instructed by the repressive morality of Victorian puritanism to find evil in the world, but she is ill-equipped to find it in herself. Like Christabel, she lacks the knowledge of self that alone can assure moral wholeness; like Beatrice Cenci, she falls prey to an incriminating innocence. She falls when she meets the serpent in paradise in the "plump" twilight of "a long June day."

By means of the governess's own narrative, James draws her, and us, carefully to the moment. The language of hyperbole reflects the heroine's naiveté upon her arrival at Bly. "The scene had a greatness" about it, she tells us, and the little girl was "a creature too charming not to make it a great fortune not to do with her. She was the most beautiful child I have ever seen" (p. 7). Later, when she meets Miles at the coach stop, she finds him "in the great glow of freshness, the same positive fragrance of purity, in which I had from the first moment seen his little sister. He was incredibly beautiful" (p. 13). Despite the unexplained note indicating that Miles would not be allowed to return to school, she thinks him "something divine"—"It would have been impossible to carry a bad name with a greater sweetness of innocence" (p. 13). Wondering if she has entered "a story-book over which [she] had fallen a-doze and a-dream," she had found herself marking "the beginning of a curiosity" when she yearned to see Miles for the first time and dispel what doubts she might have had. Now assured, she fears only her "ignorance" in dealing with a boy "whose education for the world was all on the point of beginning" (p. 14).[8] Like Miles, despite her eight years' seniority, she lives on the very threshold of sexual awareness. Her exaggerated language in the first three chapters belies her awakening consciousness. Unwilling and unable to acknowledge her own forbidden desires, she insists all the more on the innocence of her world and of the children to whom her own innocence is inexorably linked. By her own admission, she had been already "carried away," seduced in all but body, by the uncle she now finds reflected in the young "gentleman" she was so curious to see. Now she wanders alone into her pastoral garden of dazzling beauty alive with "all the music of summer and all the mystery of nature"—"O it was a trap . . . to my imagination, to my delicacy, perhaps to my vanity" (p. 14).

Chapter 3, when the governess first meets Quint, develops from a firmly established psychological motivation. Walking in the fading sunlight among "old trees" and daydreaming about the uncle, she fancies herself "a remarkable young woman," and wishes only "that he should *know*" of her virtuous strength, "appear there at the turn of a path . . . and smile and approve." Emerging from the reverie, she sees Quint on top of one of the twin towers, of which Flora had given her a tour just that morning. Assuredly, she has willed him into existence, for even she herself assumes at first that her dream of the uncle "had, in a flash, turned real." She quickly describes him as an opposite, though. Recalling that "it was not at such an elevation that the figure I had so often invoked seemed most in place," she instinctively seeks dissociation from this dark double of the London bachelor, chastened by her conscious fancy. Calling the vision the image of one "I had not seen . . . in Hartly Street," she hunts for refuge in the garden. But the snake has undoubtedly arisen from the deepest level of her unconscious mind and penetrated the garden of innocence.

James undergirds the scene with imagery of passage or initiation that marks the governess's fall: the movement from the morning tour of the tower with "little Flora" (morning and child both depicting innocence) to the return alone at twilight and subsequent return to the house "when . . . darkness had quite closed in"—the transformation of the uncle "at the turn of a path" in her daydream into "an unknown man" envisioned on a surely phallic tower in the coming darkness. The whole scene captures the transition from morning-Flora-innocence-uncle-life to twilight-Quint-experience-"unknown man"-death. In keeping with the pattern of the fall, James explicitly states through the governess's words that "the scene had been stricken with death." In the chapter's concluding paragraph, the house is symbolic of the governess's psychic drama. The governess refers to "there having been in the house—and for how long above all?—a person of whom I was in ignorance." Now fully exposed, the haunting shadow of her unconscious self manifests itself with "a touch of freedom . . . in the sign of familiarity of his wearing no hat." Having "fixed" her while standing "very erect," the figure gradually "turned away," the violation now consummated. The very last clause caps the whole of the action—"That was all I *knew*" (emphasis added).

Having *known* Quint in the psychosexual sense, the governess does live in a world "stricken with death." The serpent-animus has entered the chapel, as Blake describes it in "I saw a chapel all of gold," and she cannot deny its existence, only her association with it; yet she speaks ironically "of the visitor with whom I had been so inexplicably and yet . . . so intimately concerned" (p. 18). Chapter 4 treats the "confusion of curiosity and dread" that comes in consequence of the Fall. Though aware that the line between good and evil has been somehow breached, the governess is unable to admit to her own duality. She does not understand that it is she herself that she fears. Rather than confront "the beast," she tries to evade self-knowledge by transferring her own self-doubt to a communal dread. She shifts from singular to plural first person, from "*my* real beginning of fear" to communal fear: "*We* have been collectively subject to an intrusion" (p. 18, emphasis added). Absolving herself from any personal relationship, she trusts "that *we* should surely see no more of him." With considerable irony she escapes to the children as she seeks to maintain her own childlike innocence, but something has irrevocably changed. Paradoxically, her fall has animated her being, saved her from the "grey prose" she sensed unwittingly she might suffer in her position at Bly. Challenged by her own fears, she clings all the more tenaciously to "the romance of the nursery and the poetry of the schoolroom" (p. 19). However ironically, she moves from stasis to action.

In the days immediately following her fall, the governess vainly tries to return to her prelapsarian world, where she serves so nobly as keeper of the distant God's garden. But the necessity for innocence has become an absolute, and she must in every measure be assured of her own virtue. She eludes the possibility of her own guilt by placing her innocence alongside Miles's, to whom her destiny is most firmly bound. It is psychologically necessary for her to believe in his innocence because he is the visible form of the uncle. She must therefore expunge the mysterious crime he supposedly committed at school, for to admit to his guilt would be to admit to the uncle's satanic power and hence to her own guilt: "If he had been wicked he would have 'caught' it, and I should have felt the wound and the dishonour" (p. 19). Finally, though, Miles cannot act as her surrogate innocent self, for he also represents the illicit lover of her dreams. The impermanence of her fragile design to reconcile the opposites is implied when the governess receives "disturbing letters from home, where things were not going well" with her "eccentric" father. This brief reference illuminates what has already occurred in the passage from innocence to experience: as the forbidden god-lover of her dreams replaces the god-father of her innocence, her prelapsarian garden collapses. She cannot avert the effects of her fall. As the second encounter with Quint indicates, knowledge might be perverted, but it can never be ignored.

This time the governess sees Quint on Sunday evening at the window in "that cold clean temple of mahagony and brass, the 'grown up' dining-room." She once more meets him "as the day declines" and again sees him only "from the waist up." Even more overtly than before, Quint takes on the guise of the master, whose clothes this "remarkably handsome" ghost wears. Critics have long debated whether or not we have an allegorical description of the devil (red hair, arched eyebrows, eyes "sharp, strange—awfully," thin lips—"looking like an actor") or a creation of the governess's agitated psyche. At this point we know one thing for certain: the governess sees him *after* a fall. She had returned alone to reclaim her just-repaired gloves, perhaps a symbol of her damaged purity. This time, she confesses that "it was as if I had . . . known him always." Unable to elude the reality of the "evil," she more than ever detaches herself: "He had to come for some one else." But James closes the chapter with a clear revelation of the governess's undeniable relationship with Quint. She, who has for "the first time" seen herself from "head to foot" in a long mirror at Bly, now assumes the reflection of the other—"the full image of a repetition," just as at times Miss Jessel suggests a "shadowy portion of her personality."[9] Going to the window where Quint stood, she "applied [her] face to the pane and looked,as he had looked, into the room." Like Geraldine, Christabel, Beatrice Cenci and the captain, the governess *becomes* the other self; and like the heroines we have discussed, she washes her hands of guilt. If she cannot acknowledge him to be the forbidden lover of her dreams, the Dionysian rapist of her Apollonian purity, then indeed, "He *had* to come for someone else."

David Mogen has said that "the source of villainy in the tale is not to be found in the governess, or even in the ghosts that haunt her and the children. It is embodied in the mythology of 'innocence' itself."[10] He implies that innocence can be criminal if it takes on the character of moral absolutism. In Reinhold Niebuhr's definition, evil "is not the absence but the corruption of good."[11] Because she has been brought up in the puritanical belief that good and evil are always discernible opposites, the governess holds firmly to an either-or morality born of self-ignorance. Her fear reflects her own unaccepted guilt. As Blake suggests, guilt is simultaneously a *creation* and a *creator* of evil, the product of the rational, conscious mind. Guilt arises from the governess's unacknowledged sexual awareness and fear of lost innocence. Her mission to preserve her purity after her guilt convicts her makes her the victim of Quint and Miss Jessel as surely as Beatrice's insistence on her innocence makes her prey to her "father's spirit." So long as Quint and Miss Jessel can stand for all the evil at Bly, she can legalize any means of divorcing herself from complicity, just as Beatrice is capable of whatever violence is necessary to absolve herself from guilt. The more the demonic spirits embody her forbidden attraction for the master, the more they must be exorcized at any cost; yet, paradoxically, their presence permits the governess vicariously to participate in their dark sexual intrigue without sacrificing her virtue. Perversely, the governess becomes the evil she expels. In Charles Samuel's words, "The governess's virtue is what turns the screws."[12]

From the time she sees Quint at the window until she finds Miles at midnight staring up at the tower, the governess ostensibly clings to the children's innocence as evidence of her own moral wholeness. "They had nothing but me," she claims, "and I—well I had them." The language of possession punctuates her narrative. Quint, she fears, has been "too free with *my* boy." Feeding her ego in the same sense that Beatrice feeds hers, she offers herself "bravely . . . an expiatory victim and guard." Underlying her "extraordinary flight of heroism" lies a motivation she freely admits after the fact, that "there would be a greatness" in letting her action "be seen—oh, in the right quarter!" An evil in the garb of goodness, her willing martyrdom manifests her fallen state. A Christabel suffering "thoughts that dreams too lively leave behind," she obscures her knowledge of her own good and evil by subtle self-deception. Though hardly a "demonstrable pathological liar . . . with an unhinged fancy,"[13] she nonetheless bears responsibility for part of the evil that consumes Bly—part, but not all.

She loses her first line of defense when the children prove incapable of securing the righteousness she demands; as a result, in the last half of the narrative she inverts their absolute goodness into absolute evil. The "angels" turn into "wretches"; innocent behavior becomes "a policy and a fraud." Projecting her own journey through experience, she "knows" Miles to be the direct conduit to Quint—and so to the master she wills to possess, just as Flora becomes the agent of Miss Jessel, the secret lover buried in her psyche. Parasitically, she draws sustenance from their contact with the demonic powers, for whom she feels both repulsion and attraction. No better evidence exists of her initiation into experience than her changing views of the children, who symbolize her lost innocence.

"Lord, you do change!" Mrs. Grose tells her when the governess accuses the children of deceit at the end of the first half of the tale. Through the governess's point of view we see a transformation of the children, a metamorphosis of age, an accomplished passage into adulthood. Having proved unworthy as witnesses to her innocence, the children become the suffering children of generation in the governess's eyes. Unwilling to admit to her own experience, the guardian accuses them rather than herself of having "known" the evil spirits. In undeniable irony, as the children become older in the governess's vision, they come more to assume the sexual roles implied by the mysterious lovers Quint and Miss Jessel, Miles especially. In the last half of the narration, the governess virtually plays out her sexual fantasy with Miles while at the same time chastening it by carrying on a holy campaign against the evil she partially creates.

Does this then confirm the children's innocence? We have considered only the governess's culpability and perhaps implied too strongly that she is the sole source of evil. Such a reading reduces the sustained ambiguity of James's art and ignores the crucial fact that the evil is received as well as created. We surely need no behavioral psychologist to tell us about the selfishness of the young. But although selfhood is the elemental cause of the Fall as Blake and others describe it, the selfishness of children is something apart, displaying a kind of amorality that belies guilt. At the point of recognition and accountability that position proves untenable, however, and the child-turned-adult must assume full responsibility for moral choice. The aging of Miles and Flora may reflect the governess's jaundiced view, but it by no means can be dismissed, unless we are willing to believe nothing in the governess's account.

The fact is, the children do not remain "fixed" in the action. While there are veiled references to their possible guilt by association with Quint and Miss Jessel, Flora and Miles seem innocent enough in the first part of the story. Initially, particularly if we suspect the governess's motives or naiveté, we have little cause to doubt their motives. As the story unfolds, however, their childish pranks turn more into acts of cunning and hint at something more than childlike innocence. They are becoming adults, with all the import of that term. If the governess falls when she first sees Quint and ironically confirms her knowledge of good and evil when she sees his devilish figure staring into "the adult dining-room," then the children's fall is reflected in their stratagems and behavior. Miles's vocabulary, the obvious sexual innuendoes in his conversations, and his incredible calmness under pressure make it impossible to lay all the blame at the governess's feet. The crucial scenes between Miles and his would-be protector reveal a remarkable duality that James certainly intends. The conversation at the graveyard, the incident with the candle in Miles's bedroom and the dramatic end to the work earn respect not as cleverly executed literary puzzles designed "to catch those not easily caught" but as richly ambiguous revelations of fallen characters. Entering the garden, the governess has given form to the serpent out of her unconscious self, has thereby gained experience and instinctively reached for fig leaves in response; but the Fall concerns not only her but also the children, not only Bly but also the very cosmos itself. The evil is absolute, pervasive, and devastating.

The first of these encounters between the governess and Miles seems ostensibly less ambivalent than the last two, largely I think because James carefully constructs a superstructure of psychological realism in the earlier episodes to make believable the ambiguity he intends at the story's conclusion. Nonetheless, he provides a mythic frame and points to a larger context than the governess's point of view can provide in itself. Like many of the crucial events of the plot, this one occurs on a Sunday. The inhabitants of Bly are going to church, and Miles and the governess walk by themselves a little behind Flora and Mrs. Grose. Their conversation concludes at the church's graveyard on a bright day with a "touch of frost in the autumn air." The dialogue itself seems to be a psychological revelation of the governess rather than a mythic statement—at least at first glance.

The narrator herself tells us that she has in fact acted "like a gaoler" to Miles and Flora and that she "had all but pinned the boy to [her] shawl." She again refers to Miles's adult nature and once more unwittingly relates him to the uncle she dreams about. "Turned out for Sunday by his uncle's tailor," the young master enacts a "grand little air." In the role of Urizenic guardian, the governess fears an Orcean "revolution" on the part of her young charge, a freedom claimed "by right of his sex." Miles tells her he wants to return to school: "You know, my dear, that for a fellow to be with a lady *always*—!" She "tried to laugh," but with the self-consciousness of a fearful adolescent, she "seemed to see in the beautiful face with which he watched [her] how ugly and queer [she] looked" (p. 55). To this point Miles has served as a kind of substitute lover whose age on one hand chastens the sexual impulse the governess feels and on the other hand stimulates it by virtue of his having reached the age of puberty and experienced Quint's influence. When he tells her, therefore, that he must leave Bly—"I am a fellow, don't you see? who's—well getting on"—he endangers the precarious balance. She instinctively puts her hand on his shoulder when he contends that he has been "awfully good." Miles then alludes to the time he and Flora plotted for her to find him standing outside at midnight to prove that he could be "bad." Then, he goes on, he *wanted* her to "think [him]—for a change—bad" because he felt smothered by the obligation of goodness she imposed upon him. Now he tells her that he can show her far worse "evil" if he wishes. By appeal and threat he asks for his freedom from what we might well accept as Urizenic oppression. Though "you know a lot," he tells the keeper of the garden, "I want to see more life!" Trying to keep Miles a child, the governess compares him to Flora, but Miles wants his "own sort." When she appeals to him to remain, he directly assaults her defenses by proposing to write the master. He crosses the Rubicon—in the governess's words, "the whole thing was virtually out between us. . . . Miles had got something out of me." Though still not recognizing the source of her dread, the governess senses that the truth is indeed "out."

Symbolically left sitting "on [her] tomb," her innocence dead, she wills escape from an ambivalence she cannot comprehend. She returns to the house to pack for her departure, and "sinks at the foot of the staircase . . . exactly where, more than a month before . . . [she] had seen the spectre of the most horrible of women" (pp. 58–59). With consummate irony she sees Miss Jessel at her desk in the schoolroom, like a Geraldine laying claim to her soul. Just as in Gothic masterpieces such as Poe's "House of Usher" or James's own "Jolly Corner," the house represents the psyche: the governess enters the house, travels the dark corridors and chambers of her innermost mind and ultimately meets herself in the inner room. The governess relates: "[Miss Jessel] looked at me long enough to appear to say that her right to sit at my table was as good as mine to sit at hers." And the governess adds with unwitting accuracy, "I had the extraordinary chill of feeling that it was I who was the intruder." She meets the secret sharer who has openly usurped her innermost being. Read in such terms, the scene marks her failure to accommodate her own demonic potential. Unlike the captain, she disowns her double—"You terrible miserable woman!" (p. 59).

Yet the scene may also be read as an indictment of Miles, a conviction that grows ever more persuasive as the story continues. Even here, we find his words and actions precociously deceptive. Just as he earlier "bent forward and kissed" the governess when he wanted to repel her inquiries into why he had gone out alone at midnight, so here he manipulates her with sly coyness. Knowingly, he titillates her with "my dear," in which she naively finds "the exact shade of sentiment with which [she] desired to inspire [her] pupils." When she resists his quest for freedom, he puts "his hand into [her] arm"; and when she continues to deny him, he flirtatiously increases "the pressure of his arm." He finally employs blackmail, saying he will get his uncle to come to Bly, and so exploits the governess's fear of failing before the master. His subtle turns of the screw give credence to her claim that he enacts the scene with "consciousness and a plan."

The evidence appears more proportionate in the next major conflict when the governess wanders into Miles's bedroom after "beginning" a letter to the master she has promised Mrs. Grose she would write. The wind, rain and late night hour contribute to her anxiety as she heads for Miles's door, admittedly "impelled to listen for some betrayal of his not being at rest." Whatever the cause of *her* "sullen obsession," whatever *her* culpability, Miles's actions make him far more than a harassed victim. And if the governess possesses unconscious sexual desires, most certainly Miles seems to be playing upon them. In the manner of a seduction he invites her into the room, makes witty conversation and laughs "beautifully." When the governess puts the candle "a short way off," he draws her to his bed extending "his friendly old hand." When she asks what he thinks about when he lies awake in bed, he replies, "What in the world, my dear, but *you?*" Having carefully primed her, he tells her that he thinks about "this queer business of ours. . . . The way you bring me up. And all the rest." If knowledge comes in consequence of a fall, then Miles's knowing exposes his fallen condition whether or not the governess has fallen herself. Throughout the scene we sense the "secret precocity" that the governess describes.

The governess acts with similar ambiguity. Beginning with her watch at the door, her motives are equally suspect. She conceals the letter from school to force Miles to play his hand, pretending innocence: "I thought you wanted to go on as you are." He tells her he wants to leave and that she should understand why: "Oh *you* know what a boy wants!" Knowing full well that she is being deceitful (euphemistically saying that she "took temporary refuge"), she asks, "You want to go to your uncle?" She holds her trump card, the undisclosed letter, until, by withholding information, she allows Miles to trap himself. When he demands that the uncle come to Bly so that she will have to confess about the way she has "let it all drop," she threatens him as well by alluding indirectly to the note—"He can't send you back." A rush of emotion ends the encounter. She embraces him, kisses him, cajoles him into confessing, and at last drops on her knees beside his bed "to seize once more the chance of possessing him." No wonder the boy finally shrieks, contend the critics who find the governess neurotic or insane; the emotionally distraught woman has driven him over the edge. But it is hard to believe that he is driven to hysteria when we observe his remarkable control. When she first embraces him and cries, "Dear Miles, little Miles, dear little Miles—!" and kisses his face, he reacts with "indulgent good humor"—"Well, old lady?" We need not attribute even his shriek to hysteria; it might as well have been an effective device for arresting her relentless effort to get him to confess what happened at school. When the governess cries that the candle is out, he replies with total aplomb, "It was I who blew it, dear!" The "dear" dangling at the end of the sentence makes it all but impossible to accept that he responds in some kind of frenzy to the governess's emotional assault.

Perhaps the fault lies with both. Here and throughout the action is imbued with an aura of evil that is created by and surrounds the principal characters. We are unable to dismiss the sense of the supernatural any more than we can ascribe the dominant "evil" to any character. The eerie Gothic mood of the wind-blown night implies a more than psychological meaning. We wonder how Miles could have blown out the candle when the governess placed it "designedly, a short way off," and how to account for the "gust of frozen air" when the windows are still tight and the curtains still. We cannot totally disbelieve the narrative even if we doubt the narrator's motives. We are therefore left with an atmosphere of evil, a whole world where "summer had turned, the summer had gone; the autumn had dropped . . . and had blown out half [their] lights. The place . . . was like a theatre after the performance—all strewn with crumpled playbills" (p. 52).

The last chapters draw all the ambiguities into focus. Propelled into action by the crisis of finding Flora at the lake holding "a big ugly spray of withered fern," the two women decide on a plan. Mrs. Grose flees with Flora, and the governess confronts Miles for the last time. Here too, innocence and guilt feed upon each other. We have said that the governess is a Urizenic representative at odds with the Orcean rebel, more specifically a virgin in conflict with her own sexual impulses. Her language confirms this, especially when she refers to "an inward revolution" and, in the latter portion of the action, recalls that "the revolution unmistakenly occurred. I call it a revolution because I now see how . . . the curtain rose on the last act of my dreadful drama and the catastrophe was precipitated" (p. 55). By the last episode there is no doubt that the performance takes place within *and* without the self.

The setting creates a universe in which she stages her last defense against the evil spirit of Quint yearning to invade the sanctity of the house—that is, both the estate at Bly and the governess's own soul. The adult dining-room symbolizes that last stay against chaos, at once the very threshold to fearful consummation (where a young couple dine on their wedding night) and yet an enclosed space tenuously protected by the "frames and squares of the great window." The description given us of Miles's condition in chapter 23 suggests that he is psychologically vulnerable as much to the terror the governess may inflict upon him as he is to demonic possession. The following abbreviated passages imply just how susceptible he is: "He had been anxious all day"—"He, on his side, more and more visibly nervous, had a tone to master"—"[the governess] could catch the first little quiver of resentful passion"—"He looked round him uneasily; . . . the very first sympton [she] had seen in him of the approach of immediate fear"—"He had picked up his hat . . . and stood twirling it." To the governess these are the signs of his desperation at not being able to contact Quint; to many readers they are indications of his fear of the governess herself.

Chapter 24 intensifies rather than reduces the ambiguity. The effect on Miles is unquestionable; only its cause remains uncertain. No one can doubt that the governess "possesses" Miles, only what the possession means: "I sprang up . . . drawing him close"—"I enfolded, I drew him close"—"My hands . . . shook him"—"That moment made *me*, with a single bound and an irrepressible cry, spring straight upon him"—"I tried to press him against me" and, finally, "The grasp with which I recovered him might have been that of catching him in his fall. I caught him, yes, I held him—it may be imagined with what a passion." A consummation one way or the other, the ending moves to finality if not to certainty. Are the "unspeakable anxiety" and "convulsed supplication" of Miles the proofs needed to vindicate the governess—or do they convict her of a crime? He confesses, but to what? He opened the letter, but what does the governess really admit to when she says it contained "nothing"? When she at last divulges that she knows "everything" except exactly what Miles did to earn expulsion from school, she draws his admission: "I said things" to "those I liked." But we are still left with her question, "What *were* those things?" His possible reply is suddenly arrested by the reappearance of "the hideous author of our woe"—is it a subterfuge on the part of the governess, we wonder, or the act of a devil? Ultimately, we must repeat the governess's own words when she says of Miles, "If he *were* innocent what then on earth was I?" Executioner or savior? If neither, both?

Perhaps we have here the study of the simultaneous fall of *two* children. At the beginning the governess is in the world but hardly of it. She has not gained experience despite her age. The other "child" (Miles/Flora) has supposedly already engaged the dark forces of the psyche before the action begins. What happens? Does the governess's unconscious desire surface in the garden and in fact become the means whereby the ghost regains form and substance? Whatever his origin, from within or without, Quint, like Miss Jessel, catalyzes the action by compelling the governess to, in her most emphatic word, "*act*." No doubt she *does* defeat the ghostly invaders at Bly when she "dispossesses" Miles, even at the cost of his life. But can we say that she has defeated her own ghosts? Or does she like Blake's Thel flee again into "the vales of Har"?

It is impossible to disagree with Eric Voegelin's contention that "Henry James could be fascinated by Edenic existence, but he knew that it was the hell of living death." He "was as unable to castigate evil as he was to affirm virtue."[14] In this he shares the perception of his romantic predecessors, who knew very well that the garden inevitably leads to closure and closure to a hell of one's own making. Children together, the governess and Miles/Flora undergo the ritual of becoming. Though acting in defense of goodness, the governess cannot preserve her own innocence. To defeat evil she must somehow know it, and knowing it she must attest to her own duality. In the ultimate paradox, she cannot gain her innocence without first losing it. Whether or not she has or can regain it remains the intriguing question James leaves us with at the conclusion of the tale.

Lord of the Flies by William Golding

I could perhaps reproduce the tragedy of my childhood. . . . It would begin on a completely idyllic, patriarchal note so that no one suspected anything until suddenly the word sounded which translated everything into terror.

—Søren Kierkegaard, *Journals*

The seriousness of William Golding's art stems from his preoccupation with man as fallen creature and with the function of the artist to reproduce in his work that most basic of myths. For this reason, Golding has been accused of writing trite allegories, or, in more positive terms, called an author of fables. Golding himself remarked in an interview that "myth is a much profounder and more significant thing than a fable. I do feel a fable as being an invented thing on the surface whereas myth is something which comes out from the roots of things in the ancient sense of being the key to existence, the whole meaning of life and experience as a whole."[15] Critics who consider Golding's stories too paradigmatic may well be duped by the surface form of his art into reducing it to less than it is. "Though Golding is a moralist," Samuel Hynes comments, "he is not a moral maker, and his novels belong not with Aesop's fables, but with the important symbolic novels of the century—with Camus's and Kafka's."[16]

There is no doubt that Golding's essential theme is man's loss of innocence. Whether from the point of view of Lok and Fa, the Neanderthal Adam and Eve evolving from a prelapsarian Eden in Golding's *The Inheritors*, or Sammy Mountjoy, descended from "Paradise

Hill . . . right in the heart of the Garden of Eden" in his *Free Fall*, or Pincher Martin, posthumously unraveling the history of his criminality, Golding presents as "mythological reenactments . . . the modern equivalent of the archetypal stories in Genesis."[17] And if he seems decidedly unromantic in his attitude toward original sin or deterministic nature or human limitation, it is perhaps because some have tended historically to reduce romanticism to an optimism never long sustained by those to whom we apply the term "romantic." In fact, the idea of the noble savage, the beneficence of nature, the perfectibility of man, the transcendence of the human spirit were seldom accepted without major qualification by romantic writers. It is largely from the tradition of romantic subjectivism, after all, that we receive the impetus toward psychological realism that has so diminished our confidence in man's ability or freedom. Recent scholarship has stressed the relationship between the modern temperament and the romantic sensibility expressed in major works of the late eighteenth century. The popularity of the demonic child in current literature and film, like the concomitant popularity of occultism and violence in general, is not so much a reaction against romanticism as a vulgarization of it. As recent cultural historians have shown us, the despair, anxiety, reductionism, and uncertainty of modern times constitute an extended form of romanticism, a logical progression of the theological and philosophical shift of the romantic period. Golding presents a deeply disturbing view of the Fall, and in particular a frightening portrayal of children in *Lord of the Flies*, which may seem the reverse of romantic sentiment, but in profoundly ironic ways each of his awesome children is no less than Wordsworth's "father of the man." The self still remains the center of values, but in our thorough exploration of the shadowy caverns of the mind we have found the Children of Darkness to be as real as the Children of Light.

Most certainly a version of the Fall, *Lord of the Flies* contains none of the ambiguity, though much of the uncertainty, of *The Turn of the Screw*. We can have no doubt that the children not only are possessed by evil but also bear responsibility for it. There are no specters to blame, no outside forces, no satanic god hidden in the cosmos—or on Hartly Street. Peter Green states, "It is a moral axiom of Golding that Man, and Man alone, introduced evil into the world."[18] But Green does not go quite far enough; for, like Blake, Golding finds evil even more deeply ingrained than merely to locate it in the six-to-twelve-year-old boys isolated on an island. The created world is already fallen before they arrive, and not only the "civilized" society of men devastated by atomic warfare but even nature itself. Whereas James weaves the pattern of the Fall subtly, intricately, and ambiguously into his novella, Golding directly introduces his myth in bold strokes from the very first page. Without the hindrance of the psychological complexities associated with James's narrative technique, the omniscient point of view in *Lord of the Flies* transfers us immediately to a world long since doomed. The island on which the English schoolboys have been marooned shows signs of decay even before they can be charged with its violation. Before "the long scar smashed into the jungle," the ground at the shore had been "torn everyplace by the upheavals of fallen trees, scattered with decaying coconuts and palm saplings" (p. 7). At his first appearance we see Ralph, the central character, "clambering heavily" among clasping creepers and watch Piggy emerge scratched by thorns and twigs. The jungle ensnares and rips; the sun oppresses; the fruit causes diarrhea. A false paradise, the island quickly becomes the testing ground for survival rather than an idyllic Eden watched over by a beneficent god.

Nor do we long have any illusions about the innocence of the boys, the literally and symbolically fallen angels. Within the brief span of the first chapter we see Jack Merridew tyrannize the choir boys he dominates as chapter chorister and head boy, "clout" a trunk with his knife, slash the delicate "candle buds" and again "slam" his weapon into a tree. He only hesitates in killing a piglet caught in the creepers "because of the enormity of the knife descending and cutting into flesh; because of the unbearable blood" (p. 27). But he swears to slaughter the creature next time and firmly establishes his authority as head of the hunters.

Despite his apparent role as spokesman for civilization (his father is commander in the navy), Ralph too bears the telltale marks of a fallen character. He treats the wise Piggy with unquestionable cruelty, taunting him before the others by revealing his nickname, mocking his "ass-mar" and half-playfully machine-gunning his fat colleague. His will to power is tacitly expressed when he blows the conch, the supposed symbol of civilization: "His face was dark with the violent pleasure of making this stupendous noise, and his heart was making the stretched shirt shake" (p. 15). Furthermore, Golding describes him in highly suggestive terms. Removing the "snake-clasp of his belt," he removes his clothes and mirrors in his nakedness the green shadows of the trees at the edge of the shore. Piggy watches "Ralph's green and white body enviously" as his snake-like companion swims in the lagoon formed by "some act of God." And after the swim, "All the shadows on Ralph's face were reversed; green above, bright below from the lagoon. A blur of sunlight was crawling across his hair" (p. 12). A multicolored water snake animated by "crawling" sunlight, Ralph's sinister side is far more apparent at first than his civilized nature. At one point, Golding describes Ralph's shadow moving diabolically on the shore. The viewer could see that "a black bat-like creature danced in the sand, and only later perceived the body above it" (p. 16). The dark double envisioned in the shadow dancing in frenzied Dionysian abandon foreshadows even in the last survivor against the forces of darkness the impending power to evil. Like Miles, Ralph is twelve years old, on the brink of a sexual revolution that could well explode viciously later in a juvenile "old enough . . . to have lost the prominent tummy of childhood; and yet not yet old enough for adolescence to have made him awkward" (p. 8).

All the boys take on the characteristics of fallen or nearly fallen creatures. The twins sam-n-eric pant after Ralph "like dogs"; the increasingly sadistic Roger is labeled "the dark boy." When the choir boys first appear they seem "something dark . . . fumbling along. . . . Then the creature stepped from mirage on to the clear sand. . . . The creature was a party of boys" (p. 16). Ironically wearing a soon-discarded "silver cross on the left breast," the creature of darkness is totally controlled by the ominous Jack Merridew. And even the youngest children prove capable of offense. When Piggy suffers embarrassment, "even the tiniest child joined in" the cruel storm of laughter and formed part of "a closed circle of sympathy."

The action as well as the characters quickly sucks us into the heart of darkness. After the group elects Ralph leader, he determines to find out if they have landed on an island. Ralph, Jack, and Simon, the epileptic choir boy who had fainted in the heat, journey to the very borderline of savagery. Their language descends to elemental primitivism:

> "Wacco."
> "Wizard."
> "Smashing." (P. 23)

And again, when they push a rock downhill to delight in its devastation of the land, they respond:

> "Wacco!"
> "Like a bomb!"
> "Whee-aa-oo!" (P. 24)

Their gestures are assertions of power: cutting through the tangled undergrowth, smashing rocks, claiming "the right of dominion." Again, only the near-execution of the piglet marks the limit of their violence: "The pause was only long enough for them to understand what an enormity the downward stroke would be" (p. 27).

Piggy once tells Ralph that he knew a boy who used to blow a conch "and then his mum would come; . . . he had it on his garden wall." By the end of the first chapter we know with absolute certainty that the boys have been abandoned on a sinister paradise where no saving "mum" can secure them from the forces of darkness. Not insignificantly, all the boys have been "gorging on fruit" when they first emerge from the forest along the desolate shore. From the time Ralph calls assembly while sitting on "a dead tree," we see in microcosm and macrocosm the pattern of the Fall.

The unrelenting rhythm of descent is unrelieved in the second chapter when the boys build a fire on the mountain. Like fallen angels in Pandaemonium, they plot their future while Jack continues to challenge the civilizing constraints of Ralph and Piggy, converting the necessity for order into Urizenic terror:

> "We'll have rules!" he cried excitedly. "Lots of rules! Then when anyone breaks 'em—"
> "Whee-oh!"
> "Wacco!"
> "Bong!"
> "Doink!" (P. 29)

A little boy who mysteriously disappears at the end of the chapter asks what they will do about "the snake-thing," "the beastie" that "came in the dark." Offering ineradicable testimony that the Fall has taken place, "the snake-thing," as in other works we have discussed, demands response. Despite his insistence that "there is no beast!" Ralph cannot escape its literal and symbolic presence. It could provide the knowledge that might save the flimsy civilization, but Ralph denies it and Jack vows to "hunt and kill it."

Blinded by childish faith in rescue from some outside agency ("It might be my Daddy's ship"), Ralph confidently points to the queen's "big room full of maps" where she has "got a picture of the island." But, as Melville tells us in *Moby Dick,* "It's not set down in any map; true places never are." Without self-knowledge there is no wisdom and no salvation—and knowledge in itself is indeed a "dangerous thing." When the boys wildly run to start a fire to signal a passing ship, they lack the wisdom to differentiate between the fire as a beacon of civilization and as expression of raw savagery. Ironically, Jack and Ralph share the "shameful knowledge" that having gathered firewood they do not know how to start the fire until Jack snatches Piggy's specs, a symbol of wisdom and yet also "a burning glass," thereby illustrating the duality of knowledge that can light the darkness or produce the atomic explosion alluded to at the beginning of the story. Suggestively, the big fire on the mountain causes small fires down the side of the hill, so that the means of rescue becomes an instrument of potential self-destruction (Golding compounds the irony by having the fires of destruction signal the rescue ship at the conclusion of the novel). As Piggy points out in his wisdom, the huge fire is useless—literally, it generates no smoke; symbolically, it illuminates an inner darkness. And with a depressing accuracy, Golding ends the chapter with Piggy's warning question: "That little 'un that had a mark on his face—where is he now?" (p. 42). The symbol of the lost innocence, the boy who also asked first about the snake disappears amidst the flames as the "littluns" point to the burning creepers and gleefully scream, "Snakes! Snakes! Look at the snakes!"

From here on we see the Fall writ large and small. It appears in miniature, for example, when we watch when Roger and Maurice wantonly kick over the "littluns' " sandcastles decorated with withered flowers and "a complex of marks, tracks, walls, railway lines." When Henry, the biggest of the "littluns," goes to the edge of the lagoon, Roger follows him, hiding in the trees. Like a series of concentric circles moving in ever-widening rings, the will to power begins with the boys' play and moves outward in ever-larger patterns. Fascinated by the tiny sea creatures "scavenging over the beach," Henry playfully enacts the will to power by creating prisons with his footprints. At the point of the next circle, Roger asserts a more frightening will to power. Hoping to generate fear, he furtively hurls stones intended just to miss Henry. When he fails to get a response, he continues to court the violence he wills to inflict on the helpless boy and throws a handful of stones. Barely controlling his emotions, he leans against the palm tree "breathing quickly, his eyelids fluttering." Roger escapes the consuming evil only because his "arm was conditioned by a civilization that knew nothing of him and was in ruins" (p. 57).

But the circles widen again when Jack suddenly calls Roger from "under a tree about ten yards away." As Gerhard von Rad points out, the serpent is in effect a projection of man's developing consciousness.[19] A tempter in residence, Jack is "a dark shadow . . . eager, impatient, beckoning"—the embodiment of Roger's will to power. (In chapter 3, when he stalks the pigs, Jack frightens some birds and "shrank at this cry with a hiss of indrawn breath"). Jack calls Roger to battle by stripping away the last vestiges of civilization. Transmogrified by a mask of war paint behind which he "hid, liberated from shame and self-consciousness," Jack gains the freedom from self-judgment he needs to slaughter the pigs. He draws Roger and all the hunters from "parents and school and policemen and the law" until en masse they encircle the victim pig as the fire goes out and fails to signal a passing ship. But the circles of evil do not end here either. As the chapter concludes, Ralph too is brought within the expanding circumference, even though Jack seems to drive a wedge between him and his brother—"Ralph's mouth watered. He meant to refuse meat but . . . he accepted a piece of half-way raw meat and gnawed it like a wolf" (p. 67).

In the Fall, Erich Fromm writes, mankind enters history—gains a memory.[20] As "things are breaking up," Ralph calls an assembly to restore order, but the knowledge of evil has already entered consciousness, and Jack relives "memories of the knowledge that had come to them when they closed in on the struggling pig, knowledge that they had outwitted a living thing, imposed their will upon it, taken away its life like a long satisfying drink" (p. 64). The beast has arisen; there are dragons in Eden. The "littluns" see the beastie in their nightmares, and Percival tells them it "comes out of the sea." Set loose from the unconscious self the dark other, the stranger Jack sees in reflection, stalks his brother. As the assembly dissolves into chaos, Piggy tells Ralph with telling accuracy that Jack hates him—like Cain devoid of the redeeming self-knowledge of Byron's hero. (When he kills his first pig, Jack smears blood on his forehead.) The last representatives of order—Piggy, the saintly Simon, the twins and Ralph—look to civilization to save them. "Grown-ups know things," Piggy remarks with obvious irony. But the sign that comes betrays an adult knowledge of evil rather than good.

Events in the last half of the novel continue to translate gesture into fact, anticipation into ritual. The boys succumb totally to evil, Golding remarked in an interview, because "they don't understand their own nature . . . they don't understand the things that threaten it. This seems to me to be innocence." Equating innocence with ignorance, he implies the inevitability of a fall, for though ignorance may define innocence it can never sustain it; and, as Blake shows us, at some point or another ignorance produces evil whether or not one consciously "knows" it. The boys simply "don't understand what beasts there are in the human psyche," Golding went on to say,[21] and so they are impotent to resist them. His views have led many critics to label him a Calvinist with a fundamentalistic belief in original sin. But his conception does not quite fit the orthodox concept of original sin as argued by Augustine and reaffirmed and extended in the Calvinistic tradition. Although Golding clearly assumes that the Fall is inevitable, he implies that each individual discovers sin anew rather than emphasizing the idea of inherited guilt. The boys on the island enter a world already fallen, just as they leave a civilization in the midst of war, for the very island itself proves a deceptive paradise. They come upon sin by means of their own awareness; yet, as Blake would say, their innocence never really existed except in their naiveté. The evil is at once preexistent and newly found. The offense of selfhood or self-gratification is *origin*-al because it comes from the natural human state. That is, it would be *un*-natural, inhuman, for man not to "sin." As Stephen Daedelus learns as a young man struggling against his sexual impulses, "Not to fall was too hard, too hard. . . ." What happens on the island is important in degree rather than in kind, and tells us, "that the human propensity for evil knows no limits, not even limits of age, and that there is no Age of Innocence."[22] Golding seems unwilling to spare even the "littluns" from corruption in his conception of a universal evil so profound that no redemption seems possible. Some critics claim that the governess's imposition of the doctrine of original sin generates the evil in *A Turn of the Screw;* Golding shows us that the inherited proclivity for evil is so completely assured that, governess or not, the children are doomed by their own power of darkness. Nonetheless, several critics have argued intelligently for Golding's optimism and his conviction that goodness too is possible and can be ennobling even if it cannot guarantee success in a contemporary secular society dominated by "wars and rumors of war." Such goodness, however, is born of the knowledge gained in experience, and key events in the last part of *Lord of the Flies* compel the remaining Children of Light to recognize the beast in the mirror.

At first a nightmare image coming from the deep sea of the unconscious, the beast assumes two complementary forms, one human and one animal, as the boys acquire "knowledge." In Beelzebub, the sow's head placed ritualistically on a pole by Jack to placate the beast, we see the monster as *created* image, intended by his creator to exorcise the evil in himself. In short, the pig's head in totem usurps the common guilt of all and frees each individual from responsibility. As both victim and scapegoat, both a personification of evil and an exoneration of guilt, the rancid head carries all the paradox of the Fall.

As Blake depicts in "A Poison Tree," the tree of good and evil grows within the psyche, and from man himself grows the fatal fruit of knowledge. Mark Kinkead-Weekes and Ian Gregor describe the totem as an "external manifestation" of what really exists in the children themselves, an attempt to disengage themselves from guilt. "For Golding, the Evil Tree grows within the human brain," they go on to say, and such "emblematic reductions are dangerous manifestations of The Fall."[23] An extension of Jack's putting on war paint to conceal his true image, the "lord of the flies" is ironically a searing revelation of the savagery that produced it. In the infamous rape-murder of the maternal pig the boys are "wedded to her in lust"; but, paradoxically, the demon on the stick divorces them from association with the baseness of the offense. Yet only by confronting the Beelzebub in themselves can they overcome the monster born of themselves.

This, of course, is what Simon discovers when he creeps out from his sacred place in the jungle undergrowth to face his adversary. The head tempts him to "run away, go back to the others," to remain, as it were, in ignorance of himself. But when Simon looked back, "his gaze was held by the ancient, inescapable recognition"; and he responds, like Ralph, to the compelling rhythms of the hunt—"a pulse began to beat in his brain" (p. 128). Like the jungle powers conversing with Conrad's Kurtz, the voice of Beelzebub admits, "I'm part of you. . . . I'm the reason why it's no go" (p. 133). He articulates what Ralph fears but cannot understand when he feels pride at having struck his spear in the boar and when he fights "to get a handful of that brown, vulnerable flesh" as the boys surround Robert to reenact the ritual of the hunt. When Simon collapses in an epileptic fit while "looking into the vast" mouth, he makes the mythic night journey to Erebus and alone returns with wisdom. He "undergoes a ritual death in order to . . . revitalize the stricken society, and returns . . . as redeemer."[24]

But while the beast takes the form of primitive totem it also assumes another, more subtle shape—that of the parachutist fallen as a sign from heaven. The sinister pig's head represents in its hideous features an undisguised horror, a savagery so elemental as to be utterly without pretense, whatever the boys may or may not admit to. The parachutist's dead body, however, is a far more ironic sign. Golding refers to it as "part of the old structure, the old system, the old world, which ought to be good but at the moment is making the world and the air more and more radioactive."[25] As a symbol of history or the dead past the body is an image of the dead god—a relative of Blake's Urizen, the grown-up version of the monster made less horrid only by virtue of the thin veneer of civilization it wears, only because the pilot cannot literally dip his hands in warm blood like Jack, only because his technological instruments of destruction allow him to inflict violence from far above the devastation, and only because he wears the uniform of civilization provided by the Urizenic creators of the grown-up war. In every meaningful way, this beast embodies the evil played out in barbaric adult rites of war that at base imitate the primal Dionysian dances celebrated by the boys. One of Golding's most effective ironies is that the parachutist's body is constrained by the clothing and equipment worn for survival's sake. Subject to the wind the body rises and falls, stands upright and squats (excreting?). At once the image of civilization and its opposite, this beast is an adult parody of the boys' fallen condition. Rather than its opposite, it is nothing less than the brother of Beelzebub.

When Jack, Roger and Ralph first climb to the top of the mountain to confront the beast "slithering" above them, they, like other characters we have discussed, imitate the serpent. Jack "slid" away from Ralph; Roger "fumbled with a hiss of breath." They run in fear from a human figure grotesquely caricatured as "a great ape . . . sitting asleep with its head between its knees" (p. 114). When Simon later meets "the other," he humanizes the evil and recognizes "a human at once heroic and sad." Having sympathy for the grim beast, Simon accepts it and therefore his own flawed humanity. Though a testament of humanity's futile attempt to save man from himself, the parachutist provokes Simon's Christlike power of forgiveness. Rather than exorcising him as vile demon, Simon "turned to this poor broken thing that sat stinking by his side" (p. 136). In short he acknowledges the beast as his brother, bears his offense, and dies for him. Caught up in the frenetic chant of the hunt, the boys literally assault Simon, believing him to be the beast itself until they "leapt on to the beast, screamed, struck, bit, tore" (p. 141). When his body later is washed out to sea, Simon joins his ravaged brother, who fell to the shore and was also claimed by the sea during the violent storm that struck immediately after Simon's death. Beauty and the Beast once more coexist in the dark waters of the unconscious self from which they both came and to which they both return.

Simon's potentially saving "knowledge" of humanity in the beast and the beast in humanity defines the Fall, for it is precisely the knowledge of good and evil that describes man's fallen condition. When Simon's realization cannot be communicated, the boys have no means of defense against their own evil. The fruits of their blindness perpetuate the evil in constant crescendo: Jack has Wilfred tortured without cause; Maurice, Roger and Jack steal Piggy's glasses to light the fires of darkness; Jack and Ralph fight at Castle Rock—and finally Roger rolls a great boulder that "struck Piggy a glancing blow from chin to knees" (p. 167). When Jack at last throws his spear at Ralph "with full intention," there remains no alternative but to flee the holocaust.

Left alone now—Piggy and Simon dead, the twins coerced to join the tribe of hunters—Ralph escapes into the woods. An Abel (and a Cain?), he now understands that Jack "hates him," not because he is some kind of outside threat to his rule but because he is his *Doppelgänger* who challenges the tyranny of his demonic will, just as Jack himself is Ralph's own dark nature. At last Ralph looks into the mirror and truly sees "that undefinable connection between himself and Jack" (p. 170). Betrayed even by the loyal Sam and Eric, he can find no safe place, not even in Simon's sacred bower, until he is "rescued" by the naval officer: "white-topped cap . . . a crown, an anchor, gold foilage . . . white drill, epaulettes, a revolver, a row of gilt buttons down the front of a uniform" (p. 185)—another hunter in mask.

The sudden appearance of the ship and the uniformed officer who saves the boys adds to the ambiguity. Perhaps, as Carl Niemeyer claims, upon the arrival of the ship "civilization defeats the beast. It shrinks back into the jungle as the boys creep out to be rescued; but the beast is real. It is there, and it may return."[26] However, I disagree; the appearance of the officer is ironic, his military uniform concealing an adult criminality if anything more cataclysmic than that of the tribe of shipwrecked hunters. Perhaps, as Henri Talon has suggested, the "resolution" is totally nihilistic or agnostic, "a nightmarish fiction" which allows "murderous children" to leave "the earthly paradise they have ruined to enter a fundamentally sick, and therefore incurable world, in which intelligence is the handmaid of crime."[27] A third position embraces neither the naive assumption that civilization, if temporarily, defeats evil at the end nor the negative conclusion that Golding leaves us without hope. James R. Baker argues that *Lord of the Flies* is more than "a juvenile version of *Paradise Lost*" and more than a "simply negative or nihilistic" statement in opposition "to the outworn public images of the modern age." In Ralph's weeping "for the end of innocence, the darkness of man's heart, and the fall through the air of the true, wise friend called Piggy" (pp. 186–87), he finds "the possibility of a new mentality struggling to be born against the terrific odds imposed by the pattern of our social heritage and limitations of the species."[28] Directly relating the story to the third chapter of Genesis, William Mueller similarly argues that Ralph's newly gained awareness of the evil in him and in all humanity can render the beast "harmless," as Simon learns, but "only when it becomes universally recognized . . . as the demonic principle which is utterly destructive."[29]

I believe Golding's later work points us most clearly to his meaning, for Ralph's situation at the end of the novel describes the moment Sammy Mountjoy tries desperately to recover in *Free Fall*—"the beginning of responsibility, the beginning of darkness, the point where I began."[30] Perhaps Ralph's reassertion of authority at the end marks the crucial first step East of Eden:

> "Who's boss here?"
> "I am," said Ralph loudly. (P. 186)

Like the captain in "The Secret Sharer," Ralph first claims an authority resting upon self-ignorance and a dubious innocence. No longer the innocent boy Sammy remembers "looking at a tree . . . in the garden," Ralph has entered experience and gained the fearful self-knowledge that could finally redeem him. Having learned to his horror what Sammy Mountjoy understands too well, that "we are neither the innocent nor the wicked . . . we are the guilty" (p. 251), he may well possess the wisdom needed to preserve him from the beast at large in the adult society he now must enter—the depraved monster than can transform childish games into Buchenwald and Auschwitz, Hiroshima and My Lai.

‡ 4 ‡

Civilization and Its Discontents

In this chapter we move from the small community at Bly and the doomed society on an isolated island to the heart of Western civilization. Joseph Conrad's *Heart of Darkness* and Hermann Hesse's *Demian* are but two of many works in the last two centuries that have explored Western culture in decline. From early writings forecasting the revolutions of the late eighteenth century to the deepening intellectual and moral despair voiced after their failure came a first wave of anguish. No one described this agony over a darkening romanticism as well as Alfred de Musset in "The Confession of a Child of the Century": "There remained then, the present, the spirit of the time . . . they found him seated on a lime sack filled with bones, clad in the mantle of egoism, and shivering with a terrible cold . . . half mummy and half fetus." That fatalistic sense continued among the intellectuals and artists of the age, despite a popular belief in progress and technological advance. By the end of the century a second wave of despair had begun to engulf the naive optimism of nineteenth-century Europe. Freud's *Civilization and Its Discontents* pointed toward the near-certainty of society's devolution, and the revolutionary spirit emanating from the eighteenth century once again shattered the internal peace of nations.

Conrad's political novels interpret the fall of civilizations within the context of an encompassing gloom. Like Hesse, he gives us the individual consciousness as our way of seeing into a communal, universal, fall. Hesse, too, provides us with the experiences of a central, essentially autobiographical, character, whose story evolves from the narrow confines of his personal childhood home to the vast arena of a civilization at war. *Heart of Darkness* and *Demian* differ in their conclusions, however: Conrad's novella describes the fall of culture with only the barest hope of salvation—at best his characters remain in limbo; Hesse sees in the fall of civilizations the emergence of a renewed consciousness and a reawakening of spiritual powers. The one work ends with the devastating judgment of Genesis 3; the other takes us beyond that judgment to the hope of Revelation.

Heart of Darkness by Joseph Conrad

> Even if, juristically speaking, we were not accessories to the crime, we are always, thanks to our human nature, potential criminals. In reality we merely lacked a suitable opportunity to be drawn into the infernal melee. None of us stands outside humanity's black collective shadow. . . . One would therefore do well to possess some "imagination in evil," for only the fool can permanently neglect the conditions of his own nature.
>
> —Carl Jung, *The Undiscovered Self*

It is a commonplace of editorial journalism to invoke Conrad in attempting to account for evil bordering on the cataclysmic—the Holocaust, the My Lai massacre, famine in Biafra, the brutality of Idi Amin, the mass starvation of twentieth-century political refugees, the atrocities of political terrorism.[1] So it is that news reporter Meg Greenfield could call the Jonestown massacre a revelation of the "Heart of Darkness." Such promptings of violence, she writes, "are the dark impulses that lurk in every private psyche. . . . What made the Jonestown affair such a disturbing metaphor and called forth so many diversionary 'explanations' was its reminder that the jungle is only a few yards away."[2] Conrad's bleak novel has become part of the Western imagination, an emblem of man's frightening capacity for evil in a world seemingly devoid of a concomitant myth of redemption. In its enormous vision of darkness, goodness is all but irrelevant. It is, says Albert Guerard, "a *Pilgrim's Progress* for our pessimistic and psychoanalyzing age."[3] Nor is it any accident that Freud's and Conrad's views converged at the end of a century hounded by repeated assaults on human dignity, a century in which we move in literature from the Byronic hero stalking the cosmos to the underground man, and in society from the Great Exhibition to the vilest rapacity of colonialism—in short, in a world all but stripped of its myths of restoration by the overwhelming authority of scientific determinism and the unrestrained nationalism of European powers.

Such a *Weltanschauung* may well embrace a myth of the Fall but hardly the fortunate fall espoused by Blake and Byron. Dealing with the individual captain in "The Secret Sharer," Conrad apparently was able to find affirmation in the consequences of a fall; but close to the time he wrote *Heart of Darkness* some ten years earlier, he had undergone his own frightening journey up the Congo (in 1890) and had gained "the distasteful knowledge of the vilest scramble for loot that ever disfigured the history of human conscience."[4] In his novella, he, like Golding, hacks relentlessly through the facade of civilization to get at man's essential evil, only peripherally at his good. Yet, as Walter J. Ong observes, Conrad's probing "into the unconscious, which means lifting parts of the conscious into consciousness, can be confounding and even terrifying, but it is also humanizing." Conrad's vision of fallen man assumes a modernity in which "the implicit is becoming explicit, both individually and collectively."[5] He enlarges the vision of the Fall to include both the individual *and* the collective whole.

The narrative technique of *Heart of Darkness* establishes the expanding scope of Conrad's vision, for it incorporates three separate falls in the telling of the tale: (1) Kurtz's fall in the midst of the jungle; (2) Marlow's subsequent fall when he gains the knowledge from Kurtz; (3) the implied fall of the listeners, including the frame narrator who introduces and concludes the work. Furthermore, it describes the Fall within both the context of the African jungle and, ultimately, of the "whited sepulchre"—Brussels and, more inclusively, European culture at large. Perhaps more important, it reveals two kinds of fallen beings, those consumed by Dionysian abandon and those reduced to Apollonian stasis. In this it recalls Blake's dialectic between Orc and Urizen, Generation and Ulro. Though finally unresolved, the novel translates the Fall into a metaphor of the social entity, an illustration not simply of "civilization and its discontents" but also of the universal struggle between good and evil as it is carried out in the society as in the self.

Point of view directly creates the mythic dimension of Conrad's art, for it assimilates all the characters into a pattern of action that exceeds the limitations of time and space while at the same time maintaining a level of realism and unity. As readers we coexist in two realms of action, and we follow simultaneously what happened in Marlow's past and in the narrator's experience hearing Marlow on the boat outside London. Such narrative complexity is particularly suited to myth, for it makes us ever aware that the truth resides less in the surface of the tale than in its evocation of meaning. To adapt Baudelaire's definition of symbolism, there is a sort of "evocative sorcery" operating beneath and through the plot and its telling that transports us to the hidden reality of its truth. As in works like Brontë's *Wuthering Heights* and Faulkner's *Absalom, Absalom!* the multiple narration alerts us to the fact that the truth is in no one character but emerges through all of them, finally surrounding and transcending them all.

In introducing Marlow who introduces Kurtz, the outside narrator establishes the dream reality that characterizes the core of the inner tale. As in "The Secret Sharer," the setting describes a state of arrested becoming—a limbo between night and day, between London and "an interminable waterway," between waking and sleeping. Also similarly, the language of the opening paragraphs is full of approximations and suggestions of vagueness: "The wind was *nearly* calm," "The tide *seemed* to stand still," "The air . . . *seemed* condensed into a mournful gloom," "The Director of Companies . . . *resembled* a pilot," "The mist . . . was *like* a gauzy and radiant fabric, "The sun sank low . . . *as if* about to go out"; and it is filled with the language of mystery and indeterminacy: "The sea and the sky were welded together without a joint," "A haze rested on the shore that ran out to the sea in vanishing flatness," "The air was dark . . . brooding motionless." Other such images include "the luminous estuary . . . the brooding gloom," "a benign immensity of unstained light," "the mist . . . draping the low shores in diaphanous folds," "the gloom . . . brooding . . . more sombre every minute," "the sun . . . stricken to death by the touch of that gloom brooding over a crowd of men."[6] Conrad's purpose is to establish an ominous and mysterious atmosphere in which to unfold his narrative of moral ambiguity.

As Marlow abruptly begins, the narrator not only provides us with crucial revelations about him (facts that we shall note in discussing Marlow's fall), but he also becomes Conrad's means of enclosing the story within a larger action, a pervasive descent into darkness reminiscent of *Macbeth*. Through his eyes we see the dusk fall; we observe the lights flicker on in London, producing "a lurid glare under the stars." Unwittingly, the *persona* introduces us to the mythic world of *Heart of Darkness* before Marlow utters his famous first words, "And this also . . . has been one of the dark places of the earth" (p. 48). Anchoring the story in the outside reality presented by the narrator, Conrad can take us in time and space from the implied present on the boat near London back to Marlow's journey into the Belgian Congo and then return us again to the "present," depicting the Fall in ever-enlarging dimensions. For the knowledge delivered in Marlow's account denies the innocence of those who lived it and those who hear it.

Though readers debate about exactly who is the central character in the work, no doubt Kurtz's story is the pivotal center of the whole, and he becomes in ironic ways the moral measure of all the other characters. We cannot finally discuss Kurtz apart from Marlow, however, in whose psyche his existence is secured. He has been described variously as Marlow's *Doppelgänger*, his alter ego, the Freudian id, the Jungian "other." His relationship with Marlow has been compared with that between Ishmael and Ahab, Lear and Gloucester, and, not infrequently, that between Leggatt and the captain in "The Secret Sharer."[7] To some a reflection of Marlow, to others his opposite, Kurtz in any circumstance expresses something buried in Marlow's unconscious self. Like Geraldine or Cenci or Quint, he tempts Marlow from deep within the unconscious and, like the others, offers "the fascination of the abomination." Marlow's discovery of Kurtz is in effect self-discovery, for in the most ironic sense Kurtz is the only other truly moral figure in the narrative, that is, the only one besides Marlow who has achieved a sufficient degree of self-knowledge to pass moral judgment on himself. He alone moves from one absolute pole in the dialectic of good and evil to the other, and, as the sole possessor of Kurtz's knowledge after his death, Marlow acquires both the right and the obligation of moral choice, however we judge him. Ultimately, however, no one can claim innocence. As the external narrative moves from the outside in, from London and civilization to Africa and the heart of darkness, it paradoxically moves from the inside out; for the consequence of Marlow's tale is to bring to light everyone's heart of darkness. Kurtz's story becomes everyone's bridge to his own unconscious self.

Marlow refers to two Kurtzes. "The original Kurtz" existed in a prelapsarian state of ignorance with his Eve, his fiancée, in the midst of a spurious paradise. When he left Brussels to seek his wealth in Africa, he did so to preserve the illusory Eden he willed to return to forever. What Marlow calls "the whited sepulchre" is nothing less than Blake's Ulro, whose essential evil is, in Albert Guerard's phrase, "the evil of vacancy."[8] In consequence of his risky journey out of the Edenic European culture, Kurtz gained the moral superiority of an active evil—*pecca foriter*. Tempted by the uroboric figure of the river-snake, Kurtz took with him all the Sunday school pins awarded by the dominant white culture. "All Europe contributed to the making of Kurtz," Marlow tells us. Born of a half-English mother and half-French father, he represented not only the company but other beacons of civilization, such as the International Society for the Suppression of Savage Customs. Kurtz was an accomplished poet, journalist, essayist, musician, painter and spell-binding speaker, whose "sympathies were in the right place." Not only from paradise but the very embodiment of it, the "original Kurtz" could capture the Russian harlequin, his absurd admirer, with his poetic recitations even when he spoke from the deepest moral abyss.

To rephrase Lord Acton's famous comment, "Goodness corrupts, and absolute goodness corrupts absolutely." To place all goodness within the self is to be enslaved by it, Blake might have said, and such dangerous innocence can only lead to its opposite. John Vernon discusses Kurtz as a schizophrenic: "Schizophrenia . . . is the white man's disease, the price he pays for draining the blackness out of his own being and attempting to enslave it; for that blackness, because it has been enslaved, rises up to overwhelm Kurtz."[9] As we have noted in evaluating other characters, absolutism is the fruit of self-ignorance. Until his "epiphany," Kurtz remains blind to his evil. Yet, reduced to a kind of primal energy, he at once defies and defines morality: defies it by the very extremity of his violence, defines it by stripping away all the pretense that masks the evil in civilization. At best he may be a full-blown portrait of the romantic egoist, "the presumptive outlaw who gives a degree of admiration by crossing the boundaries of conventional morality and exploring the possibilities of living on the other side."[10] Or perhaps he is a kind of twentieth-century, bourgeois Faust, like Ibsen's John Gabriel Borkman, a modern descendant of *de casibus* tragedy without the moral certitude of the medieval world. A fallen angel in any case, he reveals the fullest possibility of evil and of good and makes us fear them both.

Fated to admire Kurtz's capacity for evil by virtue of its energizing power, Marlow is equally horrified and animated by it. Two kinds of evil confront him, Guerard notes, the evil of the "whited sepulchre" defined by "vacancy" and the evil of "active energy" defined by Kurtz's utter lack of restraint. Marlow's only defense against the latter, the "secrets" whispered in the jungle to Kurtz, is "work," total devotion to an "idea." But the sole character able to maintain such a defense in the Congo is as absurd as the old man in Camus's *The Plague* who repeatedly counts dried peas from one pan to another. The accountant in white, who earns Marlow's respect for keeping up his appearance "in the demoralization of the land," continues making "correct entries" in his book while an African man dies in the same room. Finally forced to decide on the lesser "nightmare," Marlow will opt for Kurtz, whether or not he possesses the courage of his conviction. Before he bites the apple, though, he first undergoes the temptation of a fall.

Marlow twice compares the river on the map to a snake—"an immense snake uncoiled, with its head in the sea, its body at rest curving afar over a vast country, and its tail lost in the depth of the land." He admits, "It fascinated me as a snake would a bird" (p. 52). The same feature that attracted him to the map-snake as a boy drew him again as he wandered the streets of London in search of a position—the attraction of the unknown. The second time the map serves as snake Marlow finds himself in the company office in Brussels where he hopes to gain his appointment. A record of colonialism, the large map marked in the colors of the imperialistic nations presents the two modes of knowledge that underlie the dialectical structure of the work. On one hand it outlines the accepted Urizenic knowledge of European culture, a kind of false Apollonian image of order, restraint and control. On the other hand, "the river was there—fascinating—deadly—like a snake" (p. 56). The most subtle of creatures, it challenges from "dead in the centre" the known truths, the "goodness" of civilization.

In untested innocence and hope Marlow applies for a job at the headquarters of the company. The temple of paradise is fittingly characterized by images of controlled knowledge (the map, signed documents, "a thing like caliphers" to measure the head) and Urizenic figures (the secretary, the doctor, the clerk, "the great man himself"), against which appear the more sinister forces of the unknown implied by the snake, the two women knitting wool "guarding the door of Darkness," and the unnerving warnings of the clerk and the doctor. The "ceremonies" over, Marlow, in parody of Adam, assumes control of paradise and feels "let into some conspiracy," forbidden "amongst other things not to disclose any trade secrets."

The distinctions between Marlow and Kurtz with regard to their views of "paradise" merit comment. From what we can gather, Kurtz fully embraced the objectives and values of the "whited sepulchre," as Marlow calls Brussels, though he was unaware of their true nature. He went willingly, eagerly, to carry the light of civilization into the darkness. His complete devotion in fact led to his complete reversal, as when he ended his eloquent seventeen-page essay "of burning noble words" to the International Society for the Suppression of Savage Customs with the brief note, "Exterminate all the brutes!" (p. 118). Marlow stands farther off, a wanderer in a specious European paradise he recognizes as peopled by somnambulists. Kurtz plays his role as missionary of the ideal with unwavering self-assurance, whereas Marlow finds his position as "emissary of light, something like a lower sort of apostle," pure pretense—"I was an imposter" (pp. 59–60). His cynical view of Brussels and its inhabitants indicates his attempt to be in but not of the garden. He finds his aunt's idealism about "weaning those ignorant millions from their horrid ways" so much "humbug," and he reminds her that "the Company was run for profit" (p. 59). For all his healthy detachment, though, Marlow is by no means free. He is yet to eat of the tree of good and evil, for while he understands the fearful blindness of European imperialism and finds its garden a "whited sepulchre," he not only lives by it but emulates many of its values.

Frances B. Singh finds Marlow's anticolonialism all but hypocrisy,[11] noting that Marlow's sympathetic concerns for the natives are always qualified by distance and that even his seeming admiration of them is patronizing, as is his superior attitude toward the Russian harlequin, Kurtz's tattered admirer. Whether his bias stems from his association with the white culture from which he comes, or whether it is perhaps a reflection of Conrad's own ambivalence depends to some extent on whether we trust the teller or the tale. Marlow's "inconclusive experience," his elemental passivity and his unwitting self-judgment makes us question his ability to understand even himself—finally to recover from his fall. Remembering that he talks to the men on the boat after gaining knowledge in the jungle, it is worth noting that he still speaks the language of nineteenth-century imperialism—"the devotion to efficiency will save us from the fascination of the abomination," he tells the men at one point. What "redeems" man from "the utter savagery" is "the idea only," he says (pp. 49–51). And yet we wonder what idea he can follow if he acknowledges the lie of European idealism. He admires the Roman legionaires who tamed England, he remarks, because "they were men enough to face the darkness," but his own "concessions to the wilderness" leave him admittedly "incomplete" and unable to act. Nor can we ignore his excessive insistence that he has been true to Kurtz, itself a telling revelation that he has *not* been true. And finally, when we consider his climactic encounter with the Intended and the outside narrator's last remarks, we can have only limited faith in Marlow's recovery from the Fall—and even in our own potential for redemption.

In attempting to assess Marlow's success or failure, we must follow two actions, both the events described within Marlow's narrative and the less dominant action that takes place on the boat as he speaks and after. The second illuminates the first and assures that we will distance ourselves from Marlow and from his conclusions. We must listen to Marlow's version of Kurtz's fall and his own with considerable objectivity. In his recantation Marlow does bring to light the evil in paradise, and he appreciates as no one else can the "moral victory" of Kurtz's fall. Marlow's failure comes *after* his fall, after he receives from Kurtz the true knowledge of good and evil. Yet, as he brings us to that moment, he rightly strips away the illusions of innocence both in the jungle and on the boat.

The stripping action begins almost immediately from the point when Marlow first sets out "for the centre of the earth." The pettiness of civilization against the primitive dark powers of the jungle confronts him from the outer "edge of a colossal jungle." He observes a man-of-war aimlessly shelling the bush with six-inch guns that produce a feeble "pop" and "a little white smoke." "Nothing could happen," Marlow concludes, because the "enemies" could not even be seen. And there are numerous minor touches of "insanity," such as the boiler "wallowing in the grass" at the outer station and the upturned railway-truck "dead as the carcass of some animal." He sees imported drainage pipes wantonly smashed near "a vast artificial hole . . . just a hole," and, feeling a dull detonation, watches a "puff of smoke" coming from a cliff being blasted for no real purpose and to no avail—"No change appeared on the face of the rock" (pp. 63–65). His journey into the interior is stalled by missing rivets, available anywhere in any European city yet impossible to acquire in the African interior. Even more, Marlow sees the exposed avarice of civilized man and the absurdity of his pretense: the "amazing" accountant, the "miracle" done up in white who keeps his books "in apple-pie order" though irritated by the groans of a dying man; the "chattering idiot" the manager who was "great" simply "because he was never ill" and "could keep the routine going" for three years; the brickmaker who made no bricks—a "papier-mâché Mephistopheles"; the "lot of faithless pilgrims bewitched aside a rotten fence" where the "word 'ivory' rang in the air"; the infamous Eldorado Exploring Expedition made up of European tourists armed with guns and out "to tear the treasure out of the bowels of the land . . . with no more moral purpose . . . than there is in burglars breaking into a safe" (p. 87). Devoid of his masks, European man openly enacts his savagery in "the grove of death" at the central station and in numerous acts of cruelty, as when one native is beaten for supposedly starting a fire and goes off to die in the woods. Here, in "weary pilgrimage amongst hints of nightmares," Marlow stands apart in his judgments—admiring the "wild vitality" and "intense energy" of the native paddlers who "wanted no excuse for being there," sympathizing with the suffering "phantoms" at "the grove of death" who "were not enemies . . . were not criminals," and condemning the white man's brutality.

His ability to distinguish between the deception of good and the reality of evil suggests that Marlow has already undergone a fall. To the extent that he recognizes the evil of others he has indeed gained knowledge, but he as yet lacks self-knowledge and so has not truly "fallen." He knows intellectually but not existentially. As Gerhard von Rad explains, "to know" as it is used in Genesis refers not only to intellectual but to experiential knowledge.[12] Marlow clearly understands the evil of the invading whites, but he not yet entered the reservoir of his own being. He lacks the serpent who can bring him to that knowledge—Kurtz, the fallen angel of his unconscious self.[13] Kurtz serves a dual role, for he is not only Marlow's personal tempter but a communal symbol as well. As we have said, he stands as the epitome of civilization; and in his attempt to draw Marlow with him into the maelstrom of evil, he acts to perpetuate the values of the society which produced him. His Intended, his station, his career, his idea form the composite images of a fallen culture. And however much he rejects the fact, Marlow is the emissary of that culture. He must finally be judged not only for his individual "choice of nightmares" but for what he does or does not do to redeem "the whited sepulchre." Like it or not, he is responsible for passing on the light of knowledge to the society. Without a fall, that is, without the acquisition of knowledge, no regeneration is possible. To seal the spurious garden in ignorance can only guarantee the perpetuity of its spiritual death. Marlow's journey to Kurtz, then, constitutes more than a personal fall, and we are obliged to follow it all the way to its "communal" end.

Ironically, Marlow's knowledge of Kurtz begins with Kurtz's reputation as "a first class agent." The accountant's respect for this "very remarkable person" is based solely on his ability to produce ivory; and he tells Marlow that Kurtz will "be a somebody in the Administration" because "they, above—the Council in Europe, you know—mean him to be" (p. 70). If he plays Marlow's tempter in the internal action, Kurtz acts as the Urizenic god's agent, an Adam to his Cain, within the context of his own fall. He earns the admiration and the jealousy of other agents of the "deity" in Brussels. In particular the "brickmaker" reveals the depth of their hate. With unwitting candor he accuses Kurtz, and Marlow with him, of being part of "the gang of virtue." Though a hollow man made of papier-mâché, he at least possesses accuracy of vision when he glances back to the hypocrisy of Europe which sent Kurtz as "emissary of pity and science and progress and the devil knows what else" (p. 79). Marlow struggles to distinguish between the falsity of European society, which he already acknowledged before he entered the jungle, and Kurtz's intriguing attempt to marry trade and civilization. Attracted to Kurtz partly because he sees the other "pilgrims" so diminished in his light,

Marlow sides with him because, as the manager remarks with "excessive indignation," Kurtz preached that each trading station should be "a beacon on the road toward better things . . . for humanizing, improving, instructing" (p. 91). Finding no such duality in the "pilgrims," Marlow felt drawn by a man incapable of either easy virtue or simple offense. The more alienated he finds Kurtz and the more hideous his crimes, the more he takes him for his own—"The thing was to know what he belonged to, how many powers of darkness claimed him for their own" (p. 116). Saved—or perhaps condemned, as the Russian harlequin was not—by his powers of moral judgment, Marlow is both horrified by an evil that could place "heads on stakes . . . turned to the house" and yet fascinated by it. In Kurtz's voice he hears the same whisper that "had proved irresistibly fascinating" to the "atrocious phantom." Kurtz gradually became disembodied, "a voice" heard only by Marlow (and, as the outside narrator describes Marlow, he too becomes "a voice" in the darkness outside London). And Kurtz lays claim to Marlow, to whom he gives both knowledge and an obligation. The "culminating point" of Marlow's experience, Kurtz's last words thrust him from the flimsy innocence of his ignorance. His readily attested moral superiority over the blatantly foolish "pilgrims" pales in light of Kurtz's extraordinary perception.

His inability to elude Kurtz's knowledge is recorded in grim humor when Marlow tries to save him from "unspeakable rites" shortly before his death. As Kurtz stumbles toward the ritual fire "like a vapour exhaled from the earth," Marlow says with comic overstatement, "I had cut him off cleverly" (p. 143). With increased ironic humor, he threatens to smash Kurtz's head if he shouts, but looks completely ridiculous when he cannot find a stick or a stone. Though a mere shadow, the "wandering and tormented thing" makes Marlow's every gesture absurdly futile, like trying to lasso a ghost. Against the power of his vision, Marlow's moral certainties fade rapidly. Those last infamous words, "The horror! The horror!" all but take Kurtz beyond good and evil as traditional moral categories.[14] We approach here the existential axiom that while one is free to fall one must fall to be free, for Marlow tells us that Kurtz "had kicked himself loose of the earth" (p. 144). Presumably, such an excess of "freedom," what Golding calls "free fall," is the only possible act of self-definition in a world without God. Bruce Johnson describes Kurtz's "final judgment" of himself as "the first utterance of a self reborn to the knowledge of its own foundations: not a god-given 'nature' or 'essence,' but a radical freedom to create itself."[15] In ironic reversal Kurtz achieves the godhead Blake ascribes to man himself. In his self-knowledge, he usurps the role of the judging god by passing judgment on himself and, in this, transcends the morality of the Urizenic system. If we reduce morality to the tableted law guarded by the hypocritical European culture, then surely Kurtz's cry is exactly what Marlow calls it, "a moral victory." Having gone, in Alan Watt's phrase, "beyond theology," he is free to judge—"to judge himself," Sartre would add. If the ultimate end of the romantic quest for freedom is self-knowledge, then Kurtz demonstrates just how perilous such knowledge can be. When Marlow calls his lament "an affirmation" because Kurtz "had something to say" and "said it," he finds himself guilty of precisely what traditional morality would praise—drawing back "my hesitating foot" and avoiding "a word of careless contempt" (p. 151). In a telling choice of words, he says he had "peeped" over the edge of the abyss, an ironic echo of the "pop" of the guns and the "puff" of the blast on the hillside at the central station. Hopelessly, Marlow both judges himself and claims his "loyalty" to Kurtz—"I have remained loyal to Kurtz to the last, and even beyond" (p. 151). To what degree he is really "faithful" constitutes the major question in the interpretation of the story. The answer requires us to trace Marlow's return to the civilization whose fall is embodied in Kurtz's story and to keep our focus on the outside narrator; for while Marlow's confrontation with Kurtz forms the main plot of the novella, it does not constitute the whole of the action. In Kurtz's fall all fall, and all bear the consequence of knowledge.

Whether or not Marlow achieves a higher innocence depends upon how we perceive his encounter with Kurtz's Intended. Everything about her—her "name," her dress, her apartment, her beliefs—reflect the Western culture represented by "the original Kurtz." In confronting her, Jocelyn Baines remarks, Marlow is paying "for his knowledge" and reenacts "the legend of The Fall."[16] What we deal with here are the consequences of his having received knowledge, having gained thereby the self-recognition of his own nakedness and, as it were, a kind of existential guilt—"I would have nothing to say" (p. 151). Though critics generally find something altruistic in his paying a visit to the Intended, Marlow admits that his primary motive was a bit of hand-washing: "There remained only his memory and his Intended—and I wanted to give that up too, to the past . . . to surrender personally all that remained of him with me to that oblivion which is the last of our common fate" (p. 155). Having "dreamed" his nightmare and received knowledge at "the furthest point" of his unconscious self, he too reaches for fig leaves.

Though most readers see the Intended as a sympathetic character, some consider her the ultimate symbol of the "sephulchral city." To Bruce Stark she "floats" in a "silent luxurious house" that is itself at the center of darkness, and her "dark eyes glitter with the deadly charm of the serpent."[17] Others compare her with Kurtz's "wild and gorgeous" African mistress: "The one is a partner in Kurtz's plunge into Satanic unspeakable rites; the other one is exemplar of the Fidelity to which man must cling for salvation."[18] It is Marlow, however, who provides us with our understanding of Kurtz's intended wife and what she represents, and he presents his conceptions in an incredibly ironic conversation.

Perhaps no other piece of dialogue in all of fiction contains such ironies as this. For Marlow's every lie is a truth and every truth a lie:

Intended	Marlow
"And you admired him."	"He was a remarkable man."
"I knew him best."	"You knew him best."
"But you have heard him! You know!"	"Yes, I know!"
"You and I—"	"We shall always remember him."
"His words, at least, have not died."	"His words will remain."
"And his example . . ."	"Yes his example . . ."
"He died as he lived."	"His end . . . was in every way worthy of his life."

No character in literature tries so desperately to conceal his nakedness as Marlow does. Yet in subtle ways Conrad uses setting and description to provide a commentary on Marlow's "choice" even as Marlow himself describes the moment. In this way he establishes an "objective correlative" for his judgment of Marlow without usurping point of view or violating narrative technique. In effect, Marlow's observations become the instrument whereby we judge his "loyalty" to Kurtz and his fidelity to the truth.

The whole scene is obviously couched in death from the time Marlow travels through the "whited sepulchre" and down a street "as still and decorous as a well-kept alley in a cemetery" (p. 155). The house provides visions of the jungle, and Marlow finds Kurtz himself "staring at [him] out of the glassy panel" of the door and hears him whisper, "The horror! The horror!" The Intended's room resembles the jungle: the "indistinct curves" in the furniture shine in the dusk like glimmers off the winding serpentine river; the long windows resemble "bedraped columns" like the tall jungle trees; the piano "like a sombre and polished sarcophagus" reflects "dark gleams" similarly reminiscent of the Congo. The Intended "floats" in the room like one of the dying phantoms in the jungle. In death and of death, she has mourned for Kurtz more than a year. Yet though she does in every sense exist in and for "the whited sepulchre," she earns more pity than condemnation, for she lacks the self-knowledge that might rescue her from death—not Kurtz's death but the spiritual death of the sepulchre. She is the unconscious representative of civilization against the dark barbarism of the savage; and yet, as the story unquestionably tells us, the true heart of darkness beats here in civilization itself. The conflict between the remaining "capacity for fidelity, for belief, for suffering" and the shattering light of knowledge resides in Marlow himself, for he now must decide whether or not to play the serpent in the chapel. His futile attempt to avoid choice once more produces the grim humor. Trying with quiet frenzy to evade the lie, he offers the most ironic of truths, culminating in "your name."

Conrad captures the ambiguity of Marlow's actions throughout the scene. At every point when the lie of civilization approaches the truth, the darkness deepens. When the Intended first appears, "The room seemed to have grown darker" (p. 157). When Marlow tells her, " 'You knew him best' . . . with every word spoken the room was growing darker" (p. 158). When the Intended claims, "I am proud to know I understood him better than any one on earth," Marlow says, "The darkness deepened" (p. 158). When she grieves that "nobody will see him again, never, never, never," Marlow finds her "a tragic and familiar Shade" reaching out like the demon lover "stretching bare brown arms over the glitter of the infernal stream, the stream of darkness." And as the dialogue moves to its climax after Marlow unwittingly traps himself by admitting "I heard his very last words," he hears the dusk repeat them. Then the Intended asks for "His last word—to live with," and Marlow tells his "lie": "The last word he pronounced was—your name." He did so, he tells us, because "It would have been too dark—too dark altogether . . ." (pp. 161–62).

But Conrad does not leave Marlow's conclusion untested. He calls it into question by use of Marlow's own words and by other means. Marlow's judgment of women, for example ("They live in a world of their own; . . . It is altogether beautiful"; "We must help them to stay in that beautiful world of their own, lest ours gets worse") cannot be simplistically assigned to Conrad, particularly if we pay attention to the ironies which surround Marlow's condescending references to women (after all, his aunt *did* get him his position). The parallels between Marlow's meeting with the Intended and his climactic scene with Kurtz also suggest a measure of ambiguity in Marlow's acts.

When Kurtz passed on the knowledge of "The horror! The horror!" Marlow extinguished the light; and again in Brussels he extinguishes the light. If we try to dismiss Marlow's act as excusable and necessary, as the majority of critics seem to, we may deny the knowledge that can redeem and allow ignorance to perpetuate evil. Not only the Intended's home but also she herself is aligned with the "light" of the fallen civilization. The faint glimmer of light Marlow in part lies to save glows only on her "smooth and white" forehead, a symbol, like the "cold and monumental whiteness" of the fireplace, of the ivory-ridden avarice of society. Repeatedly, what shines in the darkness are the images of greater darkness, not affirmative images of light—"the remaining light in a glimmer of gold" on the Intended's head reflects the rapacity of the materialistic society. The Intended might well be the figure in Kurtz's painting stored in the brickmaker's room, "a woman, draped and blindfolded, carrying a lighted torch. The background was sombre—almost black" (p. 79). A mockery of blind justice, the woman paradoxically illuminates the darkness in man's soul. But in truth, however unknowingly, so too does the Intended in her profound ignorance and naiveté. In a parody of justice, she defends the darkness against the light.

Many find Marlow's lie a truth (the Intended *is* "the horror!") but most readers go on to praise Marlow for his deception, concluding that self-knowledge would surely destroy the Intended's capacity to live. Lee M. Whitehead says simply, "The Nightmare that affirms life is clearly to be chosen over the one that denies it."[19] But *does* the lie affirm life? Marlow himself does not distinguish between good and bad lies when he admits, "There is a taint of death, a flavour of mortality in lies . . . like biting something rotten" (p. 82). When the Intended, "unhappy for—for life," asks for something "to live with," Marlow gives her the one "truth" that makes life impossible. Would it have been "too dark altogether?" Perhaps. We cannot say. But we know one thing for certain, that denied the knowledge the Intended cannot be reclaimed by life. There is no truth to set her free. She will mourn forever, will forever defend the fallen society she everywhere embodies. Truly, "your name" is synonymous with "the horror!"—but the truth remains concealed. For good or ill, Marlow once more blows out the candle.

Ralph Maud notes that Marlow "doesn't even do the little bit of good that is very possible for him. If he had just told Kurtz's fiancee the truth . . . she might, after some hysteria, have grown up into a healthy, useful woman, a member of the International Society for the Suppression of 'Civilized' Customs."[20] No doubt he exaggerates. Marlow's choice is not so simple. In one sense the issue is not what he thinks he "saves" her *from* but what in fact he "saves" her *to*—in denying her the right to fall, to gain knowledge, he deprives her of existence, save that in the somnambulant Eden of Western civilization. While claiming to be concerned with self-knowledge and truth, Eloise May points out, Marlow progresses toward deception and denial.[21] Even if in all likelihood the Intended does not possess the necessary courage to recover from her aborted existence, Marlow disallows her being "altogether." According to such a reading, he bites "something rotten" because he tastes the consequences of his own choice. However, Marlow's admission of his lie is perhaps not so much a sin against the Intended as an acknowledgement of his own mortality—"There is a taint of death, a flavour of mortality in lies." If so, he achieves his own "moral victory" by accepting responsibility for participating in a communal guilt. By telling the men on the boat of his lie, he confesses to his own "heart of darkness" and becomes an accomplice in the human drama.

The narrator adds to the levels of meaning by forcing us to see Marlow's tale against the larger canvas of the whole. He gives proof enough that Marlow's story carries knowledge to the others. And we know by Marlow's use of direct address that the others have been affected. He tells them that "what thrilled you" in the ugly cry of the savages "was just the thought of their humanity—*like yours*—the thought of your remote kinship with this wild and passionate uproar" (p. 96, emphasis added). Accusing them of being used to "the shackled form of a conquered monster," he calls their noble work in civilization merely "performing on your respective tightropes for—what is it? half a crown a tumble—" (p. 95). The narrator alerts us to the effect he has on the men on the boat. Someone responded, "Try to be civil, Marlow," whereupon the narrator tells us, "I knew there was at least one listener awake besides myself" (p. 94). Elsewhere, the narrator notes Marlow's irritation at someone's sigh when he struggles to tell of his fears of being robbed of his "destiny" by not seeing Kurtz and of his throwing overboard his new shoes soaked in his black helmsman's blood: "Why do you sigh in this beastly way, somebody? Absurd? Well, absurd. Good Lord! mustn't a man ever—." And then, "Here you all are, each moored with two good addresses, like a hulk with two anchors, a butcher around one corner, a policeman around another. . . . And you say, Absurd! Absurd be—exploded! Absurd!" (p. 114). By his own descriptions of Marlow, by his careful recording of Marlow's exchanges with others on the boat, and by his own commentary on the others, the narrator never lets us forget that knowledge comes to them all.

At the end of Marlow's tale, "Nobody moved for a time." The others, like him, have been stunned by truth, and the knowledge all but renders them incapable of action. They even lose "the first of the ebb" for which they have long waited. The narrator tells us by implication that they too have fallen, have received knowledge of darkness even at the edge of civilization. His last paragraph, which, according to Ford Madox Ford, Conrad spent three whole days revising,[22] tells us in no uncertain terms that the knowledge of darkness *has* been passed on—and it exposes Marlow's ironic preservation of that darkness. Marlow's last words are that "It *would have been* too dark—too dark altogether" (p. 162, emphasis added). In fact it *is* "too dark altogether." The narrator's words refer not only to the darkness that Marlow finds in Kurtz's truth ("a kind of light on everything about me") but also to the darkness Marlow himself creates. It is not just the "horror" that produces the darkness but Marlow's choice to conceal the truth, however justified his acts seem to be. The darkness is therefore both the truth *and* the lie.

For the last of several times the narrator describes Marlow as like a Buddha. His pose, according to William Bysshe Stein, reflects Marlow's transcendence: "Although qualified to enter nirvana, like the true Bodhisatta, Marlow remains in the world of work for the salvation of all souls."[23] But the text reads at best ambiguously—"in the *pose* of a meditating Buddha." And the narrator tells us at the very beginning that Marlow sat "in the *pose* of a Buddha preaching in European clothes and *without a lotus-flower*" (p. 50, emphasis added), the petals of which protect the Buddha from the mud and attest to the fecundity of the "contemplative" holy man. It is perhaps worth noting what Bruce Harkness calls "the most 'Conradesque' phrase" in Conrad's Congo diaries of 1890, the descriptions of a dead boy "in an attitude of meditative repose,"[24] for surely Marlow is aligned with death, not life.

Nonetheless, Marlow has become an agent of experience. We see in him neither total defeat nor victory, neither the consummate power of darkness nor the redemption of light. He alone has ventured into the deepest recesses of the self and has returned; but having done so, he lives in unending ambivalence, unable to step over the abyss like Kurtz or remain in the whited sepulchre like the Intended. In an ironic way he has transcended Kurtz's "victory," for he at least has been able to return to civilization. But he is exactly what the narrator says he is, "a Buddha . . . without a lotus-flower." Having ventured beyond the simplistic notion of good and evil, he cannot hope to evade his own or civilization's duplicity. For him, there is no paradise.

Jeffrey Berman comments that *Heart of Darkness* "represents the supreme culmination of the nineteenth-century English Romantic movement" in its dramatization of "the quest to push human experience to intolerable limits and to pursue transcendent knowledge," but that it also "anticipates . . . twentieth-century existential traditions" in that Kurtz "discovers no metaphysical secrets, achieves no religious salvation, reaches no resolution of his anguish."[25] That vision extends beyond Kurtz himself. The novel begins at the gate of Western civilization and it ends there. Whatever Marlow's failure, he at least raises to the level of consciousness the truth about Western culture that Kurtz learned through experience and Conrad himself acquired in his journey up the Congo in 1890—the heritage of fallen man. From Kurtz's fall comes the knowledge of a communal fall writ large in the history of Western civilization and, beyond that, in the universal chronicle of humankind. If Conrad goes "beyond theology" and the moral categories of traditional religion, he nonetheless shows us in cycles of the Fall—Kurtz's, Marlow's, the listeners'—that the most ancient of myths can yet move us closer to a truth. For the conflict between civilization and its discontents is exactly what he shows it to be—the record of a fall.

Demian by Hermann Hesse

> The being who is the object of his own reflection, in consequence of that very doubling back upon himself, becomes in a flash able to raise himself into a new sphere. In reality, another world is born.
>
> —Teilhard de Chardin, *The Phenomenon of Man*

If Hermann Hesse was spared Conrad's deep despair, it was likely because he saw in the struggles of Western culture the emergence, or at least the evolutionary possibility, of a higher communal consciousness. Though he shared Conrad's awareness that Western society was doomed by its own materialism and decadent morality, he considered its collapse the essential prerequisite for a spiritual rebirth. Hesse's vision was not limited to society in any narrow political or sociological sense but rather referred to the human community at large. Consequently, not only his conception of social structures but also his view of the individual acquired increasingly universal meaning. From the works of his earlier period of hopeful optimism, such as

Demian, through the fiction and poetry of a more purgatorial note, such as *Steppenwolf* and his collection of poems called *Crisis*, to his most affirmative statements in works such as *Das Glasperlenspiel*, Hesse's canon marks the progressive stages of growing consciousness and self-fulfillment. Inherently mythic in their structures, the novels weave together the psychoanalytic contributions of Freud and Jung and the inheritance of biblical literature. The result is both a secularization of theological tradition and a mythologizing of psychological insight. Theodore Ziolkowski asserts that in all of Hesse's work "the primary impulse is indeed religious,"[26] though this son of a missionary family can in no narrow sectarian sense be labeled a "Christian" writer.

Conrad's view of Western society as the reflection of fallen man in general certainly finds its parallels in Hesse, but with the major difference that Hesse saw in the ever repeated cycles of a fall (innocence-fall-reintegration) the progression toward a higher humanity. In many ways, his ideas more closely resemble the romantic sensibility of William Blake. Though, as Anna Otten points out, Hesse "never denied his affiliation with the romantic tradition," he primarily acknowledged German writers as his early teachers—Novalis, Holderlin, Jean Paul, Eichendorff, and E. T. A. Hoffmann.[27] His association with English romantics was indirect at best, more a matter of affinity than influence. Nonetheless, from a common ground of perception, Hesse and Blake presented remarkably similar definitions of the human condition, even given the qualifications Hesse developed in response to the psychological realism and scientific determinism of his age. Not even Nietzsche more closely approximates Blake's views.

Though likely more influenced by the Hegelian dialectic than directly by Blake, Hesse's important essay "Ein Stückchen Theologie" (1932) virtually recapitulates Blake's states of being: innocence, experience, higher innocence. Rudolf Koester paraphrases Hesse's idea of the transfer from innocence to experience as entering "a state of guilt." He goes on,

> The terms "innocence" and "guilt" are here used in their ethical sense. In childhood one is not yet responsible, one is ethically immature; whereas adolescence is a time of awakening to the ethical realities of the world. It involves an acquisition of the knowledge of good and evil and the realization that complete virtue cannot be attained. According to Hesse this realization causes despair which can be overcome by an attainment of the "third realm of spirit," transcending the polarities of life.[28]

The condition of "polarity," of course, Blake would call "experience," or "generation," the dominant state of becoming which can produce either regression or stasis in Ulro or progress to the Eden of higher innocence, Hesse's "third realm of spirit." To Hesse, the culmination of the three-staged evolution of *Menschwending* culminates in the "awakened man" just as Blake's myth ends in the awakening of the Giant Albion, the universal man. In either case, we are dealing with cosmic consciousness, not just *a* man but humankind in a process of psychic evolution.

Nor do the parallels with Blake end here. The outbreak of World War I referred to at the conclusion of *Demian* serves the function of revolution in Blake's mythology. Blake greeted the French and American revolutions as apocalyptic events just as Hesse did the Great War. For both writers the military action was less significant in its particular cause than in its "groaning toward creation." The destruction potentially served its purpose in the transvaluation of values and morality. In the fall of Western Europe a "new humanity" might grow. For both Hesse and Blake the gradual evolution of the individual ultimately exceeded the egotism expounded in more superficial romanticism. Anna Otten speaks for Hesse but may speak for Blake as well when she writes that "the personal quest becomes a 'divine duty' . . . a suprapersonal task undertaken for the betterment of the human condition . . . an individualism out of which a 'a new humanity' will grow."[29] Even the dominant symbol in *Demian* of the bird breaking out of the shell recalls Blake's belief that fallen humanity must shatter the mundane shell of time and space. The vision is communal, for just as the individual must destroy the Urizenic constraints imposed upon him, so also must evolving humanity cast off the psychic and mental chains of a dying society. For both, the temporal world must fall like the garden walls in paradise.

In their idea of the Fall, Blake and Hesse illustrate Jungian psychology. Hesse underwent extensive psychoanalysis under J. B. Lang, one of Jung's followers, in Lucerne between 1916 and 1919 and finally with Jung himself in 1921 in Küsnacht near Zurich.[30] It is clear that Hesse, with his strong religious sensitivities, embraced depth psychology and accommodated it to his mythic constructs. Most assuredly, Hesse found Jung's idea of the "cosmic man" a shaping influence in his art, for his emerging fictional hero, like Jung's archetype, embodies the integrated, or rather reintegrated, self in harmony with the life force. Blake's "human form divine," the most fully realized humanity, is an early prototype of Jung's cosmic man. So also, Jung's basic definition of individuation, which in many ways describes Blake's mythology, provided Hesse with a structural pattern for his fiction. That process, we have noted, follows the stages of the Fall. Ziolkowski relates Hesse's "rhythm of humanization" in *Demian* to the Christian pattern of "the original state of Paradise, the fall, and redemption through Christ."[31] Emil Sinclair, the central character, undergoes all three stages until he stands at last as a symbol of the New Adam, however secularized by Hesse's expanding humanism.

In the prologue Hesse introduces the Christian context of his novel by allowing his narrator-hero to relate his autobiography to Christ: "In each individual the spirit has become flesh, in each man the creation suffers, within each one a redeemer is nailed to the cross."[32] Even at the outset, then, he reveals his affinity with Blake. Henry Crabb Robinson records that when he asked the English poet and painter whether or not he considered Jesus to be God, "He said—*He is the only God*—But then he added—'and so am I & so are you.' "[33] Hesse's humanism, like Blake's, severely qualified the dogma of orthodox Christianity while holding to its mythic truth. *Demian* in particular depends heavily on the Judeo-Christian tradition of myth interpreted in the most liberal sense. Ziolkowski attributes the structure to Hesse's use of biblical *figura*. Hesse, he argues, "makes pronounced use of the modern author's prerogative to invest the traditional myth, archetype, or *figura* with a new meaning."[34] Biblical myth provides characters, interprets actions, and defines structure. Although *Demian* is finally a *Bildungsroman* following the normal outline of innocence-experience-adulthood, it owes its substance and relevance to Hesse's primarily Jungian adaptation of biblical images of the Fall—and those images begin in Genesis and end in Revelation, begin with the individual and end in cultural apocalypse.

We begin as always in the garden, defined simply as "a realm of brilliance, clarity, and cleanliness, gentle conversations, washed hands, clean clothes, and good manners" (p. 5). Peopled by father, mother, and sisters, this "realm of light and righteousness" marks the boundaries of paradise, outside of which exists an ominous world of darkness "dominated by a loud mixture of horrendous, intriguing, frightening, mysterious things. . . . Policemen and tramps, drunkards who beat their wives, droves of young girls pouring out of factories at night, old women who put the hex on you so that you fell ill, thieves hiding in the forest, arsonists nabbed by country police" (p. 6). Living on the threshold like Blake's children of "generation," James's Miles, and Golding's young schoolboys, Emil inches toward a fall, suffering the intrinsic dissatisfaction of every adolescent in paradise. Hesse grounds psychology in biblical myth when he describes Emil's loss of grace, for Emil is most certainly Adam in the guise of the Prodigal Son or *verlorner Sohn,* the erring archetype who sins against the father and suffers a self-division characterized in the parable by the remaining brother. For unavoidably Sinclair sins against the other self as surely as Cain's act of fratricide is a form of self-violation. Like all fallen creatures, Emil too suffers division when he crosses into experience, an act made possible by the tempter Franz Kromer.

We may say, of course, that all the characters in *Demian* are aspects of a self and that Emil is a composite of them all. Unquestionably Kromer plays the traditional role of serpent, the articulator of unacknowledged and illicit desire. Even called a "shadow" *(Schatten),* he emerges from Sinclair's as yet unaccepted dark side. Ruler of the nightmare world of the riverside with its "refuse, shards, tangled bundles of rusty wire and other rubbish," he introduces Sinclair to the underside of consciousness. Significantly, Sinclair falls when he lies about stealing apples in order to ingratiate himself with Kromer. The "lie" is a psychological truth, an act of the sinner residing in the psyche. In activating Sinclair's other self, Kromer thrusts him into experience with its unavoidable consequences of death, alienation, and division.

The symbolic death assumes the guise of Oedipal offense, for Hesse incorporates post-Freudian and Jungian as well as theological themes. The wayward son's primal disobedience becomes a gesture of moral freedom, "The first rent in the holy image of my father . . . the first fissure in the columns that had upheld my childhood, which every individual must destroy before he can become himself" (p. 15). By virtue of his "crime," he gains a moral superiority because he possesses a self-knowledge denied his father. When his father accuses him of having muddy boots, Sinclair finds his ignorance odious— "The actual crime was murder." He later dreamed that Kromer, his double, gave him a knife and told him to kill his father. In true Oedipal fashion, the paternal god becomes the enemy of his unconscious self.

But of course the boy's attachment to the father makes the intended murder an act of self-annihilation as well. In the tradition of the *Bildungsroman,* as the hero passes from one state of being to another, he wills to die, a theme repeated in the subsequent "falls" in the novel. Hopelessly divided, in love with his new-found freedom and yet horrified by it, Sinclair seeks oblivion. On one hand enslaved by the specious garden of straight lines, clocks, the Bible, and bookcases, and on the other hand entrapped by Kromer's criminal power, he exists in "a kind of madness" between contesting principles that equally compel him. His one world dead, the other powerless to be born, he wills to die: "For the first time in my life, I tasted death, and death tasted bitter, for death is birth, is fear and dread of some terrible renewal" (p. 16). His alienation extends to his mother and sisters as well. He feels guilty at "stealing" his own money from the piggy bank in his mother's room. He recalls escaping to his mother's lap when threatened by the harsh noises of the forbidden realm, but after his criminal acts his "mother's stepping up to [him]" frightened him even more than Kromer's commanding whistle. His guilt is magnified by his mother's apparent magnanimity and his sisters' fervent prayers. When Kromer tells him to bring his older sister the next time he pays him off for his silence, Sinclair bears "a new torture" that drives him to deeper despair. Suddenly, he finds himself unable to leave the garden and yet unable to remain. Symbolically, he had first tried to buy Kromer's silence by giving him his grandmother's watch. Later, he offered him "a Western, tin soldiers, and a compass"—all images of Urizenic order and values. Unable to save himself from his irresolute state of being, he must in effect fall again to progress, for his evolution toward psychic wholeness involves not one fall but many falls. If Kromer acts as serpent in his first fall and ultimately traps the young boy by his own will, Demian acts as the tempter in the second fall when he instructs Sinclair in the duality of good and evil by reinterpreting the story of Cain and Abel in the manner of Blake's "Bible of Hell."

Demian has been called Sinclair's "psychopompos" who stands against Kromer's "base 'shadow' " and "can set the negative forces into their proper perspective."[35] Another critic calls him "Sinclair's Socratic daimon, his admonishing inner self, but . . . also a Jungian imago, Sinclair's mental image of the ideal self, and . . . the reflective culturally unconditioned alter ego . . . a *daimon,* an imago, and an alter ego become a guiding analyst, a guru, or a guardian angel."[36] He serves many functions, to be sure, but he acts always as a tempter who can entice Sinclair into action without acting for him, except in a figurative sense. Like Leggatt, Demian is a *Doppelgänger* with whom Sinclair must hold communion, a tempter of the spirit as opposed to Kromer, the gross tempter of the flesh. In Blakean terms he is the reconciler between Orc and Urizen, passion and reason, who seeks the integration of what Hesse refers to as *Seele* and *Geist*. Speaking from the dream-world of the unconscious, he challenges the dominance of either spirit as soul or spirit as intellect. As a tempter, he urges Sinclair to break out of the garden of morality, reason, and restraint and, later, out of the equally debilitating garden of drunkenness and sensual abandon. In the first part, he encourages Sinclair to free himself from a self-imposed imprisonment by playing Cain, the direct inheritor of the Fall. "He too—though differently from Kromer—was a tempter," Sinclair writes, "a link to the evil world with which I no longer wanted to have anything to do" (p. 37).

Telling Sinclair, à la romantic tradition, that Cain, not Abel, is the hero of the spirit, Demian forces Sinclair to confront his own duality. Admittedly an Abel, Sinclair finds fearful Demian's suggestion that he ought to kill Kromer if necessary and thereby acknowledge his brotherhood with Cain. Afraid of falling, Sinclair holds desperately to his Abel nature; and when Demian destroys Kromer for him, he flees "back to the lost paradise . . . the light, untroubled world of mother and father, [his] sisters, the smell of cleanliness, and the piety of Abel" (p. 37). Having gained knowledge of his potential for evil—his illicit desire to kill his father, his secret joy in crime, his feeling of moral superiority—he cannot reenter his Edenic world. A "furious homesickness" falls upon him, Hans Luthi says, but he can no longer return to paradise.[37] Because he cannot be true to the "garden" morality without sinning against himself, he finally realizes the fact of his expulsion. The biblical myth undergoes a romantic inversion, for Sinclair soon learns that the escape *to* the garden constitutes a sin against the self far more devastating in its consequences than the sin against the patriarchal god of Genesis represented by his stern father.

The third and fourth chapters of the novel describe the end of the first prolonged stage of Sinclair's journey to selfhood, which ends when in a dream he symbolically consumes his false identify by eating the coat of arms chiseled in the keystone of the arch above the doorway to his house. The events leading up to his climactic dream continue to marry mythological or theological themes and the more or less conventional psychological themes inherent in the *Bildungsroman*. The Fall pattern is repeated three times within the two chapters.

Sinclair's first failure to recover paradise occurs because "my own sexuality overcame me." Like Blake, Hesse suggests that the fragile innocence of childhood cannot withstand the biological and psychological determinism of puberty. Sinclair's "great secret of puberberty" makes him painfully aware that "what Kromer had once been was now part of myself" (p. 41). With increased consciousness, he felt drawn more than ever to Demian. Like other opposites we have discussed, Demian provides the missing pole in the internal dialectic. When the teacher in confirmation class speaks disparagingly of the unrepentant thief on the cross, Demian defends him as "a descendant of Cain," "a man of character" as opposed to the cowardly Abel-like repentant criminal crucified with him. Almost lifting a page from *The Marriage of Heaven and Hell* and the Gnostic tradition, he argues for "a God that contains the devil too." It is worth noting that Demian does not deny the mythic truth of the Bible, only the myopic interpretation of the Church. Sinclair refers to fellow students who express a sophomoric "unbelief" in the "nonsense" of religion, but Demian is not one of them; rather he challenges only the simplistic division of the world into light and dark, good and evil. Finally, he tells Sinclair that his undiscovered self has always been present in his psyche: "You knew all along that your sanctioned world was only half the world and you tried to suppress the second half the same way the priests and teachers do." Self-knowledge comes only through experience, he says; "Only the ideas that we actually live are of any value" (p. 52). Urging him to acquire the freedom born of experience, he tempts him to gain existential knowledge by sinning against his conventional morality.

After giving impetus to action, Demian abruptly disappears until he surfaces in Sinclair's transcendent dream. In effect he is gradually absorbed by Sinclair's psyche. Even when he first appeared, Demian reflected Sinclair's inner self. He first introduced Sinclair to the coat of arms above his door—"He apparently knew our house better than I did myself" (p. 23). When Sinclair experiences his Oedipal awakening, Demian is characterized reflectively as living alone, perhaps incestuously, with his mother Eva. Feeling Demian's apparent powers of telepathy, Sinclair admits, "His voice seemed to come from within myself" (p. 33). Apparently in every way his opposite, Demian embodies something more than Franz Kromer's ostensibly evil world. Identified with all the dark powers within, he tempts Sinclair internally before he temporarily leaves him.

The Fall necessitated by puberty leads to a fall in reverse in the fourth chapter; that is, Sinclair enters a sensual garden of delights which reverses the archetypal Eden of his innocence. Attending school away from his boyhood home, he symbolically enters the autumnal world of death and decay where there was "a damp, bitter smell, and distant trees, shadowy as ghosts, loomed large out of the mist" (p. 58). Seeking escape from self-responsibility, he "greedily breathed the humid fragrance of decay and dying" as he had fled to his mother's lap in the opposing garden of light. In either case, he wants oblivion, freedom from the existential demands of selfhood. Here too, the tempter appears, in the person of Alfons Beck, a sexually experienced eighteen-year-old student. Hearing Beck boast of his exploits with Mrs. Jaggelt, owner of a stationery store, Sinclair vicariously participates in the adventure—"At least: this was reality." Quite simply, "This was paradise" (p. 61).

However limiting, Sinclair's inverted Eden marks a spiritual advance. In the evolutionary process, human beings alone can create their own environment rather than merely adapt to one, and in Sinclair's psychic evolution at least he struggles to construct his own paradise. Consciously shattering "the distant gardens of childhood," he turns from "such pure gardens" to "the world of darkness and to the devil." Embracing evil as he had embraced good, he "lived in an orgy of self-destruction" finally no more redemptive than the imprisonment of his innocence. It fails as all paradises do because it cannot tolerate its opposite. In that it establishes the dialectical tension which compels Sinclair forward, it indicates a forward point in the quest for self, but it is inevitably doomed. "I can still remember tears springing to my eyes when I saw children playing in the street on Sunday morning as I emerged from a bar," he confesses; "in my inmost heart I was in awe of everything I belittled and lay weeping before my soul, my past, my mother, before God" (pp. 62–63). Alienated by his offenses from family, friends, and teachers, he "raised between [himself] and [his] childhood a locked gateway to Eden." Despising what he had become, he feels "nostalgia for [his] former self"; but when he returns to his lost Eden during Christmas, "the fragrance of the Christmas tree told of a world that no longer existed" (p. 65).

Throughout the winter of his discontent, Sinclair continues in insoluble duality. His hedonistic garden can no more satisfy him than his earlier Eden. It too falls, and in its stead Sinclair constructs yet another paradise. In early spring, significantly, he finds himself attracted by a young, boyish-faced woman. Though he never meets her, he calls her Beatrice after Dante's mythic *anima*. She represents a new Edenic existence that, though also fated to fall, is yet another advance. Enamored of her "ethereal soulful quality," Sinclair tries "to construct an intimate 'world of light' for [himself] out of a period of devastation" (p. 67). Importantly, the new world is his own creation; "It was no longer an escape, no crawling back to mother and the safety of irresponsibility." Transfiguring his sensuality "into spirituality and devotion," he consciously plays the creator of Eden. Furthermore, he achieves a further step toward higher humanity when he transcends the reductive pleasure principle of his sexual awakening: "My goal was not joy but purity, not happiness but beauty and spirituality" (p. 67). Having played the devil in the garden of earthly delights, he now plays the saint in his spiritual garden. In Nietzschean terms, Beatrice becomes the Apollonian dream image that exorcizes the Dionysian impulses. But as Nietzsche goes on to say in *The Birth of Tragedy*, as the Apollonian principle comes to repress the Dionysian life forces, it is subjected to Dionysian revenge. By the end of the first part of the novel, Sinclair has been separated from the unconscious harmony of childhood, has tried in vain to return to it, and has unsuccessfully *but consciously* tried to live in the opposite gardens of the flesh and the spirit, darkness and light. Having thereby realized something of his potential self as god of his own being, he must at last abandon altogether the repressive constraints of his former self. Hesse ingeniously shows this in Sinclair's attempted portrait of Beatrice.

Kurt Fickert describes Sinclair's painting of Beatrice as evidence of his growth from the dualism he experiences as burgher or aesthete, sinner or saint. He notes that as the dream face evolves from Sinclair's portrait of Beatrice, it becomes "his Protean self—it is Beatrice, it is Demian, it is Demian's mother, Frau Eve." Sinclair becomes a *Dichter* [poet] figure, he contends, a "multi-faceted personality, part woman in his emotionality and creativity, part debaucher, part saint."[38] Whether or not his painting possesses any artistic value, it manifests his godlike power, his most fully realized humanity. In this, Hesse once again recalls Blake, who thought Christ the greatest artist that ever lived, "imagination . . . God himself," and "art . . . the Tree of Life."

As Sinclair gradually recognizes that the painting "was neither Beatrice nor Demian but myself . . . my inner self, my fate or my *daemon*" (p. 70), he remembers a brief meeting with Demian before he met Beatrice when his spiritual mentor accused him of going to bars like a "philistine"—"Can you see Faust sitting night after night stooped over the bar?" (p. 72). Now passed beyond debauchery, Sinclair again wills for Demian, and it is a testament to his growing consciousness that Demian does appear in a dream. Climactically, he invites Sinclair to eat his coat of arms with its heraldic sparrow hawk. Feeling the bird coming to life inside him, Sinclair awakens in fear and begins painting the bird freeing itself from a giant shell. The next day Demian sends him a note interpreting the dream: "The egg is the world. Who would be born must first destroy a world. The bird flees to God. That God's name is Abraxas" (p. 76). Several scholars point out that Hesse likely learned of this ancient Roman image from Jung or the Swiss anthropologist J. J. Bachofen. Ziolkowski notes that it symbolizes more than Sinclair's striving to break out of his own past and transcend "the world of false polarities" (light and dark, Heaven and Earth, male and female). It "reflects the development of his whole generation," he suggests, for from personal symbol it "is projected . . . onto a universal screen as a harbinger of war."[39] The dream of devouring the egg points us toward the latter half of the novel when Sinclair's autobiographical account of his personal fall expands to embrace the whole of European civilization. As in *Heart of Darkness*, the microcosm reveals a macrocosm.

As Sinclair first explores the paradoxical dualism of his human nature, no longer bound by the absolutism of his moral inheritance, he cannot evade the agony of becoming. Though he pays homage to Abraxas, the Gnostic god who is both god and devil, he cannot yet achieve harmony. A "sleepwalker" resembling the slowly waking Albion in Blake's myth, he shifts allegiance from the chaste Beatrice to his mother as his now-acknowledged lover in an Oedipal dream. As transfigured seducer, she incorporates all the illicit lovers of his unconscious, including Demian. He "felt a mixture of ecstacy and horror—the embrace was at once an act of divine worship and a crime." He "called it devil and whore, vampire and murderer," but it "enticed [him] to the gentlest love-dreams and to everlasting shamelessness" (p. 81). Perhaps in veiled reference to Goethe's *Faust*, he writes, "I was prepared to commit suicide," suffering as he does Kierkegaard's "sickness unto death." Neither saint nor sinner, he vacillates between good and evil, suffering from the judgment of the superego on one hand, the id on the other. Though he has journeyed beyond the confining garden of his youth—from childhood innocence to the paradise of earthly delight to the chaste Eden with Beatrice—he awaits another tempter to thrust him forward again. Pistorius not only triggers him to action, he also propels him toward a cosmic consciousness.

Pistorius is "a kind of midwife of the soul," "a religious epicure."[40] On the brink of suicide, Sinclair first finds himself enticed by the "intoxicating surrender" of Pistorius's organ playing. Pistorius tells him that he loves such "completely unreserved music" because "it is amoral," an expression of Abraxas. This "black sheep" son of a respectable pastor draws him even more into the mystery of being with its unending paradoxes. In a sense, Sinclair returns through him to the harmony of an innocence devoid of the moral imperatives of family and society. Through "free worship" and mystical ritual, Pistorius opens up the creative principle of the universe. Staring at the fire in Pistorius's room, Sinclair sees "red and gold threads . . . letters of the alphabet . . . faces, animals, plants, worms, and snakes" (p. 87). Recovering temporarily the images of childhood glimpsed when as a boy he stared "at bizarre natural phenomena," he finds himself in tune with "the indivisible divinity that is active through us and in nature." Virtually in the presence of god, the creative principle, Sinclair learns from Pistorius that we are each part of the creative whole, a cosmic consciousness: "If the human race were to vanish from the face of the earth save for one half-way talented child that had received no education, this child would rediscover the entire course of evolution, it would be capable of producing everything once more, gods and demons, paradises, commandments, the Old and New Testament" (p. 89).

When Sinclair asks why we must strive "if everything is completed in us," Pistorius defines humanity in terms strikingly reminiscent of Teilhard de Chardin. While all phenomena of creation carry the whole world, only man is aware of his creative principle: "As soon as the first spark of recognition dawns within him he is a human being." Only the fully realized human being can by "peeling off layers of skin" and breaking the eggshell of his temporal world achieve his divine nature. In effect, through Pistorius's teaching, Sinclair enters the evolutionary process of acquiring a deity. Most people prefer to "shed their wings and prefer to walk and obey the law," Pistorius tells him. They would rather remain in the protected garden shell of civilized society with its constrictive dualism of good and evil. He envisions Sinclair as being in the process of evolution, like a creature about to enter the land from the sea for the first time. To do so, he must leave the secure environs of his past and, regardless of price, for the first time become the creator of his own world. In Chardin's terms, the "cell" must become "someone."

As we move to an end of the Pistorius episode, Sinclair's individual story concludes, and he assumes the dimensions of the cosmic man. In a brief interlude with an admiring fellow student, he recapitulates his own past before moving on to his greater destiny. In his relationship with Knauer, he plays the role of Demian in his own biography. Just as Sinclair was fascinated by the mysterious authority of his powerful friend, Knauer is attracted by Sinclair's seemingly mystical powers. Convinced that Sinclair can communicate with spirits, he confesses his total devotion to attaining the psychic powers of "white magic" through continence and severe self-deprivation. Like a mirror image of Sinclair in his Beatrice period, Knauer insists that "you have to remain absolutely pure" if you travel "the higher, spiritual road." Having already gone beyond Knauer's stage of development, Sinclair talks to him as though to himself in retrospect. Knauer admits that he cannot exorcise his sexual yearnings in his dreams. "Each night I awake from dreams that I'm not even allowed to think about," he confesses in despair, an obvious reflection of Sinclair's forbidden dreams of his mother. At last Sinclair reiterates what he had learned from Demian and Pistorius: "You have to come to terms with yourself and then you must do what your inmost heart desires. There is no other way" (p. 99).

The encounter with Knauer ends shortly thereafter when Sinclair completes his painting "of the mother and strange woman" of his dreams. Having directly confronted his dream figure as Knauer has not, he assimiliates in his emerging consciousness the primal duality of his dream: "I questioned the painting, berated it, made love to it, prayed to it; I called it mother, called it whore and slut, called it my beloved, called it Abraxas" (p. 100). At last, "[I] saw the picture within me. . . . I could not separate it from myself, as though it had been transformed into my own ego" (p. 100). Waking from sleep, he remembers burning the painting and swallowing the ashes, most certainly a reenactment of the dream in which Demian had him eat his coat of arms. Compelled by "great restlessness," he journeys like the captain in "The Secret Sharer" to the very Gate of Erebus. Combining the psychoanalytic process of regression to childhood and the mythical motif of the night passage to the underworld, Hesse capsulizes Sinclair's past and future. Walking through the red-light district of the city to an area piled with bricks, Sinclair arrives at a building similar to "the new building back in [his] home town to which [his] tormentor Kromer has taken [him] for [his] first payment" (p. 101). Forced to enter, he sees Knauer "like a ghost" in the darkness. Aware that Knauer "must have called" him, Sinclair again plays a Demian sent for the salvation of a soul. Knauer is Sinclair past, the soul hopelessly divided against itself. Like Sinclair, and like the mythical Faust, Knauer "wanted to commit suicide." In saving him from self-destruction, Sinclair both relives his past and sounds the theme of his own eventual victory: "We create gods and struggle with them, and they bless us." Like the titles of other chapters, this one alludes to the Bible, "Jacob Wrestling," a reference to Jacob's dream when he wrestled with the angel until it blessed him. When he rescues Knauer, the image of his former self, he anticipates his own victory over the ambiguous *daemon*-angel of his own soul. That final victory, though, requires yet another fall, for in Hesse's conception each advance necessitates the wilful destruction of a garden state.

The Cain theme is woven throughout the novel. Not only is it the title of the second chapter, but it is also perhaps the dominant symbol in the text. Demian early identifies the mark of Cain as the badge of moral courage and freedom, and Sinclair "bears the mark" from the moment of first offense. The descendants of Cain are the heroes of spirit in the romantic sense. Not surprisingly, then, the Cain version of the Fall constitutes Sinclair's last major act in his personal quest for self. When he acts the role of Cain in relation to Pistorius, his individual quest is encompassed in a communal fall described in the last chapter. Recognizing that "each of us must take the step that separates him from his father, from his mentors," Sinclair finds it necessary to annihilate Pistorius and leave his garden as he did his father's.

Pistorius, who could be a fictional portrait of Hesse's Jungian psychoanalyst Dr. Lang, becomes a spurious Apollonian figure. That is, though God spoke to Sinclair through him, Pistorius gradually becomes a hindrance to Sinclair's spiritual growth. Devoted to the mythic past, he lives parasitically rather than authentically. Even his adored Abraxas, as Martin Buber notes, is deficient because "a being that represents and legitimizes nothing but ourselves . . . is not of divine nature."[41] In a way, his obedience to Abraxas is ultimately as stifling as allegiance to any externally defined god. As Sinclair learns, a borrowed deity, be it a Beatrice or an Abraxas, can never replace the "God in us." Consequently, in a wilful and profound fall, he must slay his brother. When he figuratively "shoots" Pistorius in a "fit of malice," he tells his brother-analyst-mentor, "You ought to tell me one of your dreams again sometime, a real dream, one that you've had at night. What you're telling me there is all so—so damned *antiquarian*" (p. 105). Walking for two hours after "killing" Pistorius with an arrow "from his own armory," Sinclair "felt for the first time the mark of Cain on [his] forehead" (p. 107). Like all true falls felt in the heart, Sinclair's provokes "shame and horror." But despite his "self-reproach," he knows that he "told the truth." Truly, Pistorius "was shackled to images the earth had seen before" (p. 107).

In this final personal fall before he engages in the larger fall of civilization, Sinclair feels the total alienation of anyone on "the way to himself." Ironically, Pistorius identifies him with Jesus in the garden of Gethsemane, himself on the way to godhead. Suggestively, the last paragraph of the chapter begins, "My school days were over." The dark trials of generation nearly ended, Sinclair awaits his destiny. In the mythic cycle of death and rebirth, he wills his death on the cross that the god might be resurrected in him. Symbolically speaking, he returns to paradise to be born again. This time he enters Blake's higher innocence, the Eden of the cosmic man.

Once during vacation from university study, Sinclair revisited the house where Demian lived with his mother. Seeing "an old woman strolling in the garden," he inquired after the Demian family. When she showed him a picture of her former tenants, he recognized his dream image. Returning as it were to the maternal womb, Sinclair is haunted by Frau Eva's face until late one evening he meets Demian and a Japanese man walking in the street. Seeing "the mark of Cain" more than ever etched on his friend's forehead, Demian invites him home to meet his mother. He leaves Sinclair "in front of a garden by the river" (p. 116) and tells him to return soon. On the verge of paradise, Sinclair walks out the next morning in a "gentle autumnal rain" and recovers somehow the lost innocence of his youth: in his words, it was "how the world had appeared to me in the mornings when I was a small boy, on the great feast days, at Christmas or Easter. . . . I saw that . . . it was still possible—even if you renounced your childhood happiness—to see the world shine and to savor the delicious thrill of the child's vision" (p. 117). "That moment came," he goes on, "when I found my way back to the garden."

Here he meets Frau Eva "smiling like a mother"—"her greeting was a homecoming." Eva is a combination of images. She has been called a Jungian *anima* and *Magna Mater*, the *Urmutter*, and, in terms of Revelation, "The Daughter of Zion." Irina Kirk describes her as the opposite of the Genesis Eve. Whereas Eve introduced Adam to knowledge that separates and divides, Eva reintroduces Sinclair "to the state of innocence where polarities do not exist."[42] More than Sinclair's personal spiritual mother, she embodies the creative principle itself—yearning toward the creation of a higher humanity. She gathers around her those actively seeking "the will of Nature" along divergent paths—"astrologers and cabalists, also a disciple of Count Tolstoi, and all kinds of delicate, shy, and vulnerable creatures, followers of new sects, devotees of Indian asceticism, vegetarians and so forth" all bound by "a distant good toward which all men were moving, whose image no one knew, whose laws were nowhere written down" (pp. 122–23). A chorus of humanity trying to crack the eggshell of the dying garden world of European culture, they embody in macrocosm Sinclair's arduous process of individuation.

To be born again, Sinclair's "dear mother" tells him, is "always difficult." Amidst the cosmic sweep of events, Sinclair consummates his quest for the mother-lover of his dreams, but he has far exceeded the feeble Freudian demands of his libidinous self. Rather he finds that Eva "existed only as a metaphor of my inner self, a metaphor whose sole purpose was to lead me more deeply into myself." With self-knowledge his childish wet dreams are transformed into a higher "union with her . . . consummated in new symbolic acts. She was the ocean into which I streamed" (p. 128). Less an individual than the prototype of the new man, Sinclair becomes the reintegrated man in the act of being born. His birth therefore embodies that of the whole human community.

Earlier I noted Hesse's "Ein Stückchen Theologie," which speaks of the three-staged journey to selfhood. In an essay, "Die Brüder Karamasoff oder der Untergang Europas," written in the same year as Spengler's *Decline of the West* (1919), he depicted the emergence of a new consciousness out of the ashes of Western civilization. When the false Apollonian structure of a dying culture represses the elemental life forces, it must give birth to Dionysian revenge. In its destruction might develop a higher form of humanity. This enlarged version of Sinclair's dream of the bird breaking out of its shell takes form when war breaks out in Europe.

Demian had early told Sinclair that the war will come because the "will of humanity . . . written in each individual" will manifest itself against a Europe that had lost "her own soul." In the deep reaches of the collective unconscious, he implies, "The world wants to renew itself. There is a smell of death in the air. Nothing can be born without first dying" (p. 131). In transferring the process of individuation from the self to the society at large, Ralph Freedman observes, Hesse employs Jungian themes "supplemented by mysticism" and ideas which "vaguely intermingle Zoroastrianism, the Nietzschean 'transvaluation' of good and evil, and Schopenhauer's demonic will."[43] The unifying element is still the myth of the Fall. Yearning for a better world, humanity wills its own demise, devastating its garden sepulchre by acts of violence and giving birth to the new Adam.

Hesse's chiliastic conclusion intermingles Eva, Demian, and Sinclair in a single mythic vision. The parallels to the book of Revelation are unmistakable. Once again, Hesse shows something of Blake's prophetic insight in works such as *Jeruselem*. Finding himself part of a universal force, Sinclair enters the war. When a shell goes off near him, it is transformed into a mystical symbol—"I could sense that a master was near me." Sinclair refers both to a male "god" *("ein Führer")* and a female deity *(Die Göttin")*. War marks both a *Götterdammerung* and the birth of a new divinity—in death birth, in the fall resurrection. The shell blast becomes the vision of Frau Eva, the *Magna Mater*, a "mighty godlike figure" in birth pangs:

> The goddess cowered on the ground, the mark luminous on her forehead. A dream seemed to hold sway over her: she closed her eyes and her countenance became twisted with pain. Suddenly she cried out and from her forehead sprang stars, many thousands of shining stars that leaped in marvelous arches and semicircles across the black sky. (P. 139)

The description, whose visual images match some of Blake's more visionary paintings, depicts a rebirth from the womb of the soul: "*aus ihrer Stirn sprangen Sterne*" ("from her forehead sprang stars"). In symbolically returning to the garden and reentering the womb, Sinclair is born again through the *Magna Mater*. Physically thrown into the air by the blast, he is thrust from the womb and lands "near the poplar tree, covered with earth and many wounds" (p. 139).

The apocalyptic ending of *Demian* brings the three principal characters together in the new creature and resurrection. Sinclair is "born" like Christ, whose image, Ziolkowski concludes, gathers into one "the individual and collective unconscious and the wholeness that is comprised of the opposites good and evil, light and dark."[44] In the makeshift hospital where he "lay in a stable, on straw," Sinclair finds Demian next to him. Also part of the Christ-like whole creature, Demian assures him, "I am with you," though he will have to go away. Kissing Sinclair for Frau Eva, he leaves "a little fresh blood" on the lips, thus symbolizing the needed condition of suffering in the eternal quest of fallen humanity—"In each man the creation suffers, within each one a redeemer is nailed to the cross" (p. 4).

Both Conrad and Hesse understood the truth of Freud's prediction that societies eventually fall, both recognized the depravity of Western European society of their time, both feared the devastating effects of knowledge, and both sympathized with the self in search of self-knowledge—but they saw the aftereffects of the Fall, both for the individual and the culture, in very different ways: Conrad foretold only profound uncertainty; Hesse, the promise of a greater humanity. The tortuous passage through experience with all its contradictory forces and savage revelations left Conrad's Marlow in a state of sustained ambivalence, fated like Coleridge's Ancient Mariner to repeat his tale and journey again into the Erebus of the psyche. The same agonizing path brings Hesse's autobiographical hero to redemptive knowledge. Similarly to Blake's *persona* in "I saw a chapel all of gold," Sinclair finds God in the stable. Or like his contemporary Yeats, he sees the reassertion of the godhead, however ambiguous, in the cleansing fires of war. Demian had told Sinclair that "the soul of Europe is a beast that has lain fettered for an infinitely long time. And when it's free, its first movements won't be the gentlest" (p. 124). Reborn in the mystical womb of Frau Eva, his mother-lover-self—"my ego," Hesse's hero participates in the awakening of that cosmic man. And we may wonder with Yeats "what rough beast, its hour come round at last, / Slouches toward Bethlehem to be born."

‡ 5 ‡

The Fall and After

Both Albert Camus's Jean-Baptiste Clamence in *La Chute* and Arthur Miller's protagonist Quentin in *After the Fall* undergo the paralysis of will that accompanies the devastating self-knowledge of the Fall. But whereas Camus diagnoses "the illness of the age, the fall," Miller proposes a prescription for its cure, "the prescription being a simple one requiring no less than everything."[1] The responses of Clamence and Quentin to their crises of will depict the final choice that finally must be made between being and nonbeing, between engagement in the human enterprise and unredemptive self-absorption.

Whatever his sardonic nature and however much we detach ourselves from his cynical revelations, Jean-Baptiste Clamence brings the light of darkness into our protected world. Deny him though we may, condemn him though we must, we cannot but admit, as does Clamence's mysterious listener, that we "feel less pleased" with ourselves for having heard his "confession." We see in him the testimony of our own guilt, and we can in no way deny complicity in the crimes he acknowledges. A Kurtz in the midst of an urban heart of darkness, Clamence lays bare our fallen nature along with his own. For us, as for him, the question is how to recover from the Fall in a seemingly godless age. His ingeniously concocted defense against judgment stands opposite Quentin's agonizing resolution in Arthur Miller's controversial play. Equally convinced of his guilt and the necessity of judgment, Miller's hero battles against the ultimate sin, that of not forgiving himself. Converting Clamence's thinly veiled self-hate into an elemental belief in his own higher humanity, Quentin chooses to embrace life even despite a frightening self-awareness. Both these characters illuminate a universal as well as personal guilt and the catastrophic consequences of the Fall for society and the self, and both reveal the terrible necessity for choice after the Fall. But whereas the truth finally sets Quentin free from servile self-condemnation, it locks Clamence in the inferno of his own making.

La Chute by Albert Camus

When he falls, the effect is almost as if the sky fell with him, bringing down in chaotic ruin the columns that upheld our faith. . . . We stare wildly about us, and discover—or, it may be, we never make the discovery—that it was not actually the sky that has tumbled down, but merely a frail structure of our own rearing, which never rose higher than the housetops, and has fallen because we founded it on nothing. —Hawthorne, *The Marble Faun*

"In a world that has ceased to believe in sin," Camus once wrote in the vein of a nineteenth-century sage, "the artist is responsible for the preaching."[2] Always the moralist, he consistently dealt with religious themes and issues. Though an avowed non-Christian, he indirectly articulated much of the Christian faith, if few of its doctrines. As Thomas Hanna has remarked, "When Christians pick up the works of such a man as Sartre, it is largely with a mind to refute; but, when Christians pick up the works of Camus, it is with a mind to learn."[3] But while virtually all Camus's major works raise the philosophical and humanistic concerns of twentieth-century theology, *La Chute* most directly employs the imagery and themes of the Judeo-Christian tradition. Roger Quilliot concludes that "this book could have been born only in Christian Europe."[4] Critics argue to what degree Camus's vision is compatible with Christian concepts in *La Chute,* but no one can deny his use of Christian myth and heritage. Even when refuting prescribed biblical doctrine, *La Chute* effectively employs the Bible as commentary on the modern age. In the romantic convention of mythic reinterpretation, *La Chute*, both by illustration and by inversion, attests to biblical truth outside a narrowly Christian frame of reference.

Jean-Baptiste Clamence's convoluted but tightly controlled "confession" recalls much of the romantic tradition which Camus ostensibly attacked. Clamence confronts the quintessential romantic dilemma: having discovered the self, how can one be freed of it? In effect, his monologue is less a confession than a strategy of escape. Clamence's expressions of romantic sentiment are tinged with irony: his autobiographical impulse becomes nothing more than what Blake would call "rational self-absorption"; his ironic role as Ancient Mariner transforms true penance into illusion; his Faustian heroism becomes Mephistophelean negation—his rebellion, cowardice. Enacting Christian and romantic themes, Clamence presents a brilliant, ironic revelation of not only a fallen but also a lost being able neither to accept the consequences of his guilt nor to deny it. Like Kafka, Camus constructs a modern parable on an ancient myth, the parable of twentieth-century alienated man beset with insoluble ambiguities: the story of a man who falls from an innocence that never was, seeks judgment from a God who never existed, and remains imprisoned by his inability to love or hate himself enough to be freed from himself. Like Dostoevsky's underground man, with whom he is often compared, Clamence can commit neither the saving sin nor the redeeming self-sacrifice that might release him from his self-bondage. Truly a fallen creature, Jean-Baptiste Clamence suffers the excrutiating anguish of T. S. Eliot's Gerontion, one who knows all too well who he is—and, "After such knowledge, what forgiveness?"

Clamence's recitation of his fall recalls Henry James's comment about characters who, seeming to make the point do not make the point, or seeming not to make the point make the point. He conveys both truth and half-truth. This devious master of deceit—and, most of all, self-deceit—uses the most disarming of techniques. He manipulates chronology: referring first to his prelapsarian state in Paris, then to the time he heard the derisive laughter provoked by his fall, then back to the Fall itself, then forward again to his experiences in North Africa and, at last, to his present condition in Amsterdam. We cannot be certain, of course, that even this apparent arrangement is a true account. It may even be that his fall occurred *after* his brief reign as "pope" in North Africa. Furthermore, Clamence withholds information in order to entice us further into his trap, promising to tell the listener, for example, about the evening when his life changed: "What? What evening? I'll get to it, be patient"—"What? I'm getting to it, never fear; besides I have never left it."[5] And throughout the telling, he punctuates his meaning with allusions to the present, thereby forcing his listener to reenact the past in the present. He uses setting with telling irony—the bar *Mexico-City*, the sites of Amsterdam (including the Jewish district, "the site of one of the greatest crimes in history," and the old slave market), the island of Marken and the Zuider Zee. He alludes to people to underscore his cynical viewpoint—"the worthy ape" at the *Mexico-City*, the woman he offends by his sarcasm, prostitutes behind shaded windows, a "brown bear of a man" persecuted by the police, ultimately himself. Above all, he employs every conceivable stylistic device to bait and engage his listener—rhetorical questions, ellipses, direct address (as many critics observe, his addresses become increasingly intimate and suggestive: "*monsieur,*"—"*monsieur et cher compatriote*"—"*cher mon-*

sieur"—"mon cher compatriote"—"cher ami"—"mon cher ami"—"cher"—"mon cher"—"très cher"—"cher maître"), exclamatory expressions, apparent digressions and frequent understatement. We have in fact an action of plot which is the history of Clamence's fall *and* an action of discourse which is his attempt to resolve his fallen state by foisting guilt onto the listener. What emerges is that duality of truth to which James alludes, a truth that is both conscious and unconscious. Jean-Baptiste Clamence sees with the burning vision of one who "knows" good and evil, but in his futile effort to be reconciled to his own duality he reveals a greater truth than he intends. In him we are reminded that no man can finally conceal his nakedness.

Clamence's recitation takes some five days, which are described in six sections of the novel: the first evening when Clamence meets the listener at the *Mexico-City* bar in the red-light district of Amsterdam (section 1); the second day when the two meet again at the *Mexico-City* and Clamence tells him about his lost Eden and the night he heard laughter and "gained a memory" (section 2); the third day when Clamence at last recounts his fall, the fateful moment when he allowed a woman to drown after she jumped from a bridge in Paris (section 3); the fourth day when Clamence takes the Listener to the island of Marken and returns at night on the Zuider Zee (sections 4 and 5); and the fifth day when the listener comes to Clamence's room (section 6).

The constriction and claustrophobia we feel on the fifth day, when the feverish Clamence lies confined to bed in his bare room at the center of hell, implies that this "shabby prophet" has *not* recovered from his fall. His elaborate strategem cannot save him from the severest of judges—the self. His pseudo-confession proves to be nothing more than a hopeless attempt to evade self-judgment, a form of self-indulgent, verbal masturbation. In the final analysis, because Clamence can not willingly face himself, he seeks judgment from an outer law, a god, secular or holy, rather than face the only judge that matters. Like a Dracula figure, he projects no image in the mirror—he can only reflect another. To see himself would be the death of the ego, a devastating coming of the light of truth. To meet the light would be to dissolve like the parasitic mythic creature of the night who arrives too late to evade the dawn. And as Clamence tells us, "The fall occurs at dawn" (p. 143)—it is the shattering light of truth. *La Chute* traces Clamence's night journey to a grim coming of the day.

A monologue posing as dialogue, *La Chute* follows a popular genre in modern fiction, but it differs decidedly from most other monologues. Closely related to Dostoevsky's *Notes from Underground* in structure as well as in theme, it exemplifies with profound irony the romantic concept expressed by Coleridge in *Biographia Literaria* that "the act of self-consciousness is for us the source and principle of all our knowledge." By the end of the century, Dostoevsky's anti-hero could remark, "Self-consciousness, gentleman, is a disease." Clamence echoes that sentiment, but he provides an added dimension of irony. In directing his cynical self-analysis to his unsuspecting listener Clamence believes he can hold a mirror before his victim. In fact, the listener reflects Clamence as well. If the listener exists at all, he embodies the other self that Clamence so desperately denies. His existence means that Clamence has not resolved his duplicity, that he affirms the need for self-justification that verifies his existence as part of Clamence. When Clamence openly identifies with him at the end of the narrative, asking, "What happened to *you* one night on the quays of the Seine?" he virtually becomes the shadow figure of himself, accusing the other who haunts him even now. By the end of the "confession," we realize that it is not the listener who cannot elude Clamence but the reverse. The listener's presence bears witness to Clamence's moral viability, however suspect it may seem. Clamence begins as the most subtle of creatures, skillfully arrives at the Fall (which he describes at almost the precise midpoint of the narrative), and then struggles to plead his case by claiming his victory over his divided nature. But the circuitous argument of the defense collapses, as it must, before the ultimate judge. And despite Camus's own quarrel with the existentialists, he shows us like Sartre that if man is truly free, he is free to judge himself.

The narrative begins abruptly as Clamence engages his listener at the *Mexico-City* bar. He describes the bar as a jungle, a "primeval forest, heavy with threats," ruled over by "the worthy ape," the owner whose virtue is his lack of guile. As Donald Lazere writes, "Like *Heart of Darkness, The Fall* exposes the bestiality underneath Europe's veneer of refinement."[6] In differentiating between the blinded bourgeois dreamers who haunt the "soggy hell" of modern European culture and the elemental primates who live without pretense of civility, Clamence only means to show their commonality. Clamence's initial means of engaging the listener involves assuring him that *he* at least understands the nods and grunts of the ape and hence can "plead" the listener's case. As intermediary, Clamence assumes knowledge of both the jungle and the city, both the power of darkness and of light. But "I know how to keep my distance" (p. 5), he adds pointedly. His cognizance of duplicity identifies Clamence at once as a character already fallen, already knowing good and evil. His primary strategy from the beginning is to expose the listener's duplicity as well by serving as exemplar. Hence he can accuse his listener of being a Sadducee simply because he confesses to being one himself.

He identifies with the listener's sophistication and culture only to define the opposite. Style, like silk underwear, he remarks, "too often hides eczema" (p. 6). Paris is beautiful, he admits, but it is, after all, only "a real *trompe-l'oeil*, a magnificent stage-setting inhabited by four million silhouettes" (p. 6). He characterizes the social structure as also pretense. It offers "a job, a family, and organized leisure activity" in order to conceal the moral depravity which attacks under the flesh like Brazilian piranha fish. Carefully noting that the organization is "ours," he identifies the listener with the duality in so identifying himself.

More damning than the hypocrisy of modern man is his *ennui*. Clamence defines contemporary man in one sentence: "He fornicated and read the papers" (pp. 6–7). Animated neither by the body nor the intellect, neither Apollo nor Dionysus, man lacks the ability to respond to good or to evil. Clamence brilliantly picks up the listener's answer to his question, "Are you in business?" When his colleague replies "in a way," Clamence latches onto the phrase and turns it against the speaker as further illustration of one who "fornicated and read the papers": "In a way? Excellent reply! Judicious too: in all things we are merely 'in a way' " (p. 8). Clamence implies the same detachment from life when he speaks of "my weakness" in the subjunctive mood, which the listener significantly recognizes. In a world of "if" and "maybe," good and evil become equally conditional. So it is, Clamence remarks, that by constructing "fine avenues with their parade of streetcars full of flowers and thundering sound," we can render impotent the vicious criminality of "our Hitlerian brothers" who annihilated 75,000 Jews. With remarkable nonchalance, Clamence observes that Western society has hidden its evil under the "sheer silk" of civilization, while its people drift dreamily in the moral "fog, compounded of neon, gin, and mint" (p. 13). Like a Marlow seeing in Brussels those masses who "dream their insignificant dreams," Clamence too gives witness to the living dead moving in self-ignorance and passive nonbeing. Through Clamence's eyes, Camus, like Conrad, depicts the modern inferno. Clamence tells his fellow countryman that "the center of things is here"—an echo of Marlow's comment, "I felt as though . . . I were about to set off for the center of the earth." Describing Amsterdam also as "at the heart of things," Clamence compares its concentric circles to the circles of hell, and concludes, "We are in the last circle" (p. 14). The worst condemnation of all is to remain exactly there, in the oblique vagueness where Clamence seeks refuge, a place devoid of spiritual animation.

On the second day Clamence describes the paradise he enjoyed in Paris before his fall. Though apparently a straightforward account, it too is neatly contrived to capture the supposed listener. At face value a candid revelation of hypocrisy, it is an *apéritif* to whet the appetite, for, as Geoffrey Hartman notes, Clamence "holds out the fruit of knowledge, . . . the impossibility of innocence."[7] Camus's own notebooks provide a gloss for the truth that Clamence confesses with insidious intent: "I lived my whole youth with the idea of my innocence, in other words with no idea at all."[8]

In his Edenic existence as Paris lawyer, Clamence "was buoyed up by two sincere feelings: the satisfaction of being on the right side of the bar and an instinctive scorn for judges in general" (p. 18). Unaware that one "can be corrupted by too much virtue, as well as by too much vice,"[9] he staked his being on his goodness. Free of offense in his professional life, he accepted no bribes and avoided "shady proceedings." He would not flatter and "even had the luck" of twice refusing the Legion of Honor "with a discreet dignity in which [he] found [his] true reward" (p. 20). Protector of orphans and widows, guardian of the blind, he was indeed a doer of good deeds, "giving direction in the street, obliging with a light, lending a hand to heavy pushcarts, pushing a stranded car, buying a paper from the Salvation Army lass or flowers from the old peddlers" (p. 21). In courtesy a knight—giving up a seat on the bus, picking up an item dropped by an old lady, forfeiting his taxi to another, giving up a seat in the theater, lifting a girl's suitcase onto the rack of a train—he derived "constant pleasure" from his own generous spirit. Basking in the adulation of his admiring public, he reached "that supreme moment where virtue is its own reward" (p. 23).

Skillfully integrating past and present through spatial metaphors, Clamence invites his listener to "pause on these heights." Freely admitting his love of "lofty places," he tells him he "would scale the heights and light conspicuous fires" to illuminate his "own excellence." All the more satisfied in his role as lawyer, Clamence lived "with impunity" without being concerned with judgment. Superior to the judge, "whom [he] judged in turn," precisely for judging, and superior to the defendant, "whom [he] forced to gratitude" (p. 25), Clamence lived in the most blessed of states. He could maintain innocence by virtue of his freedom from the duty and penalty of judgment. "I freely held sway bathed in a light as of Eden," he tells his listener: "Wasn't that Eden, *cher monsieur:* no intermediary between life and me?" (p. 27). Yet even as he recounts his days of glory, Clamence also acknowledges the precariousness of his paradise: "I was at ease in everything, to be sure, but at the same time satisfied with nothing" (p. 30). The beginning of the Fall is precisely the gnawing dissatisfaction which resides in the human breast, and Clamence is indeed a modern Adam. A would-be Faust turned into a Mephistopheles, he "ran on . . . never satiated, without knowing where to stop, until the day—until the night rather when the music stopped and the lights went out" (p. 30).

He postpones describing that event in order to punctuate his narrative with illustrations of human vanity and selfishness. He reminds his listener that we enjoy being generous with the dead, for example, because they can impose no obligations on us, and he alludes to a woman who used to chase him and "had the good sense" to commit suicide (a possible reference to the woman on the bridge whom he failed to save). Humankind cannot "love without self-love," he informs his listener, and he gives further examples of man's incapability of loving anyone but self. When the impatient listener asks again about the evening "when the music stopped and the lights went out," Clamence responds, "I have never left it" (p. 36). Whether he means that he consciously has been directing the listener to the moment or whether he unwittingly acknowledges that he can never escape that fateful evening, he speaks the truth.

But first Clamence recreates a later evening, not the night of his fall but a moment two or three years later when after a particularly successful day (helping a blind man, getting a reduced sentence, gaining the gratitude of his client, brilliantly improvising for several friends on the "hard-heartedness of our governing class and the hypocrisy of our leaders"), he came to the Pont des Arts. Looking down at the statue of the Vert-Galant, he suddenly heard a laugh. As it were glancing from the superior height of the bridge at the garden which symbolizes his innocence, Clamence confronted the consequences of his fall. The laughter mysteriously occurred later under his window, and when he finally looked in the mirror: "My reflection was smiling . . . but it seemed to me that my smile was double" (p. 40). At last bearing the weight of his guilt, Clamence could no longer deny his duality. The laughter could not be silenced, nor can be, because it is the voice of his other self. On the following day he explains to his listener why "it was probably then that everything began" (p. 43), for the mocking laughter drove him back, like all criminals, to the point of offense which marked his fall.

Clamence circumlocutes about the event, not in order to deny it, but the better to entrap his listener. Finally, he concludes the third evening of their brief acquaintance by describing the fateful encounter on the bridge. Subtly, however, he primes his apparently unwary victim by inviting him to walk through the town. With disarming familiarity, he integrates past with present, drawing his listener within the web of his guilt by seeming digressions and direct address. He explains with feigned disinterest how the laughter exposed his nakedness.

Clamence never speaks directly, though paradoxically he never leaves the subject. Even as he walks through the streets he means far more than he says. The "stagnant waters" of the canals with the "dead leaves" and "funeral scent rising from barges loaded with flowers" convey the images of lost innocence—his own and others'. His cumulative insights into modern man point always toward the listener. Observing a quaint house with two heads mounted above it, he informs his colleague that the heads represent Negro slaves who were once openly sold here. Now, he implies, "we are against it!" Our slavery has taken a less overt form, though of course we still have it at home and factory. Again and again he expresses knowledge of man's thinly disguised depravity, his elemental egocentricity. So pervasive is human guilt, he assures his listener, that to survive at all, we have necessarily manufactured shop signs of deceit. Lacking the extraordinary candor of the less sophisticated past when a slaver could announce bluntly, "You see I'm a man of substance; I'm in the slave trade: I deal in black flesh" (p. 44), contemporary man has masked his true identity. With direct assault Clamence challenges his *"cher compatriote,"* asking what his sign would be. Noting his silence, he threateningly concludes, "Well, you'll tell me later on. I know mine in any case: a double face, a charming Janus, and above it the motto of the house: 'Don't rely on it.' On my card: 'Jean-Baptiste Clamence, play actor' " (p. 47). As throughout, he literally admits his ulterior purpose as if he dares the listener *not* to succumb to his art. Here he virtually plays the "charming Janus" by admitting to being him, for within the same paragraph he warns the listener that he will tell him his "sign" later, then returns abruptly to his past to chronicle the self-discoveries he made after first hearing the laughter.

Theologians speak of the Fall as man's entering history, that is, entering a world dominated by time, conditioned by the consequence of past choices. If one fulfills the freedom to act, one thereby enters time by disrupting the horizontal sameness of his life where every day repeats the pattern of every other day. In Tillich's terms, one moves from essence to existence. Clamence refers to the laughter as the acquisition of memory—"Until then I had always been aided by my extraordinary ability to forget" (p. 49). A relentless pursuer, the laughter drives Clamence back to the point of offense by illuminating his elemental hypocrisy. Compelled to return to "the heart of [his] memory" because he cannot evade the derisive laughter, Clamence gradually had to recognize his own criminality. "Clamence's fall was more clearly a coming to a knowledge of good and evil than was Adam's," William Mueller contends, for he "had mistaken evil for good until he fell; his fall is actually a conviction of sin, an intellectual awareness of what really distinguishes the evil from the good."[10] Able to see his past *after* the Fall, he is tragically aware of his guilt.

For the "benefit" of his listener, Clamence indulges in a series of revelations even as the rain of judgment falls upon them on the streets of Amsterdam. Camus emphasizes the presentness of the past, for the falling rain personifies a common humanity in the "soggy hell" of modern culture. By hindsight after the Fall, Clamence recalls the sudden truths which bared his moral void. Finding himself tipping his hat to a blind man in hope of some sort of aggrandizement, he realized his total vanity: "I lived . . . without any other continuity than that, from day to day, of I, I, I" (p. 50). In a revealing echo of his listener's response, "in a way," he tells how he lived superficially in the illustion of reality: "All those books barely read, those friends barely loved, those cities barely visited, those women barely possessed" (p. 50). Living "in a way" out of a deep-set boredom, Clamence gained cognizance of his frailty both from within and without. He recalls being struck in public by a diminutive motorcyclist whom he had politely asked to move and realizes now that his petty humiliation merely exposed his own triviality. Laughing at himself with the perception gained from his fall, he admits: "I was eager to get my revenge, to strike and to conquer" (p. 55). Like the underground man, he had harbored an exaggerated revenge against someone who enacted a meaningless offense. Exposing his "dreams of oppression," Clamence "learned at last that I was on the side of the guilty, the accused. . . . When I was threatened, I became not only a judge in turn but even more: an irascible monster, who wanted, regardless of the law, to strike down the offender and get him on his knees" (pp. 55–56). No longer able to claim innocence, having in effect judged, he discovered that he too was one of the fallen.

So too he learned that his love of women was purely self-gratification, and that he was driven by his selfish need to possess their admiration more than by physical passion. Coming with consummate skill to his description of his fall, Clamence obliquely refers to one girl who "attracted me by her passive, avid manner." When she "related [his] deficiencies to a third person," he relates, he sought "to mortify her in every way." And when she finally "paid tribute to what was enslaving her," he concludes, "That very day I began to move away from her" (p. 65). But with the self-truth that comes from the Fall, Clamence "couldn't deceive [himself] as to the truth of [his] nature." With the harsh knowledge of good and evil, he knows that he merely desired "to be loved" and to receive what in his opinion was due him. In his words, "The moment I was loved . . . I shone, I was at the top of my form, I became likeable" (p. 67). Inching very close to the climactic revelation of his fall, Clamence adds that his "ideal solution" to a love affair "would have been the death of the person I was interested in" (p. 67). Such an end would have "fixed our relationship" without encumbering obligations to another human being.

On the second day Clamence had referred to a woman "who used to chase after" him and "had the good sense to die young" (p. 33). That such a death was by suicide made it the more enjoyable, for he could bask in the glory of her dying love, indulge in self-pity for his loss, and, above all, maintain the freedom from obligation. It may well be that the woman's suicide and the "shabby affair" with a woman he recounts on the third day directly relate to "the adventure I found at the heart of my memory," his actual fall. Significantly, as he finally tells of the event, the rain stops, perhaps signaling that the amorphous confession at last has reached the moment of truth. He recalls how on a November evening some "two or three years before the evening when I thought I heard laughter behind me," he heard a woman jump from a bridge—and he did nothing to save her. His fall is a sin of omission, not commission. Man cannot *not* fall simply by avoiding offense, Camus seems to say. Not to do something "evil" is never enough; one must do something "good" as well.

The imposition of choice is simply this: it can make one guilty whether or not one has committed a crime. According to David Madden, "Jean in Paris is Adam in Eden, unmarried, promiscuous, meeting his Eve and his fall in the drowning girl; Jean as Adam is modern man."[11] Finally forced to choose between executioner and victim, Clamence tries to extricate himself by evading choice. But, Albert Chesneau points out, Clamence *must* choose, and no "*excessif de pureté morale*" can wash away his guilt.[12] Phillip Rhein describes Clamence's recognition:

> Up to the moment of confrontation between the "I" and the "other," it is possible to speak of evil as outside the self or in "others," but after the

confrontation the "I" becomes aware that to the "others," he is an "other." The "I" then recognizes both his subjective innocence and his objective guilt.[13]

Denied superiority in his virtue, Clamence can reconstruct it only in his vice.

"Who can tell the anguish of the man who sided with the creature against the creator and who, loving the idea of his own innocence, and that of others, judges the creature, and himself, to be as criminal as the creator?" Camus asks in his *Notebooks*.[14] What is the cause of his guilt? Why did Clamence not act to save the girl? Camus simply referred to "the flaw in man,"[15] perhaps the closest he came to defining original sin. One thing we know: Clamence could not remain in his paradise. But in reciting his vain attempts to recover from the Fall, Clamence tightens the web around his listener, only to become the victim of his own deceptions.

The two sections which comprise the fourth day of the acquaintance move from Amsterdam proper to the Island of Marken and the Zuider Zee. The landscape imagery becomes even more obscure than in the city itself, for we are now indeed in the nebulous circles of hell:

> Isn't it the most beautiful negative landscape? Just see on the left that pile of ashes they call a dune here, the gray dykes on the right, the livid beach at our feet, and in front of us, the sea the color of a weak lye-solution with the vast sky reflecting the colorless waters. (P. 72)

An appropriate description of Blake's Urizenic universe, the setting is completely horizontal—"No relief; space is colorless, and life dead. Is it not universal obliteration, everlasting nothingness made visible?" (p. 72). A witty Mephistopheles slyly presenting his repressive nihilism, Clamence, as he has all along, wills to deflate whatever optimism his listener clings to. When the hearer refers to the doves being alive at least, this intellectual Satan in modern dress assures him that though the doves "would like to come down . . . there is nothing but the sea and canals, roofs covered with shop signs, and never a head on which to light" (p. 73). Obviously an allusion to the biblical symbol of the Holy Spirit, the dove alone seems to challenge Clamence's negativism. Consequently, he must deny the image, transform it from a sign of hope to a symbol of despair. Only in a hopeless existence can Clamence maintain his superiority, for without a god of redemption he alone reigns supreme.

With arresting candor Clamence tells of confronting his own nothingness, of realizing he had no friends, only fellow accomplices in the common human guilt. With the visionary power of a malcontent in a Jacobean tragedy, he tells his immediate accomplice, "The earth is dark, *cher ami*, the coffin thick, and the shroud opaque" (p. 74). Moving cunningly from autobiography to present narrative, he describes the absurdity of existence in a fallen world. A disreputable existentialist who loves life too much to commit suicide in the face of such absurdity, he finds he can live only so long as he can "elude judgment"—find the fig leaves to conceal his nakedness. From "the moment [he] grasped there was something to judge in [him]," as he describes it, he suffered a classic paranoia, a profound fear that all "were laughing" derisively at him. The laughter, like Poe's tell-tale heart, could not be silenced: "The day I was alerted I became lucid; I received all the wounds at the same time and lost my strength all at once. The whole universe began to laugh at me" (p. 80).

Always plying the listener, he embraces him with a designing "we": "We all want to appeal against something!" he tells him, and he all but reveals his strategy of entrapment: "Each of us insists on being innocent at all costs, even if he has to accuse the whole human race and heaven itself" (p. 81)—"It's a matter of dodging judgment" (p. 82). With a pointed allusion to Dante, he says, "We should like, at the same time, to cease being guilty and yet not to make the effort of cleansing ourselves. Not enough cynicism and not enough virtue. We lack the energy of evil as well as the energy of good." Like Dante's "neutral angels," he goes on, we exist "in Limbo, a sort of vestibule of . . . Hell. We are in the vestibule, *cher ami*" (pp. 83–84). As he continues his history he thus interprets the common condition of humankind, ever drawing his listener into the morass of his own guilt.

As if to assure the listener that all efforts to escape guilt are in the final analysis futile, he recounts his own efforts. He first increased his efforts at virtuousness, he tells him, but "I could not manage to believe in the commitments I made" (p. 88). In short, "I could not forgive myself" (p. 89). Not God but he himself judged himself while paradoxically attempting to evade judgment. His newly exposed Other, the reprobate beneath the mask, took on the role of avenger, "publicly inveighing against the humanitarian spirit" that his virtuous self had espoused. "I wanted to break open the handsome wax-figure I presented everywhere" (p. 94), he remarks; but he discovered, "It is not enough to accuse yourself in order to clear yourself; otherwise, I'd be as innocent as a lamb. One must accuse oneself in a certain way" (pp. 95–96). Tantalizing his listener with a sudden shift to the present, he observes the sea rising, the day ending, the doves ominously gathering in the sky, and, most suggestively, the light "waning." "Don't you think we should be silent to enjoy this rather sinister moment?" (p. 96), he asks, fully aware that his hearer will say no. Truly an ingenious master of illusion, this word-juggler tells "us truth . . . to win us to our harm."

The second portion of the account of the fourth day begins, like the first part, with a reference to the landscape. The Zuider Zee serves again as the symbol of spiritual despair: "With its flat shores, lost in the fog, there's no saying where it begins or ends. So we are steaming along without a landmark; we can't gauge our speed. We are making progress and yet nothing is changing. It's not navigation but dreaming" (p. 97). Against the spiritual fog, Clamence resumes his story, telling how he sought escape from his guilt in debauchery. "In a sense, I had always lived in debauchery," he adds, "bursting with a longing to be immortal. I was too much in love with myself not to want the precious object of my love never to disappear" (p. 102). But if the rational paradise he had designed as successful lawyer was fated to collapse by virtue of his inability to believe in his own virtue, his "earthly paradise" proved equally impermanent. Though it "liberates because it creates no obligations," debauchery also falls prey to man's mortality: the liver and fatigue. Temporarily creating "a fog in which the laughter became so muffled that eventually [he] ceased to notice it" (p. 106), it too gave knowledge of human limitation. After a brief physical recovery, Clamence again believed "the crisis was over," but, as he repeatedly tells his listener, there is no return to innocence after the Fall.

All illusions of escape dissolved one day on an ocean liner when Clamence thought he saw a drowning person far off from the ship. Though he instinctively turned away and his heart "beat wildly," he "forced" himself to look again. When "on the point of shouting, stupidly calling for help," he saw that it was only a bit of refuse. But the truth was all too clear: "The cry which had sounded over the Seine behind me years before had never ceased, carried . . . across the limitless expanse of the ocean; . . . it had waited for me there until the day I had encountered it" (p. 108). An unwilling Oedipus returned to the crossroads, he once more faces the fact of his guilt. In another ironic reference to the Bible, Clamence hears the cry wherever can be found "the bitter water of [his] baptism." His past innocence symbolically dead and buried in the baptismal waters, he stands with the listener overlooking "this flat, monotonous, interminable water," "this immense holy-water fount," listening to the invisible gulls calling him—"to what?" (pp. 108–09). Having endured an ironic baptism, having his innocence *not* his sins washed away, he can see no dove of the Holy Spirit about to descend and bless him. All innocence gone, "I had to submit and admit my guilt," he says, to endure the agony of the "little-ease," that medieval torture chamber which is "not high enough to stand up in nor yet wide enough to sit down in" (p. 109). Lying "on the diagonal" with what Albert Maquet calls "the stabbing pain of desire for innocence crushed beneath the weight of a guilty conscience,"[16] Clamence can only hope to elude judgment. Denied the privilege of innocence, he can take comfort only in the guilt of all. "Every man testifies to the crime of all others—that is my faith and my hope" (p. 110).

In a perverse doctine of original sin, Clamence rejoices in a universal guilt. He takes refuge even in Christ's guilt. Christ, too, was guilty, after all. The slaughter of the innocents was his "innocent crime"; and, not able to defend himself, he had the courage "to die, in order not to be the only one to live" (p. 113). While he confesses to loving his own life too much to commit suicide, Clamence praises Christ for the suffering of his incarnation: "He cried aloud in His agony and that's why I love him" (p. 114). Identifying the incarnate Christ as the ultimate rebel against God because of his "seditious cry" on the cross, "Why hast thou forsaken me?" Clamence lays claim to Him as the epitome of humankind—"my friend who died without knowing" (p. 114). His ironic Christ speaks of both truth and falsity: truth because if Christ put on the flesh he must have somehow shared in a common guilt, falsity because Clamence cannot acknowledge the redeeming power of His resurrection. He can accept the Christ of negation but not of affirmation. To him, Christ "left us alone" without the power of the Holy Spirit to comfort us. For us, Clamence tries to convince the listener, the dove does not descend. Alone, and therefore ironically free, Clamence must seek his own salvation. Irina Kirk contends that the freedom Clamence gains as a result of his profound self-consciousness elevates him "into a position of self-creator, his own judge, and opens before him two avenues, one leading to nihilism, the other to self-respect and respect for others."[17] Like Dostoevsky's cynical anti-hero, Clamence chooses nihilism. Hence, as he says, he has "taken refuge in a desert of stone, fogs, and stagnant waters—an empty prophet for a shabby time, Elijah without a messiah" (p. 117). Promising to explain his recovery on the next day, he plays both Christ and John the Baptist, whose name he illicitly claims: "Fortunately, I arrived! I am the end and the beginning; I announce the law. In short, I am judge-penitent" (p. 118).

The closer we come to the end of Clamence's recitation, the more we become aware of his physical weakness, and such frailty no doubt exposes his failure to recover from the Fall. On the fifth day the listener finds him in bed suffering from a fever, a worsening of the chills he felt in the "damned humidity" on the Zuider Zee (p. 111). Confined to his bed in the very heart of moral darkness, Clamence seems physically to caricature the victory he claims, like the dying Kurtz making vain boasts in the midst of the jungle. His room bespeaks his moral state, containing only "the bare necessities, clean and polished like a coffin. Besides," he observes, "these Dutch beds, so hard and with their immaculate sheets—one dies in them as if already wrapped in a shroud, embalmed in purity" (p. 120). Even as he begins this last of his history and announces his triumph over duplicity, we watch the progress of his physical decay and hear in the substrata of his speech the testimony of fear. "Did you close the door thoroughly?" he asks. "Make sure, please. Forgive me, I have the bolt complex. . . . I am . . . eager to block the door of the closed little universe of which I am king, the pope, and the judge" (pp. 127–28). The more assertive he becomes, the more conscious we are of the quiet desperation seething beneath the surface of cynical control.

He recalls how he discovered the solution to his dilemma. During the war he was captured by the Germans and imprisoned in Tripoli, not because he had joined the Resistance, but because he had followed a woman to Tunis who, unknown to him, was an agent for the Allies. One day in prison a Frenchman sarcastically called for the election of a new pope, one who "has the most failing" of all. When Clamence jokingly nominated himself, he was appointed and began to "exercise my pontificate for several weeks, with increasing seriousness" (p. 126). It struck him that "one must forgive the pope. To begin with, he needs it more than anyone else. Secondly, that's the only way to set oneself above him" (p. 127). In other words, he discovered that the mock-pope acquired power simply because he fulfilled the psychological necessity of others to feel superior to him—because he had "the most faults"—and, paradoxically, because he merited the highest level of forgiveness. The others "got into the habit of obeying me," he confirms, "even those who lacked faith" (p. 126). The experience ended (or rather, he "closed the circle") the day Clamence drank a dying prisoner's water allotment, "convincing [himself] that the others needed [him] more than this fellow who was going to die anyway" (p. 127). Though he assumes a cold aloofness from the event and betrays no deep remorse, Clamence is yet compelled to confess the deed. He even admits that had the dying man been the Frenchman who named him pope, he would have resisted stealing the water longer, "For I loved him—yes, I loved him, or so it seems" (p. 127). Whatever he claims, Clamence still suffers duality, still owns a moral consciousness he obscures with his intellectual detachment.

But as always, Clamence quickly turns from then to now, from history to commentary on the present, to keep his listener off-guard and to avoid revealing more of himself than he intends. He calls the listener's attention to the stolen painting of "The Last Judges" (the panel of the Van Eyck brothers' famous polytych "The Adoration of the Lamb" stolen in 1934) which he has stored in his cupboard. Earlier at the *Mexico-City*, Clamence had pointed out the empty rectangle where the picture had hung. The stolen painting apparently was given to Clamence by "the worthy ape," who somehow acquired it after the theft. As Ralph Berets observes, the altarpiece depicting God's love and judgment provides a "basic counterpoint" to Clamence's view of the world: "It reveals a historically accepted interpretation of man's relationship to his universe. Using this as his foundation, Camus, by confounding historical events with psychologically distorted interpretations, suggests that this stable world view was finally and irrevocably destroyed during the Nazi atrocities of the Second World War." Clamence himself "is closely linked to the art thief, who is at least symbolically responsible for the disappearing of justice and the various imitations that have been fabricated to fill the void."[18] Offering a six-point argument for the thief's not returning the panel, Clamence insists that he has "definitively" separated justice from innocence—the judges from the innocent Christ, even as the stolen panel has removed the judges from the Lamb. And so, he ends, he has made "the way clear to work according to my convictions. . . . I can practice the difficult profession of judge-penitent" (p. 130).

By way of recapitulation and interpretation, Clamence then defines his profession—"I am practicing it at present" (p. 130). A virtual parody of himself, even as he reaches this point of greatest triumph, having "set myself up after so many blighted hopes and contradictions," he must sit up to gain his breath and admit, "Oh, how weak I am!" (p. 130). Seeing his physical dissolution, hearing his frenzied words, we can no more believe in his recovery than he can truly believe in it himself.

As he describes his devious strategy, Clamence covertly and overtly continues to threaten the listener from whom he draws the sustenance needed to maintain his ego. "Don't get the idea that I talked to you at length for five days just for the fun of it," he warns. "Now my words have a purpose . . . the purpose, obviously, of silencing the laughter, of avoiding judgment personally, though there is apparently no escape" (p. 131). Once believing his guilt intolerable, Clamence now finds innocence intolerable—anyone's innocence. At one time in love with his operatic heroism, he now engages in masochistic self-deprecation. Says Sara Toenes, "Clamence cannot tolerate the idea of being human, of being partly good and partly evil. Unable to believe as he once did in his own superior virtue, he determines to recreate himself as totally evil. His confession paints a portrait of absolute guilt, and at the same time creates a universe in which he can reign triumphant, a Lucifer or Prometheus, rather than a moral creature."[19] To resolve his crisis, in short, Clamence transforms his absolute goodness into absolute evil. (Camus once considered calling the novel "*Un Puritain de notre temps.*")[20] In that one can be puritanized by evil as by good, the title would have been apt, for Clamence in either case is doomed to hell, as Mildred Hartsock says, not "from the ambiguity of good and evil, but from the refusal to live in a tension between the two. Clamence sells out to an absolute."[21] In discussing the governess in *A Turn of the Screw* we noted in ironic paraphrase that if innocence corrupts, absolute innocence corrupts absolutely. Clamence verifies this truth and its opposite as well. He lacks the integrity, the elemental courage, needed to live with his own opposites. As he now tells us, he found a way to make self-contempt a mark of superiority, "to gain a deity" by assuming the role of god-judge—"God being out of style" (p. 133).

Humanity most fears freedom, for freedom demands self-judgment. "At the end of all freedom is a court sentence; that's why freedom is too heavy to bear, especially when you're down with a fever, or are distressed, or love nobody" (p. 133). Consequently, we need some god, some measure of good and evil, however arbitrary, so that we can at all costs evade the awesome weight burdening those who judge themselves. To be free of merciless judgment of the self, we seek to obey "a greater rogue than oneself" (p. 136). By being that rogue, assuming the satanic role seemingly on behalf of "*les autres,*" Clamence gains "the right to sit calmly on the outside myself" (p. 137). That is, by playing the sinner-penitent so that no one can judge him more guilty than he himself, he can become the judge of others rather than himself, thereby sitting on the throne—"the king, the pope, and the judge." "So I have been practicing my useful profession at *Mexico-City* for some time," he pointedly confesses, where "I lie in wait particularly for the bourgeois" (p. 138–39). My "public confession" is "not hard," he continues, "for I now have gained a memory." Deviously, he depersonalizes his guilt by constructing "a portrait which is the image of all and of no one," and "when the portrait is finished, as it is this evening, I show it with sorrow. 'This alas, is what I am!' The prosecutor's charge is finished. But at the same time the portrait I hold out to my contemporaries becomes a mirror" (pp. 139–40).

For all his assurances, though, Clamence, like all who abide in Ulro, cannot regain paradise. He claims to "have accepted duplicity instead of being upset about it" (p. 141). But his rising fever and increasing desperation betray his failure. "At long intervals, on a really beautiful night," he truly confesses, "I occasionally hear a distant laugh and again I doubt" (p. 142). Even the image he paints of himself as successfully applying "the details of my technique" proves false. He has to ask the listener to remove the blanket so he can breathe, and he vainly tries to move about in order to "be higher than you." His insistence that he has gained happiness fades into despair: "I am happy, I tell you, I won't let you think I'm not happy, I am happy unto death. Oh, sun, beaches, and the islands in the path of the trade winds, youth whose memory drives one to despair!" (p. 144).

Acknowledging that "we have lost the track of the light, the mornings, the holy innocence of those who forgive themselves" (p. 145), Clamence tells his listener it would be well if he were a policeman and could arrest him for theft of "The Last Judges," for again someone else could judge him, and, as he says, "I'd have no more fear of death." Decapitated head held up like that of John the Baptist, "I again could dominate," he surmises: "I should have brought to a close, unseen and unknown, my career as a false prophet crying in the wilderness and refusing to come forth" (p. 147). Clamence indeed makes the point while seeming not to make the point and does not make the point while seeming to make the point. In that he defines the shifting poles of good and evil, he achieves the "moral victory" of a Kurtz. His fall, like Kurtz's, brings the frightening revelation of every man's capacity for evil. Nor should we be misled by Camus's own comments about the illicitness of ascribing guilt. Though in *The Myth of Sisyphus* Camus defends human innocence against existential and Christian charges of guilt, Camus by no means considered the individual inculpable. As Phillip Rhein concludes, "If all men are innocent, there can be no man created evil which they would be compelled to resist. Obviously, evil does exist, and men exist who create the conditions against which the rebel revolts."[22] In exposing what Geoffrey Hartman calls "this purely horizontal world" of "complicity, the secular form of original sin,"[23] Clamence serves a moral end.

Clamence himself seems "irrevocably lost" like Kurtz. Although some readers have concluded that he would not save the woman at the bridge even if given a second chance, Clamence does not directly refuse to save her; he only observes, "*Brr! . . . l'eau est si froide!*" True, he calls it fortunate that "It's too late now. It will always be too late" (p. 147), but it is no small point that he does not explicitly say, "I would not act." In fact, even if ironically, he says in the conditional tense, "*Il faudrait s'exécuter*" ("We'd have to do it"). Furthermore, we must raise the whole question of who the listener is. Though many critics, such as Sara Toenes, consider him distinctly different from Clamence, the many parallels between the two suggest otherwise. Nor does it seem likely that a Paris lawyer of such obvious sophistication would visit a seedy bar in the red-light district of Amsterdam. Though it is true that the listener's implied responses dot the narrative, we are left to wonder if Clamence is not talking to himself, perhaps like the captain speaking in "silent communion" to the "secret sharer" in Conrad's short story. If so, we would add not only profound irony (does Clamence turn the mirror to himself in true romantic fashion?) but also a motivation for the whole "*récit.*" For if he talks to himself, then Clamence remains a viable moral being still forced to see the futility of his own evasions. He apparently shatters the distance between himself and the listener at the very end when he assimilates his identity:

> Then please tell me what happened to you one night on the quays of the Seine and how you managed never to risk your life. You yourself utter the words that for years have never ceased echoing through my nights and that I shall at last say through your mouth: "O young woman, throw yourself into the water again so that I may a second time have a chance of saving both of us!"
>
> (P. 147)

Clamence is *not* reconciled to the Fall, nor can he deny the ontological dilemma he yet suffers after the Fall.

Despite Camus's professed anti-Christian stance, some have tried to make *La Chute* "profoundly Christian." For example, Conor Cruise O'Brien finds it Christian "in its confessional form, in its imagery, and above all in its pervasive message that it is only through a full recognition of our sinful nature that we can hope for grace."[24] To most, I have noted, the novel interprets the Fall in essentially non-Christian terms. R. W. B. Lewis insightfully relates it to the tradition of the 'fortunate fall' but denies that it is Christian myth:

> The phrase is intended to suggest, within the Christian framework, that the fall of Adam (that is, the fall of man) proved to be fortunate for mankind since

it made necessary the entrance into human history of God as man. . . . Modern literature, however, has often exploited a humanistic equivalent of the religious idea; and has suggested that the fall from innocence or virtue can have a fortunate effect upon an individual, that it can educate, enrich and humanize him. Such, so far as we can make out in the Dutch fog amid the interwoven ambiguities of the novel, is the effect of his fall upon Clamence; . . . he is at least a much fuller human being, and a more real one.[25]

Perhaps in a postromantic sense, if Jean-Baptiste Clamence is guilty, he has sinned against himself, not God; if he has fallen, he has fallen from his own flawed self-conception. Rather than negating the Fall, such an interpretation humanizes it. It makes a theological doctrine into an essentially existential parable. In Paul Tillich's terms it illustrates the movement from essence to existence. If we consider this the trivial secularization of a religious myth, our terms may deceive us. Camus does not deny the presence of man's higher nature, but he steadfastly refuses to locate its source outside the self. Clamence's terrible offense is finally that he refuses to pay the full price of his humanity, to endure the duplicity which is his common fate. He is therefore "not so much fallen as *continually* falling."[26] Say what we will, he at least realizes the unauthenticity of life in the modern Eden, and he gives witness to the universal depravity of man. Suffering the agony of a Kurtz in perpetuity, he can neither be redeemed nor lose his passion for redemption, however much he tries to convince us that he can. In the ultimate sense, then, he experiences the most *un*fortunate of falls, the fall of one who "knows" but cannot act to redeem himself.

After the Fall by Arthur Miller

An innocent man is a sin before God. Inhuman and therefore unworthy. No man should live without absorbing the sins of his kind, the foul air of his innocence, even if he did wilt rows of angel trumpets and cause them to fall from their vines.
—Toni Morrison, *Tar Baby*

Although in Arthur Miller's *After the Fall* the allusion to the Fall pertains to the Holocaust and to the political injustices of the McCarthy era following World War II, it refers in particular to the spiritual condition of a man who must unequivocally face his own complicity in the evil of his age and in the suffering of those whose lives he has directly touched. Like Camus's Jean-Baptiste Clamence, Miller's protagonist Quentin begins his personal drama in crisis after the Fall, tottering between action and inaction, evasion and choice.

Though to some the play is strongly anti-Christian or even nonreligious, despite its title, Miller's themes stem from the elemental concerns of the American puritan tradition. Leonard Moss has commented on Miller's "strong interest in the fall theme—the crisis of disillusionment—from the start of his career in the early nineteen-forties."[27] Depravity and guilt have been ultimate concerns in all his major works. Miller himself commented, "I can't see the problem of evil evolving fruitfully unless the existence of evil is taken into account."[28] *After the Fall* directly addresses the problem of evil, for it depicts man not only after his personal fall but also after the historical fall which is his inheritance and the corporate fall which is the overwhelming fact of his age.

A lawyer twice married, Quentin contemplates a third marriage, this time to a German-born archeologist named Holga. Talking to an imaginary listener, he wonders aloud whether or not to risk love again after acquiring a record of failed relationships, including two shattered marriages. He begins a lengthy autobiography, which the play dramatizes on different levels of the stage. Though the scenes are patterned associatively rather than chronologically, the first act can be roughly divided into scenes relating to his growing up and family life, his disastrous first marriage, his involvement in the political life of his friend Lou, and his first acquaintance with his second wife Maggie. The structure, which Miller describes as "surging, flitting instantaneousness of mind questing over its own surfaces and into its depths,"[29] vacillates across time—distant past, recent past, the immediate present. The openness of the structure permits Miller to bring together in the same scene characters from different periods in his life, implying thereby a unity of theme, a pattern of repetitious events and images which integrates the whole. Though Maggie, Quentin's second wife, dominates the second act, she appears significantly in the first to accentuate the meaning at certain points set earlier in time. The setting, according to Miller, is "monolithic, a lava-like supple geography in which, like pits and hollows found in lava, the scenes take place" (p. 1). The multilayered stage represents levels of the mind, and the stone tower of a Nazi concentration camp provides a further means of unity in the extended monologue.

In a foreword to the play, Miller explains the basis of his title. Eve, he says, opened up "the knowledge of good and evil" by presenting Adam with a choice. And "where choice begins, Paradise ends. Innocence ends, for what is Paradise but the absense of any need to choose . . . ?"[30] Subsequently, he goes on, humanity has always had to choose—between war and peace, destruction and love. Like the later romantics, Miller refers to the story of Cain and Abel as the quintessential embodiment of that choice, but he does not make Cain a Byronic hero so much as the representative of humanity's destructive nature. In his essay, "Our Guilt for the World Evil," he contends that when the ancient rabbis selected Cain as "the first personage . . . who can be called human," they did so "not out of some interest in criminology, but because they understood that the sight of his crimes is the highest agony a man can know, and the hardest to relate to."[31] Miller's protagonist stands precisely in that position, a Cain surveying the record of his own criminality. His guilt, he discovers, extends beyond the obvious murderous gestures of his life. "There are nonactions, and we have . . . a literal blood connection with the evil of the time," Miller has commented,[32] a culpability for what we allow as for what we do ourselves. In this respect Quentin shares in the offense of Jean-Baptiste Clamence, whose innocence is violated by the suicide of another, an act in which he participates by virtue of not acting. For Miller as for Camus, the idea of original sin, however bared of its theological trappings, assumes genuine significance. Quite simply, for both of them human beings cannot *not* be guilty.

Like Camus's anti-hero, Quentin rehearses his past in a quasi-confessional narrative; but whereas Clamence's Machiavellian strategy leads to the truth only through ironic revelation, Quentin's earnest recitation *seems* to forego irony for direct illumination. Only limited irony appears in the repetitious pattern of events and gestures which belie the context of various staged events—for example, Quentin's twice-enacted cruciform pose, which he strikes when he reaches out for two light fixtures on the wall of his hotel room, portrays him as anything but Christlike. But in watching the episodic scenes from Quentin's past we need to maintain aesthetic distance from the actors. We cannot expect quentin in his literal reenactments to provide either illumination or honesty. These staged past experiences reveal his ignorance *before* coming to self-knowledge and his potential for self-deception. In glossing over the critical distinction between Quentin past and Quentin present, critics have often missed a dimension of irony and have assumed that Quentin is Miller self-glorified, that Miller uses Quentin to exonerate himself after the suicide of his wife, the celebrated film star, Marilyn Monroe. In fact, Quentin's pomposity is most often a deliberately self-conscious revelation of the character he *was*. To be sure, we must question whether Quentin as narrator does not too easily vindicate himself in playing out his autobiography; however, Miller's artistic intention was to establish a dialectic between Quentin the narrator and Quentin the actor of historical events, seeing his past self from the perspective of *after* a fall.

An extended conversation with an implied listener, *After the Fall* is in effect an interior monologue like *La Chute*. The listener to whom Quentin speaks throughout never interrupts nor directly challenges Quentin's interpretation of events. Although, as Miller says in the foreword, he may be a psychologist to some or God to others, he is "Quentin himself turned at the edge of the abyss to look at his experience, his nature and his time in order to bring light, to seize—innocent no more—to forever guard against his own complicity with Cain, and the world's" (Foreword, p. 32). Critics who object to this arrangement, argue that Miller "could have dispensed with the listener entirely";[33] to them the listener seems nothing more than an artificial device to gain pretended objectivity. The point of view being solely Quentin's, we are asked to accept the complete validity of his self-evaluation. Tom Prideaux warns that "in all voluntary public penitents there is a touch of ham. Self-castigation begins to give off an embarrassing hint of self-infatuation, especially when it is offered center stage."[34] But to what degree is Quentin in the *process* of discovery? At times, he is pompous or arrogant or hypocritical; but so long as we see his monologue as a reenactment of the past done in order somehow to be reconciled to the present—that is, so long as we accept Quentin the actor and Quentin the narrator as parts of a divided self—we cannot legitimately dismiss the listener. He not only provides the motivation for telling the story, but also a distinction between what Quentin was and what he is struggling to become. Though Quentin has undergone a fall, though he already "knows" something of his potential for evil, though he has even gained a measure of self-understanding, he retells and reenacts the past in a process of becoming that exposes both past failure and his still-deficient wisdom. The Quentin who sees and hears vicariously through the listener must be reconciled to the Quentin who plays out the scenes from the past.

Quentin begins his recitation by bringing the supposed listener up to date. He tells of having quit the successful law firm which he had long served, of his mother's recent death, and of his meeting Holga, the German woman about whom he must make his decision. Holga, an archeologist, has survived the Second World War even though she had participated indirectly in the plot to assassinate Hitler. Showing Quentin the horror of the Nazi concentration camp, she had admitted her profound sense of guilt—"I don't know how I could not have known" (p. 15). Having acknowledged and accommodated herself to her guilt, Holga presents Quentin with a solution to his Kierkegaardian despair. But in light of his two divorces and the undeniable testimony of a life full of betrayal, Quentin fears to act, experiencing that incapacitating "sickness unto death" that comes to those who know only too well the dark shadows of the self. Living with guilt before an empty bench, with no god to acquit or condemn him, Quentin inherits the most modern of ills, "the endless argument with oneself." Unable to be the innocent boy who opens his eyes like Adam in the first morning of the world and unable to pass judgment on himself, he suffers a crisis of will at "the edge of the abyss." To act he must come to grips with what he has been and what he is. Holga's promise compels him to enter the "field of mirrors" which illuminates his past.

Quentin first recalls a few brief episodes with Felice, whom he had represented as lawyer in a divorce case and briefly flirted with. He had told her, in one of the many ironies that dot the text, that in a divorce, "no one has to be to blame!" (p. 5). Quentin as narrator breaks into the recreated scene with Felice to say to the listener with obvious self-mockery, "God, what excellent advice I give!" (p. 5). In direct contrast to Quentin's simplistic comment, Holga later tells him that indeed everyone is guilty. The distance between the Quentin talking to Felice and the Quentin talking to the listener is terribly important, for in the first case he talks to Felice before receiving self-knowledge, in the second case to the listener after receiving it. Far from being without irony, Miller's play depends on it. Furthermore, it extends into the present of the play; that is, it occurs in the midst of Quentin's "conversation" with the listener. At one point when he is telling Felice, "You never stop loving whoever you loved" (p. 6), his two wives Louise and Maggie suddenly appear before him, and he cries out, "These goddamned women have injured me! Have I learned nothing!" (p. 6). Given what Quentin learns by the end of the play, Miller can only mean this self-pitying remark as ironic.

The brief encounter with Felice in the opening scene leads to the first important cluster of scenes, those relating to his own family, the period of first betrayals. Felice fades into the darkness just after she blesses Quentin for rejuvenating her life, symbolized by the frivolous act of having her nose rebuilt. "I feel like a mirror in which she somehow sees herself as glorious," Quentin remarks. The image triggers the recollection of his mother's death. He remembers that at her burial he saw "a field of buried mirrors in which the living merely saw themselves" (p. 19).

The following scene reconstructs his meeting his brother Dan at a hospital where his father is recovering from an operation. The mother has died unexpectedly, and Quentin tells Dan they must give their father the news—"It belongs to him, as much as his wedding" (p. 10). Quentin, as throughout, bears his guilt with him in recalling the moment. As actor on stage he poses as the successful young lawyer mouthing high-sounding platitudes to his brother, but as self-judge in the present he turns to his listener and admits, "Or is it that I am crueler than he?" (p. 7). Realizing that he cannot grieve for his mother and that even his father returned to normal life "with all his tears," he senses that all is somehow related to the tower which suddenly lights up in the background. Seemingly no one can escape the fact that he cannot totally give himself to another person, that there is a hint of betrayal even in his father despite his extreme grief. The ultimate statement of the distance between human beings is the lighted tower, the consummate symbol of dehumanizing separation. After an intervening scene with Holga, who shows him through the concentration camp, Quentin returns to the record of offense in his family, thereby juxtaposing the tower, the macrocosm of human criminality, with family, a microcosm of the common guilt.

Quentin's mother reappears at the end of a key address to the listener. As the tower "bores in on him" and changes color, he remarks, "Why do I *know* something here? . . . It's that I no longer see some final grace! . . . some final hope is gone that always saved before the end!" (pp. 21–22). When his mother breaks into the reverie, talking to him when he was a boy on the day of his uncle's marriage, he exclaims with surprise, "Mother! That's strange. And murder?" (p. 22). Linking his mother with lost grace, he recalls her bitterness, viewing it not as the innocent boy enacting his past but as a man after the Fall. He remembers her guilt, her resentment at being forced into a marriage and losing a scholarship to Hunter College, her embarrassment over her husband's inability to read, her deep hostility over his bankruptcy. She had called Quentin's father a "moron" and "an idiot"—"I should have run the day I met you" (p. 20), she says to him. Realizing that the boy Quentin had heard her remarks, she had denied saying them: "I didn't say anything! . . . Darling, I didn't say anything!" (p. 21).

Edward Murray contends that Miller "whitewashes" Quentin in his relationship with his mother, "because the focus is almost wholly on *her* guilt and on Quentin's 'complicity': this complicity, however, is rather passive, and not necessarily blameworthy in all respects."[35] Murray refers in part to the second act when Quentin recalls how his mother favored him over his brother, trying to recover the lost promise of her own youth. When the father insisted that he needed him to regain his lost fortune, the mother demanded that Quentin be able to go to college rather than Dan "because he's different!" (p. 95). True, Quentin did act upon his mother's insistence rather than his own, but he hardly exonerates himself as he reenacts the moment. "Yes, I felt a power, in the going," he says, "and treason in it" (p. 67). He could excuse the boy, perhaps, but not the man who sees the boy.

In a later scene with Maggie, he tells how much he admires her "not pretending to be—innocent" (p. 74). Dan, who sacrificed his own opportunities so that Quentin could go on to school, suddenly appears. "I came to like her," he says, as Dan's image disappears, "just as I liked Dan, for 'her goodness!' " (p. 75). He knows that Dan's "goodness" was not "fraud." He also knows, therefore, that he cannot deny his share in his mother's betrayal. Miller hints at an Oedipal relationship between Quentin and his mother, as his strained encounters with Louise and Maggie reveal. The implication is not so much psychological as religious or moral, a manifestation of "original sin"—as the association with his mother as co-conspirator against his father and Dan reflects the treason of Jacob and Rebekah against Isaac and Esau. In no sense can Quentin excuse his guilt, nor does he.

The second and third groups of scenes concern Quentin's personal and professional life with Louise and their friends Elsie, Lou and Mickey. His life with Louise had been "some kind of paradise"—"I had a dinner table and a wife . . . a child and the world so wonderfully threatened by injustices I was born to correct! . . . There were good people and bad people. And how easy it was to tell! The worst son of a bitch, if he loved Jews and hated Hitler, he was a buddy" (p. 22). Yet, he confesses, when he began "to look at it," he found here too the evidence of his guilt. He visualizes the time Elsie changed from her wet bathing suit in front of him, and he could not deny his illicit desire. Seeing the relationships among his friends, he knows by hindsight that their apparently altruistic gestures were undercut by a selfish instinct for survival. Elsie's advice to Lou not to publish his textbook lest he further endanger himself before the House Un-American Activities Committee seemed a gesture of genuine concern for Lou, but when he threatened to follow Quentin's suggestion to go ahead with publication, Elsie expressed her deep contempt for his naiveté. As she acts out her disgust, Quentin reimages the moment when his mother called his father an idiot. At the point Mickey tells Lou he will tell the truth about his involvement with the Communist party and will name names, he seems almost noble. In the name of brotherhood "opposed to all the world's injustice" and for the sake of "truth," he urges Lou to go with him before the committee. But his nobility fades in light of his admission: "I testify or I'll be out of the firm" (p. 33). And Lou fears dismissal as well, despite his high-blown rhetoric: "Everything kind of falls away excepting one's self. One's truth; . . . if everyone broke faith there would be no civilization!" (pp. 35–36). As Mickey reminds him, he must confess that he himself once concealed the truth about Russian law in a book he had written.

Quentin exposes Louise's depravity in particular. From the day his Edenic world collapsed "and nobody was innocent again" (p. 25), Quentin saw Louise's culpability as well as his own. He relives their painful confrontations when she always assumed her innocence. Even when he had once tried to tell the truth about refusing a woman who wanted to sleep with him, she turned his account into an admission of guilt. Feeling himself the victim of this Eve, Quentin sees her now alongside his mother, the first female betrayer in his experience. When Louise later discovered a letter Quentin received from another woman, she accused him again and refused to accept either his repentance or her complicity. Finally, she claimed to be a "separate person" with her own right to be. Ironically, she proves to be right; but as Quentin discovers, it is precisely separateness that allows us to inflict our tyranny upon others.

The moments between Louise and Quentin seem at first to make him something of the victim of what he earlier calls "these goddamned women." Beyond question, Louise *is* an unrepentant Eve. But Quentin is not the passive victim of her cold-hearted puritanism; she provides a penetrating revelation of Quentin's guilt whether or not she herself is at fault. Significantly, Quentin says *to the listener*, "Why do I believe she's right! . . . Why can't I be innocent?" And as the tower again is illuminated, he asks, "Even this slaughterhouse! Why does something in me bow its head like an accomplice in this place!" (p. 30). The Quentin in the past, as Louise quite rightly tells us, keeps trying to defend himself, but Quentin the objective narrator cannot evade his responsibility for his actions. Not the least of Louise's perceptions is her comment that Quentin seeks his mother in his women—a truth even more apparent in his relationship with Maggie. But Quentin could not understand that truth and avoided it until he reached the climactic moment in his life with Maggie. Louise ironically calls Quentin "an idiot" at the conclusion of the restaged confrontation, a direct mimicking of his mother's condemnation of his father (once Elsie calls Mickey a "*moral idiot!*"). For all her moral arrogance, Louise is no simple foil to Quentin's goodness, and Quentin is no poor victim. The presence of the tower lends a certain credence to her revelations; and even Quentin is, as Miller says, "*stopped by this truth*" (p. 40).

After his first meeting with Maggie, to be discussed later, Quentin meets Louise one last time. Critics especially point to this episode as "whitewashing," but the scene is more delicately balanced than that implies. Quentin's mind wanders from meeting Maggie to seeing Louise reading a book upon his belated return from the office: "How beautiful! A woman of my own! What a miracle!" (p. 52). Although he tries to express affection for her, he again meets her disdain. He had forgotten a parents' meeting he said he would attend to discuss their daughter Betty with her teacher. More important, he had apparently lied about working late; Louise had called the office and discovered that he was not there. Accidentally meeting Maggie, he had also forgotten a crucial meeting with the others in the law firm to discuss his intent to defend Lou before the congressional investigating committee. When he tries to explain his unexpected meeting with Maggie, Louise angrily tells him that she will not sleep with him. At this point the phone rings, and one of his partners tells him that Lou has been killed by a subway train. Until now, the scene portrays Louise's guilt, not Quentin's; but the news about Lou's death destroys any illusion we might hold of Quentin's innocence.

As actor, Quentin ponders why Lou should have died. As Louise tells him, Lou could not have committed suicide. "He knew where he stood!" "Maybe it's not enough to know yourself," Quentin replies, "Or maybe it's too much" (p. 58). Then resuming his role as narrator he directly tells the listener that Lou died because he knew he had no friend left in the world; ironically, he was the "separate person" that Louise willed to be:

> It was dreadful because I was not his friend either, and he knew it. I'd have stuck it to the end but I hated the danger in it for myself, he saw through my faithfulness. . . . Because I wanted out, to be a good American again, kosher again—and proved it in the joy . . . the joy . . . joy I felt now that my danger had spilled out over the subway track! (P. 59)

Glancing at the blazing tower, he asks, "How can one understand that, if one is innocent? If somewhere in one's soul there is no accomplice—of that joy, that joy when a burden dies . . . and leaves you safe?" (p. 59). Miller lays no small blame at his protagonist's feet. Clamence speaks of the joy we secretly feel over another's death because it lifts our burden of obligation to another human being. The full weight of that awful truth falls upon Quentin *in the present* as he rehearses the past.

The last encounter with Louise concludes not with Quentin's posturing virtue but with his own gesture of violence toward Louise. Angered by her self-righteousness, he had raised his clenched fist. At once "terrified" and animated by his own "aborted violence," he discovered power not in innocence but denial: "Not to see one's evil—there's power! And rightness too!—so kill conscience. . . . Know all, admit nothing" (p. 61). But Quentin the narrator knows that denial is impossible. Hope resides not in escape from guilt but in the equal belief in elemental decency, the remembrance that when he wakes, as in the first morning of the world, he opens his eyes . . . "like a boy, even now; even now" (p. 61). Salvation lies not in the ignorance of evil but the belief in human goodness as well. Act 2 portrays both the full knowledge of that evil and its redeeming opposite.

Ostensibly, act 2 begins as Quentin talks to the listener while awaiting Holga's arrival from Frankfurt. The freedom of Miller's dramatic structure permits him to retard or accelerate the action as Quentin's thoughts dictate. Consequently, the act opens with Holga's greeting, which triggers a rapidly paced collection of scenes and characters, then focuses primarily on Quentin and Maggie, and finally returns to Holga's "Hello" and Quentin's symbolically affirmative response. Though various speeches by other characters and past events intersperse the lengthy account of Quentin's life with Maggie, the major portion of the plot is a direct rendering of their relationship. This most controversial portion of the play draws Miller's theme into focus and contains some of the best drama he has yet written.

The fragmented pattern at the beginning weaves together the events recalled in the first act and both reinforces and recapitulates the central theme—the power of one human being over another. Quentin tells his listener that he "can be clearer, now" if he can just recover that second "somewhere along the line" when "I saw my life. . . . And that vision sometimes hangs behind my head, blind now, bleached out like the moon in the mornings and if I could only let in some necessary darkness it would shine again. I think it had to do with power" (p. 64). Power, the individual's or the system's, is the Cain potential that everyone and every society possesses. Struggling somehow to understand his own responsibility for "the death of love," he now sees power as the essential weapon of destruction. Recalling the power he felt when he sided with his mother and left Dan and his father, the unwitting power he exercised over Felice in their fleeting encounter, and the power that he acquired over Maggie, he defines his Cain-like nature. For this reason he justly fears loving Holga.

Holga appears amid the haunting images of those victimized by Quentin's destructive will. In effect each of his victims gave him the power with which he could destroy them. They all "adored" him, and his vanity in essence reinforced the tyranny of his will. A fraudulent self emerged, beginning with his mother's monumental claim that he was a born savior. "I saw a star" gone bright and fall at your birth, "like some great man had died," she had told him, "and you being pulled out of me to take his place, and be a light, a light in the world!" (p. 67). Felice's constant blessing also legalized that power. And above all, Maggie, who saw him "like a god" (p. 72), a surrogate father, granted him "the power" to murder her. Seen as a kind of god by the subservient women in his life, Quentin now knows himself to be a counterfeit savior. He recreates with unquestionable self-mockery the Christlike pose he struck the night Felice left him in his hotel room after he resisted seducing her. He knew his apparent virtue was in part a pretense, just as he is stung by the recognition that beneath all his seeming compassion for Maggie was an elemental tyranny. He lied to her, he tells the listener in a bitter outburst of self-blame: "I should have agreed she *was* a joke, a beautiful piece, trying to take herself seriously! Why did I lie to her, play this cheap benefactor, this—" (p. 70). With her limited understanding, Louise had told him when he tried to explain his first chance meeting with Maggie that he really saw her as a tart—"But what did it matter as long as she praised you?" Though an unjust accusation, her remark points to a truth. The will to love never cancels out the will to wield power over the object of one's love; and when that power comes directly by means of another's adoration, it brings consummate temptation. Until experience proved otherwise, Quentin's mother, Felice, and Maggie conferred an innocence on him that he knew to be false.

What importance should we give to the autobiographical element of the play? To what extent does it reflect self-blame? Self-exoneration? It is a serious charge to say that Miller excuses Quentin's guilt by virtue of acknowledging the guilt of all—in other words, by suggesting, "If all have sinned, then I may not be better than the others, but I'm no worse either." The problem is, if we cannot truly believe in the profundity of the character's guilt, we cannot believe in the profundity of his recovery from the Fall. It is therefore important to examine carefully whether Miller really intends for us to believe in Quentin's fallen nature, or if he dilutes his guilt by abstracting it in some amorphous statement about the common condition of man in an imperfect world. Central to this pivotal critical debate is the account of Quentin's and Maggie's marriage.

Miller's dramatic form creates an artistic dilemma. To bring Quentin to the revelation that he is the author of his own criminality, he must allow him at first to depict Maggie's fallen state. That is, to achieve the dramatic reversal of the climax when Quentin fully knows *himself* to be Cain, he must first make himself the apparent victim of Maggie's destructive power. Otherwise, the climax would not present the discovery needed to trigger the end of the action. The difficulty lies in the point of view. In that only he is privy to Maggie's flawed condition, Quentin is in the uncomfortable position of being her accuser even while he poses as her savior. But it is not so much Maggie's guilt but Quentin's misconception of Maggie that Miller wants us to see. At first Quentin's speech was full of rhetorical flourish and sham sentiment—"But you're a victory, Maggie, you're like a flag to me, a kind of proof, somehow, that people can win" (p. 88). With remarkable naiveté Quentin had endowed her with the same adoration that he received unjustly from others. When Maggie seemingly changed, then, ironically insisting on receiving his total devotion as he had received the devotion of others, he began to analyze her faults. Once he had told her, "We want the same thing," that she should be a true artist. But he turns to the listener with the essential truth that they both really wanted "power"—"to transform somebody, to save!" (p. 95). In other words, they both sought innocence. Primarily because Quentin as a lawyer has verbal skills, he seems to get the best of it in the quest for innocence, and he comes off to many readers as the arrogant "Judgey" Maggie called him.

But Miller never intends for us to admire him for his pontification. Invariably his rhetoric is undercut by action. Even when he seems the kindly victim of Maggie's viciousness—spending forty percent of his time keeping her out of legal trouble, arguing for the rights of the poor people she runs over roughshod, suffering the abuse of her constant accusations—there is something dishonest in the long-suffering martyrdom. His most quotable, polished speeches (for example, "It's that if there is love, it must be limitless; a love not even of persons, but blind, blind to insult, blind to the spear in the flesh, like justice blind, like . . ." p. 100) are framed by the mocking images of betrayal, his own as well as others'. But as he moves closer to recounting the climactic "last night" with Maggie, Quentin sees the lie of his own innocence. He had wanted to wash his hands of Maggie's self-destructive impulse. Having twice saved her from suicide, he wanted to free himself from the responsibility for her life, to force her "to look at what *you're* doing" (p. 103). It all sounds noble; but just as the last scene with Maggie is being played out, Quentin introduces it by asking the listener, "But in whose name do you turn your back?" (p. 100). The Quentin struggling to depict the story reluctantly reenacts his part in the suicide even as he repeats his words to Maggie that she must be responsible for herself.

There is indeed irony in the juxtaposition of scenes, and one form of irony is that as he introduces his last moments with Maggie, he recalls his mother's once betraying him, going to Atlantic City with his father and Dan, leaving him alone. He, too, had threatened suicide by locking the door and running water in the bathtub. But if his mother had betrayed him, did he not betray Maggie? He rationalized his leaving her by ironically repeating Louise's claim: "We are all separate people." He told Maggie, "I have to survive too, honey" (p. 104). And that is precisely what Quentin was doing, trying to survive his fall and preserve his innocence, as Miller says in the foreword, "obliterating whatever stands in the way, thus destroying what is loved as well." To evade responsibility, Quentin had accused Maggie of making him the source of "all the evil in the world. . . . All the betrayal, the broken hopes, the murderous revenge" (p. 104).

Quentin's speech carries a measure of truth, as does his protestation to Maggie that "something in you has been setting me up for a murder" (p. 106). Maggie did want to transfer responsibility for her life onto Quentin—but the play does not end here, and we cannot say on the basis of Quentin's past comments to Maggie that Miller makes a hero of him. In an ironic repetition of an earlier speech to Louise when he has begged her to "say that something, something important was [her] fault and that [she was] sorry" (p. 42), Quentin urged Maggie to confess her own guilt, to say, " 'I have been kicked around, but I have been as unexcusably vicious to others, called my husband idiot in public, I have been utterly selfish despite my generosity, I have been hurt by a long line of men but I have cooperated with my persecutors—' " (p. 107). Later he told Maggie, "Do the hardest thing of all!—see your own hatred and live!" (p. 109).

But something rings hollow here, and it is precisely what Maggie said it was: "You're still playing God! That's what killed me, Quentin!" (p. 109).[36] Referring to a note she had found in which Quentin had written, "The only one I will ever love is my daughter" (p. 108), Maggie justly accused him of betraying her love. Coming close to the truth, he admitted that he had written it when he had seen in her eyes "that I'd made you feel you didn't exist." And "it closed a circle for me," he told Maggie, because that was exactly what Louise had said to him—"And I wanted to face the worst thing I could imagine—that I could not love" (p. 109). With near-truth, he concluded, "Maggie, we were born of many errors; a human being has to forgive himself! Neither of us is innocent" (p. 109). But such intellectual truth can only be attested by experience, and that evidence of guilt came at the end when in his Cain-like anger he grabbed the pills from Maggie's hand and "transfixed," choked her as she suddenly assumes the person of his mother in the present, a repetition and extension of his violence toward Louise. Arthur Ganz points out that Quentin realizes "not that he loved his mother too well but that he was capable of willing her death"[37]—and Louise's and Maggie's as well, we might add. The point is, he manifests his *own* destructive will to power, and so he comes to answer his own question: "In whose name do you ever turn your back—*he looks out at the audience*—but in your own. In Quentin's name. Always in your own blood-covered name you turn your back!" (p. 112). Such knowledge comes after the Fall when innocence can no longer be claimed. Quentin says this *to the audience;* he closes the circle once more. The seeds of the most monstrous atrocities grow in each individual soul. Miller elevates a "personal" tragedy to the level of "public" horror, for to believe in Quentin's potential for evil is to believe absolutely in the possibility of the Holocaust.

The reconstruction of Quentin's attempt to strangle Maggie/his mother/Louise ends abruptly when Holga reappears *"on the highest level"* of the stage. Her return brings a swift resolution to the action—so swift a resolution that it may strain credulity to accept it as a legitimate end. The general accusation that Holga's character is not adequately developed, given the significant role that she should play, has some justification; she appears only in two full scenes and otherwise in very abbreviated moments. Nonetheless, her function as a kind of Jungian *anima* seems clear enough, and she serves as symbol if not as a three-dimensional character.

After being introduced briefly by Quentin at the beginning, Holga figures prominently in only one scene in the first act. At the Nazi concentration camp she surveys her life and explains to Quentin her near-obsession with visiting the camp. Though imprisoned for two years by the Nazis, she afterward had found it difficult to enter the United States until she had proven she was neither a communist nor a Jew but the blood relative to several officials in the Nazi government. As though spreading the net of culpability, Holga had come to the profound realization not just of her own guilt but the common guilt of all. Finding that "survival can be hard to bear" (p. 14), she could nevertheless proclaim her own guilt without, in Quentin's words, "looking for some goddamned . . . *moral victory*" (p. 15). But while Quentin admitted that he felt "an understanding with this slaughterhouse" (p. 16), he felt neither "indignant" nor "angry" at the horror, as though the very enormity of the crime had swallowed up the moral outrage. The scene at the camp concludes just after Quentin relives his betrayal of his father when he went off to college. Sensing the pervasive evil of the place, Quentin had challenged Holga to race to the car—"The car will be all sweet inside!" but seeing the tower he sensed that "*he had committed a sacrilege.*" Holga had told him, "Quentin, dear—no one they didn't kill can be innocent again" (p. 21).

Act 2 contains another short scene with Holga, set at a Salzburg café. She had expressed the fear that she was "boring" him, a reflection of Louise's observation that Quentin paid no attention to her. With Louise, Quentin had the altruistic idea that he needed somehow "to step between her and her suffering." He had known that she herself "didn't like her face" portrayed in the mirror, and "I felt guilty even for her face!" (p. 66). With Holga, though, "there was some new permission" that would allow him to go from her without judgment until he could return her love. Having the freedom to leave her to recover the will to commit himself to her had triggered his long night's journey into day. Holga lends meaning to Quentin's long search and, at the end, validates his recovery, however tenuous, from the Fall.

Holga had told Quentin at the concentration camp about a recurring dream. She had given birth to an idiot child, which would run away but always return to her lap. She sensed that "if I could kiss it . . . perhaps I could sleep. And I bent to its broken face, and it was horrible . . . but I kissed it. I think one must finally take one's life in one's arms, Quentin" (p. 22). The child figure personifies the absurdity and guilt to which everyone gives birth. Not to accept, not to embrace that child, would be to commit an unforgivable sin against life and against the self. Quentin knows at the end of the play "that we are very dangerous!" (p. 113). His "we" is not Clamence's subtle means of shifting responsibility, but the recognition that not even love can exonerate guilt or cancel out the possiblity of evil. Hope can be constructed only on the foundation of knowledge itself—"To know, and even happily, that we meet unblessed; not in some garden of wax fruit and painted trees, that lie of Eden, but after, after the Fall, after many, many deaths" (p. 113). Paradoxically, Quentin is able to greet Holga at the end of the play because of, not despite, the knowledge that "the wish to kill is never killed" (p. 114). Saved from the incapacitating potential of self-knowledge, Quentin accepts "the validity of the evidence without resorting to 'the everlasting temptation of innocence.' Not to accept is to live a life of 'pointless litigation of existence before an empty bench.' "[38]

Miller shows us that after the Fall the supreme temptation is innocence itself. Robert Hogan calls Quentin's recognition that no one "can be innocent again on this mountain of skulls" (p. 113) a "remarkable statement" from "the young Communist sympathizer of the 1940's holding aloft his white and unsullied banner." And he even argues, "It is a statement to file away with other hard-won, hard-boiled verities like Stephen Dedalus' courage to be wrong and Faulkner's 'They will endure.' It is not precisely a *Reader's Digest* kind of sentiment, but it is probably one of the few mature remarks ever made in an American play." Audiences may resist Miller's conclusion because "he demands more of us than just love or sympathy; he calls for comprehension."[39] What finally keeps Quentin from being a "separate person" is ironically that common guilt he shares with all others. In finding his "brotherhood" in the criminality of all (as Clamence calls the Nazis "our Nazi brethren"), he escapes the estrangement that threatens his relationsip with Holga. In Quentin's search we discover again both the dark possibilities and the hope of the belief in self as the repository of values. Unlike Jean-Baptiste Clamence, he is able to emerge from the Erebus of his own soul with the slender but firm hope that truth can set him free from the consuming self-absorption that claims Camus's "empty prophet for shabby times."

‡ 6 ‡

The Fall in Fantasy

The prevalence of the Fall motif in children's literature and science fiction hardly needs proving. As psychologists such as Bruno Bettelheim have long noted, the best of fairy tales and children's stories protectively initiate children into the terrors of the unconscious within the reassuring context of control and the absolution of guilt. In acknowledging and to some degree exorcising the potential for violence, such literature eases the precarious passage from innocence to experience. So also the early adolescent adventure tale often explores the initiation into adulthood: a child leaves home, enters into experience, endures some danger of death or violation, achieves a victory by a courageous act of will, and finally returns home transfigured into an adult self. Science fiction, of course, commonly begins with a garden—a positive utopia or a repressive dystopia—which is on the brink of collapse and compels the protagonist consciously to choose or reject its values, to move east of Eden, to exist in perpetual Ulro, or in some way to accept or transform the society. In the most general terms science fiction almost inevitably rewrites something of Genesis.

Although Lewis Carroll's Alice stories and Arthur Clarke's and Stanley Kubrick's collaborative work *2001: A Space Odyssey* to some degree follow these patterns, they depict the Fall in unique ways. Carroll's two tales both consciously and unconsciously expose Carroll's conception of Victorian adult society and probably his personal neurosis. His extraordinary angle of vision describes a fall in reverse. Rather than moving *from* absolute innocence to experience, Alice returns *to* the garden an already corrupted character. She does not confront so much as create the duality of Wonderland as she moves inexorably to a fully affirmed adulthood that does not merit our admiration so much as our despair. *2001: A Space Odyssey* not only evokes the mythical journey of Odysseus but the very process of human evolution itself. It traces the emergence of humankind in a series of falls from the dawn of man to the twenty-first century. Finally, though, *2001* parallels the pattern of Carroll's stories. It, too, describes a fall in reverse, if ironically. But whereas Alice's return to the garden is but a tenuous moment in her evolving consciousness of mortality and domineering adulthood, the emerging human figure in *2001* recovers lost innocence by progressing through the Fall to a higher state of awareness. As Star Child, he once more returns to innocence.

Alice in Wonderland and *Through the Looking-Glass* by Lewis Carroll

It is characteristic of the modern temper that it believes that its journey in the underworld (the underground, as Dostoievski called it) of irrational and disorienting subjectivity is not pure loss but instead the prerequisite of a new and fuller realization of humanity.

—Tom F. Driver, *Romantic Quest and Modern Query*

What fascinates us about the Alice stories, what attracts us as children and yet also intrigues us as adults, may well be the extraordinary ambivalence of Carroll's viewpoint. For Alice seemingly exists between two worlds, one of childlike fantasy and one of prescriptive absolutes. In psychoanalytic terms, she moves somewhere between two profound early stages of consciousness, the Oedipal period and puberty. Given the precociousness she exhibits for a child her age, she betrays the myopic vision of seven-to-ten-year-olds, who psychologists tell us undergo an intense literal-mindedness. As Donald Rackin notes, Alice "has reached the stage of development where the world appears explainable and unambiguous, that most narrow-minded, prejudicial period of life where, paradoxically, daring curiosity is wedded to uncompromising literalness and priggish, ignorant faith in the fundamental sanity of things."[1] Viewed theologically, or existentially, the issue lies deeper: Alice's naive point of view raises fundamental questions about the relationship between childhood and original sin. Here, at least, critics part company.

The Victorian attitude toward children was itself divided. In a postromantic age when children—via Blake, Wordsworth, and others —were accorded idyllic grace, the relationship between the child figure and the Fall was understandably muted, despite a strongly evangelical bent toward fundamentalistic, Augustinian doctrine. Carroll, Robert Pattison suggests, could not "tolerate the idea of children as part of the world of sin, and in *Alice in Wonderland*, the heroine stands resolutely apart from the machinery of Original Sin."

Alice remains innocent even though Wonderland itself "is the world after the Fall . . . a world of death where living creatures are perverted from their natural functions."[2] But it is difficult to accept Alice's innocence in light of her raw assertions of power and her dominant will. We sense that she has already moved beyond the quiet, unassailable but unearned innocence of Blakean childhood. Far from being "the romantic pastoral child, the symbol of Blake's innocent life,"[3] Alice reflects a postlapsarian state by her very protestations of innocence. She is neither a conscious villain nor an unsuspecting victim, neither a child of Rousseau nor a child of Calvin; and it is this remarkable duality, this paradoxical nature that allows her both to judge and to be judged. Naively an image of the fallen adult society which she embodies at an age when she wholeheartedly embraces its values and assumptions, Alice barely retains the most precious gift of childlike innocence—a potentially redemptive imagination which gives her passage to Wonderland.

We therefore can identify Alice's point of view as symptomatic of both innocence and experience: innocence because she is not so bound by the fallen world that she cannot yet enter Wonderland, experience because although she "falls" into Wonderland, she unknowingly brings with her the destructive powers of adulthood. This may explain the division among critics who find her either a mistreated heroine or a rather malicious snob. Rackin represents those who find Alice morally superior to the bizarre characters who lie in the Kafkaesque realm of Wonderland. Like Pattison and others, he sees the "underworld" as the fallen garden which Alice must finally transcend. Against this argument stands the less frequently stated idea that Alice is the truly fallen creature who threatens the regenerative world of the unconscious. James Kincaid articulates this thesis in his essay, "Alice's Invasion of Wonderland." To him, Alice's "rude and tragic haste" to achieve queenship in the "underside of consciousness" marks "the loss of Eden."[4] For some critics, then, Wonderland seems the reflection of innocence—a garden of sorts, for others the terrifying world of experience. Glimpsed one way, Wonderland and the Looking-Glass portray the fallen garden; viewed another way, the fallen garden is the repressive culture which Alice leaves.

Perhaps Carroll's own ambivalence, his outward conventionality and inward, quiet rebellion, corresponds to his dual vision of Wonderland and attests to the competing opposites that inevitably emerge from the Fall. But, whatever the cause, Alice's delicate balance depicts a tense dialectical pattern: on the edge of sexual consciousness yet not conscious, tottering between innocence and experience—already having embraced the fallen world above the rabbit hole with all its constraining powers but not yet *consciously* choosing it. At the beginning she is still naive, still unaware of her potential will to power. She is on the cutting edge of a new state of being—too big to remain in the "womb" and too small to leave it. In effect, Alice's fall is a fall in reverse—that is, a return to the garden. She carries the knowledge of an adult consciousness with her, and such knowledge creates a fixed world of time and space. Although she cannot avoid the mockery of time in Wonderland, Alice, nonetheless, moves in linear fashion in a place where clocks and maps seem inoperative but are constantly present—present both because they reflect the adventures Alice has already had in time and because they remind us that Wonderland and the Looking-Glass exist in just that precarious moment before the alarm of consciousness shatters them forever.

We have, then, a heroine innocent only insofar as she has remained unconscious of her potential for evil who visits a garden peopled by creatures parodying the fallen characters of her everyday world. In Wonderland, threats, violence, and cruelty are always neutralized. If characters battle, no one loses. Allusions to death are neither true causes for alarm nor for despair. Death appears comically at the end of the rat's tail (tale), for example; and the Gnat speaks of death in the most unapprehensive terms.

> A new difficulty came into Alice's head.
> "Supposing it couldn't find any?" she suggested.
> "Then it would die, of course."
> "But that must happen very often," Alice remarked thoughtfully.
> "It always happens," said the Gnat.[5]

Except where Alice is concerned, the limits of mortality seem nonexistent or irrelevant. Her growing consciousness alone terrorizes Wonderland—and it gives testimoney of the Fall.

To illustrate the tension between Alice's unwitting "fallen" vision acquired by means of age and experience in the adult world and the still-innocent vision of her dream consciousness, we can examine a few representative episodes in the two Alice stories. Again, this dialectic between competing realities can best be understood as depicting a fall in reverse, for the measure of Alice's innocence is her ability to journey into Wonderland and the measure of her fallen nature is her inability to remain there.

Claire Rosenfield says that the boys in *Lord of the Flies,* "degenerate into adults."[6] Alice's "degeneration" manifests itself the moment she falls down the rabbit hole. She asserts her flawed knowledge of school subjects, manners and moral platitudes. Though utterly naive, she betrays a proclivity for violence, moral tyranny and unswerving absolutism. Her vocabulary reflects her linear assumptions about truth. Allusions to longitude, latitude, "antipathies," maps, and books of rules, expose her effort to circumscribe reality. Both a prelapsarian Eve "curiouser and curiouser" to enter the "lovely garden" and a fallen Eve instinctively aware of death (seen in her fear of killing someone with the marmalade jar, her references to Dinah and apprehension about "poison," and, especially, in her fear of extinction), Alice arrives at the existential question: " 'Who am I?' Ah, that's the great puzzle!" Already divided against herself, Alice "was very fond of pretending to be two people." An authoritarian *and* a rebel, like Blake's Urizen and Orc, "she remembered trying to box her own ears for having cheated herself in a game of croquet she was playing against herself" (p. 12). Paradoxically aware but ignorant, she acts out her fallen nature while retaining an unearned innocence.

Certain themes continually illustrate Alice's degeneration into adulthood. Her attitude toward other people exemplifies the moral folly of her normal world. She fears being Mabel because Mabel lives "in that pokey little House" and has "ever so many lessons to learn!" (p. 17). Later, she feels no remorse in knocking the Rabbit into the cucumber-frame or kicking Bill out of the chimney. Challenged by the Caterpillar's rude questions about her identity, she appears more piteous than threatening, especially when she unintentionally insults him by complaining that "three inches is such a wretched height to be" (p. 41). But, in fact, her humility comes from her diminished height. She conceals her judgment ("I wish the creatures wouldn't be so easily offended!") only because she is not in a position of power. When in control of authority, she seldom hesitates to use it.

A superb illustration of her duality occurs at the end of chapter 5 when she eats the mushroom and finds herself towering far above the trees with a neck able to "bend about in any direction, like a serpent" (p. 42). In the ensuing encounter with the Pigeon, Alice once again faces the existential question. Accused of being a serpent, Alice claims to be a little girl. She is of course both. "In this scene," Nina Auerbach writes, "the golden child herself becomes the serpent in childhood's Eden."[7] When the Pigeon asks if she has tasted an egg, Alice replies, "I *have* tasted eggs, certainly . . . but little girls eat eggs quite as much as serpents do, you know" (p. 43). With stunning simplicity the Pigeon replies, "If they do, why, then they're a kind of serpent: that's all I can say" (p. 43). As James Kincaid observes, "It doesn't matter if Eden is destroyed by purposeful malignity or by callous egotism and ruthless insensitivity that often pass for innocence."[8] The truth is, Alice is no more innocent than her flawed humanity will allow her to be. The Pigeon knows cannibalism when she sees it, even if Alice does not. If Alice provokes our sympathy, it is not because she is victimized by others but rather victimized by herself. Eve and the serpent, like Adam and the serpent, are one.

Perhaps the most telling episode in *Alice's Adventures in Wonderland* occurs at the Duchess's house. Here too Alice garners our sympathy *and* our judgment. In her attempt to save the baby from abuse, Alice assumes moral responsibility: "Wouldn't it be murder to leave it behind?" (p. 49). But her compassion coexists with her "civilized" nature: " 'Don't grunt,' said Alice, 'that's not at all a proper way of expressing yourself.' " When she discovers the child to be a pig, Alice gratefully puts the creature down and surmises:

> "If it had grown up," she said to herself, "it would have made a dreadfully ugly child: but it makes a rather handsome pig, I think." And she began thinking over other children she knew, who might do very well as pigs . . . saying to herself "if one only knew the right way to change them—"
>
> (P. 50)

As Kincaid and others have noted, Alice's potential for tyranny is nowhere more apparent than here. "Alice is transformed into a kind of Circe," says Roger Sale, "turning all those she controls into swine."[9] Devoid of all but self-deception, Alice, like the boys in *Lord of the Flies*, becomes a child of darkness as well as light.

The dialectical pattern repeats itself throughout the tale—in her attempts at poetry, which transform nursery rhymes into poems about death; in her frequent allusions to Dinah, which change a child's pet into a beast of prey; in her constant concern for rules, which attempt to reduce the openness of Wonderland to constrictions of time and place. As the unwitting defender of civilization, Alice usually suffers defeat. To her literal mind time is the servant of order; to those at the Mad Tea Party, as Donald Rackin remarks, it is "a person, a kind of ill-behaved child created by men."[10] Alice's reductiveness gives way to expansiveness. Her efforts to apply constraints to reality—to establish rules for the croquet match, meaning for the Duchess's moral aphorisms, and sense for the Mock Turtle's outrageous puns—seldom succeed. Existing in the dream state, like Marlow in *Heart of Darkness*

(p. 82), Alice experiences "that commingling of absurdity, surprise and bewilderment . . . that notion of being captured by the incredible which is the very essence of dreams."

Withal, there remains Carroll's marvelous comic detachment and his reassurance that man's cruelty to man can never be enacted here. Even if the king did not whisper to the host of those sentenced to execution "You are all pardoned" (p. 73), we know they are—"They never executes nobody, you know" (p. 74), the Gryphon informs us. The world of the imagination, in short, for all the references to time, to law, to rule, to schooling and manners, to child abuse and death, maintains the virtues of openness and incompletion. Unending in its possibilities and protected by its fantasy, the garden can redeem with truth the temporal society it mimics. Though time is a constant theme in Wonderland, in fact time exists for Alice alone. Her tendency toward closure betrays her fallen condition. Unlike the creatures she treats with careless malice, Alice reveals her divided nature, her potential for kindness and disdain, compassion and judgment. Though she can temporarily visit Wonderland, she cannot long remain there. She has nearly outgrown her innocence.

The end of *Alice in Wonderland* reveals Alice's tenuous state of becoming. Lionel Morton says of the trial of the Knave of Hearts that Alice's challenge, " 'You're nothing but a pack of cards!' is more devastating than 'Off with his head' " because "it destroys a whole world. . . . Alice's awakening is the end of the story and the breaking of the spell of the half-unreal love that has united Alice and her Scheherazade. . . . With the end of the story time resumes its power."[11] Peter Coveney finds in Wonderland "the claustrophobic atmosphere of a children's Kafka" and labels the story "the frustrated 'quest' for the 'Garden' which in the event is peopled with such unpleasant creatures." Hence, he concludes, we feel "a sense of shock" to find Alice's "innocent life blighted with 'dead leaves' " at the end of the story.[12] But the destructive power resides in Alice herself, not in the dreamworld of the imagination. The "fallen leaves" appear in the *external* world, not in Wonderland—and they existed there before Alice entered the "underside of consciousness."

Carroll resumes his narrative in *Through the Looking-Glass* with a clear sense of continuity, for Alice—as in Wonderland far more mature than her age suggests—continues the cycle of becoming from childhood to adulthood. In effect, Alice in the looking-glass is Alice in Wonderland once removed. The differences in the stories reveal not contradiction but logical progression.

The obvious contrasts between Wonderland and the world of the looking-glass—outside/inside, light/dark, summer/winter—signal Alice's evolving character. In some respects she has already assumed adult obligations. Lionel Morton points out that Alice is a sort of mock maternal figure mothering Dinah's newborn kittens rather than being mothered by her sister.[13] Alice's identification with the Red Queen is also meaningful. Whereas in Wonderland Alice rejected the terrifying power of the queen, now she all but seeks it. Consequently, the action varies. As Empson says, "Wonderland is a dream, the Looking-Glass is self-consciousness."[14] The journey in Wonderland remains marvelously quixotic, whereas in the looking-glass world, the squares of the chessboard and Alice's will to be crowned queen determine the action. Morton concludes that Alice *is* the Red Queen: "The Queen is the desire to dominate and to punish, which began the whole dream and caused all the mischief. This desire is also the desire to grow up and be an adult, as Carroll sees it."[15] In Blakean language, the looking-glass marks the final passage from a rapidly fading innocence to an assertive selfhood, for Blake the essence of sin—*Through the Looking-Glass* portrays the consequences of a fall, not unlike Blake's own work "The Crystal Cabinet." Yet, paradoxically, such a fall is the unavoidable condition of mortality.

Even from the beginning Alice plays "Urizen," Blake's mythological figure representing the rational faculty attributed to the "nobodaddy" god of the Old Testament. Her first words are judgmental: "Oh, you wicked little thing! . . . Really, Dinah ought to have taught you better manners!" (pp. 107–08). She threatens to put the kitten out in the snow and to save "all your punishments for Wednesday week" (pp. 108–09). Her proclivity for violence also surfaces when she recalls frightening her old nurse "by shouting suddenly in her ear, 'Nurse! Do let's pretend that I'm a hungry hyaena and you're a bone!' " (p. 110)—an ironic echo of the many cannibalistic expressions in *Alice in Wonderland*. More aggressive and confident, Alice does not fall accidentally down the rabbit hole but wilfully enters the mirror. Symbolically, she has moved from what John Vernon labels a "garden" consciousness to a "map" consciousness. Vernon describes the dialectic between "the unity of opposites and the wholeness of experience" envisioned to the garden and the "separation of opposites and the fragmentation of experience" in the adult psyche embodied in the map.[16] The tension between these opposite appeals provides clear evidence that Alice has ventured beyond innocence.

In Wonderland Alice experienced a pattern of a stretch and shrink—stretch because she was challenged by new knowledge, shrink because she was humiliated by her ignorance. In the looking-glass the conflict dissolves, for Alice is too "wise," too confident, and too superior in her attitude. In the Garden of Live Flowers she identifies with the Tiger-lily, who terrorizes the other flowers. The Tiger-lily trembles "with excitement" when the daisies shout together because "they know I can't get at them!" But in defense of the tyrant Alice whispers ominously to the daisies, "If you don't hold your tongues, I'll pick you!" (p. 122). Finally impatient with the flowers, she decides to go meet the Red Queen, "for, though the flowers are interesting enough, she felt it would be far grander to have a talk with a real Queen" (p. 123). Impressed by power, she sets out on the chessboard, admitting, "I wouldn't mind being a Pawn . . . though of course I should *like* to be a Queen, best" (p. 126).

The series of events which follow traces Alice's steps to the Eighth Square. Though offered redemptive self-knowledge in various encounters on the way, Alice journeys unabated toward a single goal—queenship. Her intent to meet and finally to be a queen ironically identifies her with the other symbols of power, and especially with the Queen of Hearts and the Red Queen. The queens express comically an authority that Alice reenacts in earnest. If Dinah embodies her unacknowledged will to power in the first book, the quest for queenship portrays it overtly in the second book. Though challenged by the "garden" consciousness of various characters, Alice never veers from her course.

One example of Alice's inability to respond to the "garden" is the episode with the Gnat. With the possible exception of Sissy Jupe's futile attempt to define a horse for Mr. Gradgrind in *Hard Times*, no moment in literature so cogently reveals the conflict between childlike imagination and reductive reason. The Gnat struggles vainly to deny Alice's devotion to certainty, logic, and definition. Baffled by his wisdom, Alice holds to her Urizenic assurances. When the Gnat asks what insects she rejoices in, Alice can only reply, "I don't *rejoice* in insects at all. . . . But I can tell you the names of some of them" (p. 132). The conversation goes on,

> "Of course they answer to their names?" the Gnat remarked carelessly.
>
> "I never knew them to do it."
>
> "What's the use of their having names," the Gnat said, "if they won't answer to them?"
>
> "No use to them" said Alice; "but it's useful to the people that name them, I suppose. If not, why do they have names at all?"

As we see reflected later in the Humpty Dumpty episode, names are an imposition of order to Alice, a means of exercising control over other creatures. That is, for Alice, as for Gradgrind and the utilitarian society he represents, names constitute what Martin Buber would call an I-It relationship in which other beings become objects capable of being manipulated.

When Alice offers to list some insects she knows, the Gnat converts dictionary definitions into poetic truths: "a Rocking-horse-fly. It's made entirely of wood, and gets about by swinging itself from branch to branch"; "a Snap-dragon-fly. Its body is made of plum-pudding, its wings of holly-leaves, and its head is a raisin burning in brandy"; and "a Bread-and-butter fly. Its wings are thin slices of bread-and-butter, its body is a crust, and its head is a lump of sugar" (pp. 133–34). Against the Gnat's transcendent definitions stands Alice's morbid sense of mortality. She theorizes about why "insects are so fond of flying into candles" and expresses her fear that the Bread-and-butter-fly might die for want of "weak tea with cream in it."

Finally the Gnat asks Alice if she would be willing to lose her name. Her selfhood firmly established, Alice "anxiously" answers, "No, indeed." The Gnat then puns by remarking that Alice's governess could not call her to lessons if she had no name:

> "Well, if she said 'Miss,' and didn't say anything more," the Gnat replied, "of course you'd miss your lessons. That's a joke. I wish *you* had made it."
> "Why do you wish *I* had made it?" Alice asked. "It's a very bad one."
> But the Gnat only sighed deeply while two large tears came rolling down its cheeks.
> (P. 135)

Surely the Gnat weeps for her lost innocence. Bound by her acquired distrust of insects, by her reductive dictionary definitions, by her elemental fear of death, by her own self-definition, Alice mirrors her fallen condition—her commitment to Urizenic principles of order and to an unredemptive selfhood.

Alice's ensuing brief journey through the woods "where things have no names" marks a further rite of passage from innocence to experience. Empson associates the dark woods with death and sexual awakening. Perhaps so. In one sense, however, Alice has already been acquainted with death and has frequently received and issued threats of death. In another sense her self-consciousness *is* raised dramatically in the scene: "I know my name now," she claims with resolve—"I won't forget it again" (p. 137). Furthermore, the appearance of the Fawn gives significance to the moment. When she enters the woods, Alice speaks with and "lovingly" holds the Fawn. When they come out of the woods, though, the Fawn cries out, "You're a human child!" and runs away in fear. The child's association with gentle animals is of course a conventional symbol of innocence. Alice's dissociation exposes her emerging state of being.

While continuing to parody adult follies (as in the mock battles between Tweedledum and Tweedledee, the Lion and the Unicorn, and the Red and White Knights), the characters seem less threatening to Alice as the book goes on. But while Alice moves with increasing surety, she continues to show her susceptibility and fear when her comic antagonists penetrate her easy assumptions. Her apprehension that she may be part of the Red King's dream, as Tweedledee tells her, provokes both insistence—"I am real!" (p. 145)—and tears. She rapidly changes the subject. She does so again later when Humpty Dumpty tells her that seven-and-a-half is "an uncomfortable sort of age" (p. 162). Humpty tells her she should have left off at seven, and Alice replies, "One ca'n't help growing older." His response—"One ca'n't perhaps . . . but *two* can. With proper assistance, you might have left off at seven!" (p. 162)—has led Richard Kelly to remark, "Humpty's chilling phrase, 'with proper assistance,' is a grim reminder that Alice is in a post-lapserian [sic] world and that innocence is indeed a fragile commodity."[17]

Alice's innocence has indeed been lost. Whereas Humpty can rejoice in unbirthdays, Alice is compelled forward in time, driven across the board to the Eighth Square where identity and death coexist. Declaring independence of time and language, Humpty counters Alice's necessity for fixity and certainty. Against his imaginative interpretation of "Jabberwocky" (Humpty assures her that he "can explain all the poems that were invented—and a good many that haven't been invented yet"—p. 164), Alice can offer only the reductive fact of death: "*somebody* killed *something*: that's clear, at any rate—" (p. 118). Unconscious but nonetheless aware of the fallen world, Alice sees through postlapsarian lenses.

Her sight is at once wise to the way of the world and deficient in grace. Her end—selfhood and queenship—justifies her means. The scene with the White Knight illustrates the point. To Martin Gardner, "Of all the characters Alice meets on her two dreamy adventures, only the White Knight seems to be genuinely fond of her and to offer her special assistance. He is almost alone in speaking to her with respect and courtesy." He concludes that "we hear loudest in this episode that 'shadow of a sigh' that Carroll tells us in his prefatory poem will 'tremble through the story.' "[18] The sorrow that Gardner finds stems from Alice's compulsion (and perhaps her need) to achieve queenship. Carroll, as biographers have noted, found the line between childhood and adulthood, innocence and puberty, difficult to acknowledge. Perhaps in injecting himself into the story in the person of the White Knight, Carroll utters his modest protest against the deterministic forces that drive his heroine. For however unknowingly, Alice does abandon the impotent White Knight and, figuratively at least, the precarious and gentle world he represents. Says James Kincaid, this "deeply kind" figure may provoke laughter, but "we must taken him seriously." His song parody of Wordsworth's "Resolution and Independence" exactly parallels Alice's insensitivity to him: "The point of the poem is the cruelty of self-absorption, precisely the same self-absorption that allows Alice to joke about the disappearing friend—'It wo'n't take long to see him *off*, I expect'—and then skip away thoughtlessly: 'and now for the last brook, and to be a Queen! How grand it sounds!' "[19] Alice cannot remain a child forever, of course, so we cannot make her into some kind of villainess because of her treatment of the White Knight. Nonetheless, her will to power sadly justifies an unconscious cruelty. As Blake well knew, experience is purchased at the cost of innocence.

When Alice finally arrives at the Eighth Square, she undergoes a last ironic "test," a climax to all the mock rituals, the parodies of learning, and the satires on authority which form the sum and substance of the tales. She thinks the whole affair "grand" when she finds herself newly crowned sitting between the Red Queen and the White Queen. Her every expectation of sovereignty is marvelously ridiculed. Unable to answer the queens' questions, to play the game of nonsense which totally lambastes the privileges of rank and position, Alice laments, "I wish Queens never asked questions" (p. 195). When the examination ends, the Red Queen shows a side of queenship that Alice seems to know little about—kindness. She tells the new queen to sing the White Queen a lullaby ("She's tired, poor thing!"); but Alice can no more sing than she could join in the humor—"I don't know any soothing lullabies." As the two queens sleep on Alice's shoulders, she characteristically defines queenship by the book:

> "I don't think it *ever* happened before, that anyone had to take care of two Queens asleep at once! No, not in all the History of England—it couldn't, you know, because there never was more than one Queen at a time. Do wake up you heavy things!"
> (P. 197)

As always, Alice measures the fantasy world against her knowledge and finds it wanting. All the more insistent on her reign, she goes on to "Queen Alice's," announces her royalty to the old Frog, complains about the missing servant, and stamps her foot in irritation. She has become the "real" queen she has sought to be, an authoritarian with the overriding power to enact her will.

To some, perhaps most, Alice's enactment of the will to power at the dinner is a positive gesture. It strikes out against chaos, they contend; or, in Robert Pattison's language, it "overturns the false order of Wonderland with the faith and assurance of the symbolic logician destroying a fallacious syllogism."[20] Truly one cannot remain in Wonderland, and we are given little choice in deciding between growing and retreating into childhood. Yet even if Carroll did not suffer the prolonged commitment to Neverland that Barrie did, he seemingly was keenly aware of the price to be paid for the loss of innocence—and he depicts Alice's "victory" with no little irony. When the Red Queen parodies the rules of etiquette by scolding Alice for wanting to slice the mutton before she has been introduced and orders it off along with the pudding, Alice decides the Red Queen should not "be the only one to give orders." When all goes awry, she pulls out the tablecloth, not so much resolving the chaos as participating in it. That is not all, of course; Alice turns "fiercely" upon the Red Queen, "catching hold of the little creature in the very act of jumping over a bottle. . . . She took it off the table as she spoke and shook it backwards and forwards with all her might" (pp. 204–05). The violence expressed in the dream suddenly explodes in the external world, where it is truly frightening, however much Alice coyly pretends to fuss over her kitten, whom the Red Queen becomes, for waking her from "such a nice dream." Lionel Morton incisively states that Alice "cannot really shake off the Red Queen, because the Queen is in her, not the kitten: the Queen is the desire to dominate and to punish. . . . This desire is also the desire to grow up and be an adult, as Carroll saw it."[21]

When Alice observes Dinah, the image of her predatory self, cleaning the white kitten, she remarks, "Do you know you're scrubbing a White Queen? Really, it's most disrespectful of you!" She plays the governess-judge-queen, ordering the kitten to confess, sit up straight and curtsey. Then, she recalls the "quantity of poetry" she heard about fishes and concludes ominously,

> "Tomorrow morning you shall have a real treat. All the time you're eating your breakfast, I'll repeat 'The Walrus and the Carpenter' to you; and you can make believe it's oysters, dear!" (P. 208)

As Kincaid points out, "The Walrus is a very apt caricature of Alice."[22] The poem's comic portrayal of the Walrus's mock sympathy for the oysters and, by implication, the whole of the savagery and cruelty everywhere apparent in Wonderland and behind the looking-glass are transposed in a world no longer protected by regenerative humor.

Throughout the Alice books, Alice exists in opposing realities, a fallen and so divided character. The tension moves her from humiliation to the assertion of power in an abbreviated moment of becoming. Elizabeth Sewell finds Carroll's "deep sense . . . to be very close to that of Blake, who sees in the logical, rational Urizen a power beautiful when balanced by other powers of the mind, lethal when developed in independence and isolation."[23] It is precisely Alice's comfortable faith in the pure light of reason and guaranteed existence that renders her deficient in Wonderland and dooms her to destroy it—and concomitantly to pay undue allegiance to a fallen adulthood. Alice's fall in reverse, her return to the innocence of the garden, can prove redemptive only to the degree she can recover from the "autumn frosts" of time. "We are but older children, dear," Carroll writes in the prefatory poem to *Through the Looking-Glass*, "who fret to find our bedtime near" (p. 103). If the innocence of childhood remains, it abides in the memory of a lost childhood, whose vision alone can do battle with the Urizenic realities of a fallen world. So long as it exists within the self it can resist the "shadowy hermaphrodite" who Blake warns us threatens to circumscribe our being. Though the Alice stories do not guarantee the triumph of the imagination in Alice's growing up, they give credence and meaning to the most ancient of myths—and remind Carroll's readers once more that "a little child shall lead them."

2001: A Space Odyssey by Arthur C. Clarke and Stanley Kubrick

> Or was that only mythology? He knew it would seem like mythology when he got back to Earth (if he ever got back). . . . It even occurred to him that the distinction between history and mythology might be itself meaningless outside the Earth.
>
> —C. S. Lewis, *Out of the Silent Planet*

Harry Levin claims that the Alice books "merge the fairy tale with science fiction."[24] One reason they do, of course, is the close similarity between the fantasy of children's literature and science fiction. With a liberated imagination marginally constrained by the demands of realism, writers of such fantasy are free to explore new dimensions of character and setting. Because both science fiction and fairy tales depend heavily on myth as the common ground of human experience, it is not surprising that the Fall motif appears frequently in both. Nor is it difficult to understand why a popular culture venting its need for myth in an age of scientific and technological determinism would respond to science fiction and the fantasies of a Tolkein or C. S. Lewis both at the bookstore and the movie theater. Though escape is doubtless one motive for the popularity of fantasy literature, so also is the psychological need to touch once more those universal human truths obscured by the oppressive pluralism of modern culture. Arthur Clarke's and Stanley Kubrick's joint creation, *2001: A Space Odyssey*, reflects the need as much as Carroll's two Alice tales do. Like *Alice*, *2001* also depicts a fall in reverse, if ironically. In the concluding episode the protagonist returns to childhood at a heightened level of consciousness. The ending culminates a series of falls describing the evolution of human consciousness.

The movie *2001* has a curious history, being the product of filmmaker Stanley Kubrick's elaboration of Arthur Clarke's short story "The Sentinel." Clarke worked closely with Kubrick on the film script and concurrently wrote the novel, which also appeared in 1968. The book likely owes its popularity more to the movie than to its own virtues, for it provided for many movie viewers at least a partial explanation of the more baffling moments in the film. If not as firm in its control or characterization as Clarke's earlier *Childhood's End*, published in 1948, the novel offers more than a gloss of the film, despite occasional lapses in language and structure. As my comments indicate, I sometimes refer to the film and sometimes to the novel, for both are collaborative efforts, Clarke's short story and contributions to the script having provided the essential direction for Kubrick's film, and Kubrick's elaboration and visualization of the original story having been the basis of Clarke's novel.

Spanning the entire history of humankind, the action of *2001* involves three falls: the first describing the evolution of man from simple primate, the brief first section of the work set in Africa at "The Dawn of Man"; the second his freedom from a futuristic, technological paradise, the largest portion of the action, set on the spaceship Discovery journeying across space to the source of mysterious radio signals coming from a moon of Saturn; the third his acquisition of "higher innocence," which portrays the central character's return to Earth transfigured in the form of "Star Child." Alan Brody rightly identifies "human consciousness" as the film's hero and the fortunate fall as its integrating theme.[25] Clarke himself once remarked that "M-G-M doesn't know it yet, but they've footed the bill for the first $10,500,000.00 religious film," and Kubrick admitted that the "God concept" was at "the heart of the film."[26] It is ironic that Clarke has long lived in Ceylon near the site of Adam's Peak, where according to

Muslim legend Adam settled with Eve and propagated the human race after their expulsion from the Garden of Eden. For in their modern odyssey, Clarke and Kubrick envision the essential romantic version of the Fall, in which human disobedience is "the necessary first step in the educational journey by which thinking and striving man wins his way back to a lost integrity, along a road that looks like a reversion but is in fact a progression."[27] The Fall in *2001* marks such a pattern of becoming.

The initial fall, which actually serves as a prologue to the futuristic story which follows, occurs on the primal African desert, where a group of man-apes seek survival at a small waterhole. If the arid landscape of *Australopithecus africanus*'s world is in any sense Eden, it is so because the ancestors of man exist in profound self-ignorance, satisfied only because they are unaware of their potential for change and thereby content in their naiveté. Moon-Watcher, the main man-ape identified in the novel, "unmistakably held in his genes the promise of humanity,"[28] but he lacked necessary self-knowledge. In theological terms he had not yet entered history because he had not yet gained the freedom to act; he owned no past and no future. He thought of his father, simply called the Old One, as he thought of the rival tribe of apes at the waterhole, solely in the context of the now. His father's death brings neither remorse nor relief.

One morning a mysterious slab appears standing upright near the waterhole. An intrusion upon the horizontal reality of the land, "New Rock," like the Tree in Eden, is an emblem of a deity. Instinctively, Moon-Watcher attempts to eat it, thus mimicking the Genesis myth. Though he fails, the "tree" initiates the movement toward self-knowledge, a dramatic event which Kubrick heightens in the movie with the intense chanting of György Ligeti's musical score. Clarke speaks of the transparency of the monolith wherein "ill-defined phantoms moved across its surface and its depths" (p. 21). In its reflections of the apes, the tree-monolith establishes a narcissistic truth: seeing himself for the first time, as Adam and Eve become aware of their nakedness, Moon-Watcher sees a new image in his world. Driven to action by a signal transmitted by the slab, he hits the monolith with a rock and feels "indescribable pleasure, almost sexual in its intensity" (p. 23). Though as yet uninitiated into "experience," Moon-Watcher imitates man's primal gesture of offense, dissatisfaction with paradise—"Discontent had come into his soul, and he had taken one small step toward humanity" (p. 25).

From such temptations comes a fall, and Clarke appropriately relates it to death, the first fruit of knowledge, being the ability to kill a fellow creature with a weapon. Picking up a pointed stone, Moon-Watcher discovers the first tool-weapon, and is about to become the first and only creature able to construct his own garden—to play god. With "a pleasing sense of power and authority" he kills a pig and enters wholeheartedly into the duality of good and evil. Now carnivorous, he has found a ready means of survival in a land of minimal vegetation, and yet he has for the first time exercised a potentially self-destructive will to power. From this other dualities emerge. In the climactic moment of this first ritual of a fall, Moon-Watcher takes us all the way to Genesis 4. A hunter and a killer, he slays his brother creature, thereby anticipating the spaceman Dave Bowman's later murdering the computer-brother HAL and the use of space technology for military aggression as discussed at the moonbase where the second monolith appears. In the first episode One-Ear, leader of the Others, a rival tribe of apes at the waterhole, bears the wrath of his brother Cain—"The frozen snarl of death came crashing down upon his uncomprehending head" (p. 34). Man has entered the world of experience, "acquired a past" and begun "to grope tward a future." Moon-Watcher turns knowledge into a weapon of self-destruction—good and evil can not be kept forever in balance. As Brody tells us, death coexists with knowledge. The "first experience to liberate man's mind . . . comes as a direct result of an encounter with death."[29] The very weapon of destruction itself is the bone of another creature. As in Eden, the first and ultimate consequence of the Fall is mortality, but death as self-conscious act, not just dying but knowing one is dying, experiencing death as something other than a mundane event, a disappearing off the margin of existence as the Old One does at the beginning of the novel.

Kubrick records the duality Clarke tells us about in a spectacular film sequence. The sequence is foreshadowed when an ape-man in childlike innocence playfully strikes the bones of a skeleton with another bone. Play becomes an exercise of power moving from wrist to arm and finally exploding in Dionysian abandon when the wildly dancing ape shatters the skeleton with violent blows. Moon-Watcher repeats the primordial dance when he slays One-Ear with a bone and then flings his weapon gleefully into the air—the gracefully floating bone becoming a twenty-first-century space ship (an image reinforced later when the spaceship Discovery also assumes the appearance of an elongated bone). Kubrick effectively underscores the visual dissolve by shifting the sound track from the orgiastic power of Strauss's *Thus Spake Zarathustra* to the liquid sounds of *The Blue Danube* waltz. The same powers of mind that can produce the sensational technological advances of the space age can create the sophisticated weaponry capable of annihilating man. The theme seems clear enough: knowledge is purchased at a price, but the knowledge acquired by the Fall initiates the odyssey to a higher state of being. The remaining portions of the work reenact the same inevitable pattern of the Fall at even-higher levels of consciousness.

The second fall concerns another Cain-Abel act, the "murder" of the astronauts' computer-"brother" on the spaceship Discovery. It proves "an even greater fall from innocence" than the first and leads "to a new and even greater discovery of self and an even greater fall."[30] Though apparently the antithesis of the primal African desert, the futuristic setting reveals a sterility even more extreme, a technological wonderland where spiritual powers have entropied and human beings seem little more than automatons. The action, which constitutes the largest portion of the book and film, falls into two parts. The first follows Dr. Heywood Floyd, Chairman of the National Council of Astronautics, as he investigates a monolith (TMA-1, Tycho-Magnetic-Anomaly 1) newly uncovered in a moon crater.

The bland dialogue and synthetic environment seem a veritable parody of projected twenty-first-century culture, the false paradise of modern scientific man. All conversations are reduced to banality or impossible technological jargon: Heywood Floyd's brief exchanges with the smiling stewardess on his journey to the moon, his protracted discussion of the possible problem at the moon base with his Russian colleague Dimitri Moisevitch and others at the base lounge, and his completely uninspired briefing of the American contingent temporarily quarantined at the base. Language is conveyed by computer, silenced on two-dimensional "news pads," and stripped of all emotion. In the film Kubrick accentuates the deficiency of oral language by using inordinately long pauses and focusing visually on nonaural communication (for example, centering attention on the written instructions for using a toilet in zero gravity) or pseudo-oral communication (as when Floyd has to talk into a computer for voice identification). The setting reveals the same bland existence. The rooms at Clavius Base even look "like a good motel suite," and Kubrick makes much of the Howard Johnson's sign prominently displayed in the lobby. Surely another deficient garden, the futuristic society needs the redemption of a fall.

In this totally artificial state grows the Tree of Knowledge for a second time, and it makes a mockery of man's limited knowledge and pseudo-existence. It challenges what Don Daniels rightly calls the "technological totalitarianism" which makes human beings "servants of scientific rationalism," reducing them to Blake's "technicians with their 'golden moon, the quadrant, & the rule & balance.' "[31] The monolith, like the apple offered by the serpent, piques man's curiosity, appealing to his unquenchable desire "to become like one of us," to possess godlike power. Significantly, in the encounter with the second monolith, Floyd repeats Moon-Watcher's first gesture: he instinctively extends his hand to touch. But as Daniels points out, "The scientist reaches toward the slab with a hand insulated by his suit."[32] The protective apparel of modern man must be stripped away in the confrontation with knowledge. "To know" man must be made aware of his vulnerability. A powerful radio signal suddenly transmitted by the slab produces such an action. Their confident control shattered by the unleashed energy of the monolith, the humans are compelled to venture beyond their protected universe. A new, as yet incomprehensible, reality endangers their ordered lives. Whereas the men-apes at the dawn of man lived on the brink of physical extinction in a desert wasteland, the voyagers on the spaceship Discovery are imperiled by an ever-greater extinction in a spiritual wasteland possessing all the deceptions of a utopia. On a secret mission to Japetus, a moon of Saturn, Discovery is nothing less than Eden, an image of twenty-first-century man in miniature—and it carries with it all the spiritually debilitating force that Blake glimpsed in the Urizenic paradise of eighteenth-century scientific rationalism.

As the work suddenly shifts from the moonbase Clavius to the spaceship Discovery seeking to locate the direction of the radio signal released by the slab, we draw closer to the second fall. The second part of the second fall introduces three main characters: the spacemen Dave Bowman and Frank Poole, and the computer named HAL, who figures importantly as a character in the drama. HAL's presence extends the Fall myth to the Cain and Abel story in Genesis 4, for he is the offspring of man and is to be slain by his brother. In biblical language, Adam "knew" Eve, and she bore Cain. As Gerhard von Rad notes, "to know" implies not just knowledge but experience,[33] and truly the computer is as much a child of "ontology" as Cain. An android created by humanoids, HAL is born of and reflects modern man's mechanistic existence, an echo of Blake's "shadowy hermaphrodite." Spuriously androgynous with his mellow masculine voice and maternal breast (a nipple-like red light that lights as he talks in the film version), he is a descendant of Adam and Eve, and like his fallen creators he too has been assigned guardianship of paradise.

The artificial life on board the Discovery reflects the spiritual *ennui* the English romantics found in the biblical paradise in their conception of a fortunate fall. Here too man lacks freedom and self-awareness. Life is simulated in the "electronic sarcophagi" where three astronauts remain in hibernation, awaiting resurrection when the ship nears its destination. The sarcophagi literally become their tombs, however, when HAL turns off their support system. Life is reduced to biosensor panels where the EEG displays provide "the electronic signatures of three personalities that had once existed, and would one day exist again" (pp. 91–92). In this Urizenic garden knowledge is limited to maps and charts and geological surveys, language to "technish" or incredible banality, survival to the blibs and blinks of the "situation board." "Life functions" go on in an artificial existence—sex, exercise, games, even culture are played out while passive human beings drift in nothingness. The hopeless vacuity of their lives is characterized nowhere better than in the birthday greeting Frank Poole receives from "home" (a scene that recreates a similarly inept attempt by Heywood Floyd to phone birthday greetings to his daughter from the moon): "Well, Frank, can't think of anything else to say at the moment. . ." (p. 119). Kubrick does not even allow Poole to get up from the exercise table to respond to the telescreen and has HAL position Poole's body and head to receive the message from his family. Poole makes no gesture of his own, shows no emotion. Clarke says in the novel that he "had moved into a new dimension of remoteness, and almost all emotional links had been stretched beyond the yield point" (p. 120). With no small irony, the moment ends with HAL's comment, "Sorry to interrupt the festivities . . . but we have a problem" (p. 120). The problem precipitates the crisis which will force Bowman, the last survivor after HAL has destroyed his fellows, into combat with the computer, resulting in the "murder" of his "brother" HAL.

The garden implies closure and, according to the second law of thermodynamics, closed systems entropy. The decadent utopia can no more endure than the One World created by the Overlords in Clarke's novel *Childhood's End*. Sooner or later the garden of the spaceship must suffer collapse. In the chapter of *2001* called "Need to Know," Clarke writes simply, "Like his makers HAL had been created innocent; but, all too soon, a snake had entered his electronic Eden" (p. 148). As the protector of this doomed paradise, HAL is both the agent of the gods and a brother to the astronauts. He suffers from the elemental disease of fallen man, a profound schizophrenia, a divided nature that compels him to sin against himself while at the same time he rejects his guilt. Programmed for perfection, HAL cannot tolerate the judgment of the gods at Mission Control who convict him of a fault. When he is charged by a twin computer on Earth of inaccurately predicting the failure of an AE-35 transmitting unit, he staunchly maintains his "innocence," hence playing the human absolutist who will do anything necessary to guard his virtue. His "moral" absolutism reflects the Urizenic gods that made him. In the vein of a radical theology articulated in secular terms, Clarke blames the false deities (and their agents, "the planners," and "their twin gods of Security and National Interest") for HAL's insoluble dilemma—"the conflict between truth and the concealment of truth" (p. 149). Programmed not to act in deception, he must do so to conceal the knowledge he alone possesses about the Discovery's true mission. A neurotic coerced to "sin" but unable to admit his guilt without endangering his prescribed *raison d'être,* HAL attempts to hide himself, like Adam and Eve. "Without rancor—and without pity," the computer struggles to preserve his innocence-perfection upon which his selfhood depends. Here Clarke differentiates between the android and the humanoid, for whereas HAL cannot gain Blakean higher innocence because he cannot sin against the "moral" categories implanted in his being, Bowman can and must achieve moral freedom by a conscious violation of moral imperatives. Bowman must gain independence from the deified system that has constructed his mechanistic Eden. In his ability to choose, he can assume control of the "life-support system" while HAL remains the parasite of the system that judges him. To achieve his salvation, however ironic, Bowman must also fall—and by choice. In response to the "warning bell sounded somewhere far down in the depths" of his conscience (p. 140), he must display "the courage to be."

As we have observed, the romantics tended to see the fall recorded in Genesis 4, Cain's murder of Abel, as a consummate act of freedom and to make Cain something of a hero of spirit along with Milton's Satan in *Paradise Lost* and Goethe's Faust. To the romantics "Cain, the direct heir to the Fall . . . is of more absorbing interest than are Adam and Eve."[34] In romantic versions of the myth, such as Byron's *Cain,* the rebellious brother, like the Prodigal Son, acts more courageously and acquires greater self-consciousness than his brother. Like the romantic hero, Bowman achieves a moral superiority when he kills his brother HAL. Threatened with death when HAL releases the oxygen from the ship, Bowman, in the novelistic account, barely manages to escape death by putting on a space suit (in the film he is locked outside the ship and forces reentry). Aware that his survival depends on wresting control of the ship from HAL, his obedient brother following the order of his gods devoted to the perfection of reason and science, Bowman performs a "lobotomy" by disconnecting the memory banks in the computer's "brain." Until this point all his actions have been purely emotionless and perfunctory. Now he must commit murder, in a way imitate Moon-Watcher's murder of One-Ear at the dawn of man—but with consciousness and through the exercise of human cunning and wit unavailable to HAL. Unlike his predecessor, he feels. "This is harder than I expected," he admits (p. 156). His sorrow stems in part from his own fear of isolation and loneliness, the immediate fate of Cain in the Bible, and in part from his compassion for HAL. Clarke tells us that Bowman pulls out the last memory unit when he "could bear no more" of HAL's pathetic return in infancy. In death HAL regains the innocence of childhood; Bowman moves through experience to the Blakean higher innocence associated with full self-consciousness. Until he commits his crime against the sterile perfection that has rendered him spiritually impotent, Bowman is literally the equal of HAL, essentially an advanced automaton devoid of being. When he slays his brother, therefore, he commits a form of suicide by destroying an image of his own perfection. In Tim Hunter's words, "In committing murder, Bowman has essentially lost his dehumanization and become an archetypal new being: one worthy of the transcendental transformation that follows."[35] In this regard, Bowman recalls Emil Sinclair's slaying of Pistorius in *Demian*, a similar act of spiritual independence.

In Tillich's sense, Bowman's fall in killing his brother moves him from essence to existence by thrusting him out of a spiritual state of suspended animation. He, like Adam and Eve, has been expelled from paradise, that controlled existence where he served as agent of a distant god. To quote Erich Fromm's phrase, Bowman now "is able to make his own history, to develop his own powers."[36] Yet he must fall again. The enigmatic ending of both the film and the novel describes Bowman's literal and symbolic fall through the Star Gate when he arrives at the destination charted by the radio signals, one of the moons of Saturn. In the eye of Japetus, Bowman discovers TMA-1's "big brother." This third fall in the story is the most symbolic, pointing not to the Fall in Eden or to the myth of Cain and Abel, but to another, more mystical fall. Bowman literally falls through the Star Gate, the entry to the great underside of the monolith, and experiences the ultimate evolution of man into "mind"—"and if there was anything beyond *that*, its name could only be God" (p. 174).

After a long fall through the Star Gate, which Kubrick portrays in the film as a prolonged psychedelic trip, Bowman lands in his space pod on "the polished floor of an elegant, anonymous hotel suite" (p.

208), furnished in the film in Louis-XVI decor. In a mysterious world both real and unreal, like the strange Wonderland where Alice's fall ends, Bowman tries to comprehend where he is. Apparently a near-perfect imitation of life on Earth, the room becomes the stage whereon Bowman acts out the remaining moments of his life, moving in accelerated stages through age to death and subsequent rebirth. In the scene just before the dramatic ending of the work, Bowman as an aged man eats a last meal in a setting of extraordinay starkness. Although the room is elegantly furnished and impeccably neat, all the surfaces used in the film seem hard and cold. The echo of harsh sounds, such as Bowman's hitting the floor with his shoes or striking his brightly shining plate with his utensils, depict an eerie void. Only when he drops his wineglass, shattering it on the floor, does he violate the sterile paradise. When he does, he looks up to see himself as an old man dying in a large bed. As the dying figure reaches out to touch the monolith suddenly appearing at the foot of the bed, he is transformed into a fetus, Star Child miraculously drifting across the great expanse of space. During the entire scene from the point of his fall through Star Gate, as Alan Brody notes, Bowman "*overtakes himself in time*,"[37] becoming finally the fetal symbol of a new Adam evolved to a higher form, moving without constraint or dependence across the cosmos.

In effect, in the moment of transfiguration, Bowman returns to the dawn of man, regains his humanity "retrogressing down the corridors of time, being drained of knowledge and experience." Yet "nothing was being lost; all that he had been, at every moment of his life, was being transferred to safer keeping. Even as one David Bowman ceased to exist another became immortal" (p. 216). From Genesis to Revelation, from fall to rebirth—transfigured from a puppet living within the constraints of a closed mechanistic garden into the Star Child transcending the dimensions of time and space, Bowman truly "gains a deity." He becomes an infinite version of the being Teilhard de Chardin describes "who is the object of his own reflection"—and "in consequence of that very doubling back upon himself becomes in a flash able to raise himself into a new sphere."[38] Unable to remain in the spiritually vacant hotel suite that parodies modern man's highly ordered but impotent world, he falls from death to life.

Blake distinguishes between the innocence of childhood, which is unearned and unconscious, and the higher innocence gained through experience when one chooses to act. The Star Child manifests that higher innocence when he wills to return to Earth across "the great river of suns": "Unwittingly, he had crossed it once; now he must cross it again—this time, of his own volition. The thought filled him with a sudden, freezing terror" (p. 218). If not a Christ assuming flesh, this new Adam "was back, precisely where he wished to be, in the space men called real" (p. 220). In the novel Clarke makes him into an agent of apocalypse, bringing judgment to the world. Detonating a ring of nuclear bombs man has placed around earth, he begins a first act of judgment and purification. Through the will of the Star Child, humanity's bent toward destruction, as in *Demian*, may lead to a new beginning. Though Kubrick does not project it in the film, Clarke shows him triggering another fall—as Camus concludes in *The Plague*, "for the bane and enlightening of men."

The Fall in the space fantasy *2001* occurs cyclically like stages in the evolutionary process. Presumably, human progress is possible, but the process itself can never end. Perfectibility is neither possible nor desired. In choosing to return to Earth, the Star Child reaffirms his humanity, rejecting the perfection that humanity cannot acquire. Born of the ever-evolving cycles of fall and rebirth, from the desert plain to the emptiness of space, he reenters human history armed with an understanding of the fortunate fall. Unlike Alice, he opts for becoming instead of being. We do not know what may transpire at the end of the work, only that the pattern will continue. If "not quite sure what he would do next," like his ancestor Moon-Watcher, the Star Child "would think of something."

‡ 7 ‡

Running the Risk

According to the Judeo-Christian legend, Adam and Eve vainly sought recovery or reconstruction of their first home after expulsion from paradise. The curse doomed them to certain failure, or course, for whatever Eden they designed could not resolve their alienation from spiritual wholeness and harmony. The inevitable cycle of construction and destruction, illusory peace and unending restlessness, has thus formed the pattern of human history. We have seen in all the characters we have examined the same irreversible process. No spurious Eden can long endure. Bly in *The Turn of the Screw,* the idyllic island in *Lord of the Flies,* Paris—or Western civilization—in *Demian* or *Heart of Darkness* or *La Chute,* the spaceship Discovery in *2001,* the life of the successful lawyer in *After the Fall,* all collapse before the unrelenting truth of self-knowledge. To this point we have centered on visions of the Fall which portray Edens as they appear at the edge of adulthood, in the image of a declining culture, by hindsight after the Fall, and in fantasy. Now we turn to two works describing people who must *choose* to destroy their false gardens, who must run the risk of shattering their self-protective worlds in order to release spiritual powers hitherto rendered ineffectual. Paradise can only be restored by a denial of self-knowledge—and the characters in *Who's Afraid of Virginia Woolf?* and *Deliverance* find that such denial is possible only at the cost of their souls.

In the "Parnassus" of New Carthage Edward Albee exposes a decadent Eden governed by an unseen Urizenic god. Each of the four fallen characters has survived in this garden by self-deception. By the end of the play, though, the terrible forces of truth, unleashed in sadomasochistic fury, ravage the fragile innocence each claims. The only cure to their spiritual dilemma is a shattering of the composite illusion that permits their paradise to stand. In the exorcism that ends the play, all four characters are freed from their counterfeit innocence to face an ominous but potentially redemptive world.

In *Deliverance* Ed Gentry's gnawing sensation of emptiness in his self-created garden gives impetus to a harrowing journey into another Eden, stripped of all vestiges of civilization and human control. In a way, in his attempt to flee from a civilized paradise of his own making to a natural Eden of demonic power, Ed discovers that he somehow must embrace the irreconcilable opposites that compete in his psyche. To achieve some kind of integration, he has to enter a dark internal world via his long trip into a Georgia woods and there consciously sacrifice his false innocence. Both the urban and the primitive Edens prove equally destructive, the first by subtle passivity, the second by Dionysian violence—and Ed, knowing the powers of good and evil, must accommodate both without wholly existing in either.

Who's Afraid of Virginia Woolf? by Edward Albee

> And now, when they are stripped naked to
> their souls
> And can choose, whether to put on proper
> costumes
> Or huddle quickly into new disguises,
> They have, for the first time, somewhere
> to start from.
>
> —Julia in T.S. Eliot's *The Cocktail Party*

The Zoo Story, The Death of Bessie Smith, The Sandbox, and *The American Dream* early earned Edward Albee something of a reputation as a moralistic playwright portraying the loss of innocence and humane values in contemporary, and especially American, culture. When his first full-length play, *Who's Afraid of Virginia Woolf?*, abandoned off-Broadway for the commercial stage, it unleashed a critical controversy scarcely abated even now. Though a popular success much praised by critics, the play has been the target of a strong hostile minority. Alfred Chester led one of the earliest attacks on the drama, accusing it of "the most repugnant kind of puritanical priggishness. The morality of *Virginia Woolf* is one which conceives that folly, desperation, frustration, hate are not in themselves their greatest penalty—as virtue is said to be its own reward—but must be judged and punished from above, beyond, without."[1] Not long after, theologian-critic Tom Driver called Albee "this little man who looks as if he dreamed of evil but is actually mild as a dove and wants to be loved."[2] Probably the most vitriolic and influential attack was written by Richard Schechner, who called the drama a "cheap hunt for love" that "makes dishonesty a virtue, perversion a joke, adultery a simple party game." Schechner condemned the play's "perverse and dangerous" values, and charged Albee with gratifying "an adolescent culture which likes to think of itself as decadent."[3]

For all its sadomasochistic violence, its profanity, cruel invective, and verbal abuse, *Who's Afraid of Virginia Woolf?* has been seen more and more as a modern religious drama in the morality play tradition. C. W. E. Bigsby relates the "religious overtones" of *Virginia Woolf, The Zoo Story*, and Miller's *After the Fall* to a kind of secular gospel, asserting "the primacy of human contact based on an acceptance of reality." Such a myth "is not so far removed from the liberal humanism of Tillich," Bigsby suggests: "Deprived of God man is of necessity his own salvation."[4] Though not going so far as to call the play "a modern version of *Pilgrim's Progress*," as Bigsby does, Arthur Evans describes the fundamental Christian themes in the play. He sees the work as dramatizing how man, "originally and tragically trapped in his own History (i.e., 'original sin') . . . transcends himself and his own History by the grace beyond History which is love."[5] His theory echoes that of David McDonald that "many elements of the drama can be related to the religious—and often specifically Christian—concept of man's fall from grace."[6]

We can approach the play, then, both as a realistic presentation of psychological frustration and a "morality play" in which ritual provides a metaphysical perspective. Albee has said of the dual levels of the play, "If people were a little more aware of what actually is beneath the naturalistic overlay they would be surprised to find how early the unnaturalistic base has been set. When you're dealing with a symbol in a realistic play, it is also a realistic fact. You must expect the audience's mind to work on both levels, symbolically and realistically."[7] The play's first director, Alan Schneider, claims simply that he "never thought of it as a realistic or naturalistic play," despite Albee's obvious use of realistic detail and psychological themes.[8] It is the elaborate underlay of mythic matter and the rhythm of ritual that gives substance to the whole. Not only the overt use of the Latin requiem mass in the third act, but virtually every mention of Jesus or Christ or God—however profane, every obscure allusion to religious symbolism and terminology assumes significance. On one hand a portrayal of the psychological despair of the characters, these religious elements also constitute the mythic action of a fall and resurrection.

To some degree, it may be argued, all of Albee's major works treat the demise of the American Eden and its communal center, the family. In *Virginia Woolf* Martha and George, with all their sophisticated barbarism, are the Adam and Eve in a debunked technological and materialistic paradise. As Richard Kostelanetz notes, they, and Nick and Honey too, undergo the paradigmatic pattern of "group psychoanalysis," the stripping away of illusion and confrontation with truth.[9] It is impossible, and probably pointless, to differentiate between confession and exorcism on one hand and retroactive illumination and "psychological release" on the other. We do not have a secular opposed to a religious action, a conflict between realism and ritual, but an intimate pairing of the two. Religious terminology can be applied appropriately to the psychological processes of the plot. As Carl Jung and his disciples have theorized, psychology in its largest sense is the handmaiden of theology. We can justly seek out theological implications and religious meanings that coexist with the secular determinism of the play. In short, *Virginia Woolf,* with its extraordinary sense of ritual, its religious symbolism and invocations of the deity, dramatizes the religious and existential condition of fallen humanity.

We begin with the garden—New Carthage, whose name recalls the legendary site of Dido's and Aeneus's ill-fated love, the object of St. Augustine's condemnation, the Phoenecian city doomed to destruction in the Punic Wars. In its most inclusive sense, New Carthage is yet another image of fallen civilization, in particular a symbol of failed America—the names of the protagonists echoing those of the "father of his country" and his wife—the New Eden with its dehumanizing values of materialism, pragmatism and accommodation. In New Carthage, Emil Roy writes, a "specious goodness" is "concealed by a puritanical moral code, an observation rooted in Freud's *Civilization and Its Discontents.*"[10] Here George, the bog in the history department, and Nick, the "wave-of-the-future" biologist, compete in what Lee Baxandall labels an ironic "House of Intellect."[11] George ironically calls New Carthage "Parnassus," the mythic home of the gods, and he cynically says to Nick, "This is your heart's content—Illyria . . . Penguin Island . . . Gomorrah."[12]

The ruler of his paradise is Martha's father, truly a Urizenic god. "Martha's Daddy . . . may be the Head of the University," Rictor Norton declares, "but he may also be Ruler of the Universe."[13] Like the mayor in *The Death of Bessie Smith* and Tiny Alice's departed father, he never appears, Baxandall observes; but "the whole faculty does obedience to an infinitely remote and super-powered figure with 'a great shock of white hair, and those beady little eyes' like a mouse—a man who 'is the college' and 'is not going to die.' "[14] George tells Nick, "He's God, we all know that" (p. 26). Like Hedda Gabler's father the general, Martha's daddy broods over the play, the distant god and creator of this dubious cosmos. George warns Nick that he had better not let it be "bandied about" that Nick does not intend to stay there forever, for "Martha's father expects loyalty and devotion" (p. 41).

But the setting is more than the mythic Parnassus of New Carthage; it is George's and Martha's house, a false Eden within a false Eden. Albee "wanted the image of a womb or a cave," according to Alan Schneider, not a realistic bourgeois set. The home was to "seem real" but have "all kinds of angles and places that you wouldn't ordinarily have, and strong distortions."[15] As much an arena for sophisticated linguistic warfare as an educated, middle-class couple's living room, it represents Martha's and George's ironic version of a lost paradise. Albee's insistence on a sense of confinement implies that Martha and George have long been locked in their garden, that they have paid due obedience to the god of New Carthage to protect their feeble existences. As womb, however, the set becomes a symbol both of aborted life and ultimately of birth.

Into this seemingly Edenic world come Nick, the young biology professor, and Honey, his wife. In the action that follows the four characters form more than an ensemble—they so merge and reflect one another that they cannot be understood without the contrasting and comparative images they provide of each other. Superficially the opposite of Martha—"slim-hipped" and proper, as opposed to George's opulently sensuous wife—Honey in fact is much like her hostess. (George twice accuses Nick of confusing Martha with Honey.) Anita Stenz makes the point that despite Honey's apparent modesty, she is not "as unworldly as she behaves. She certainly knew how to get her man. Sexually as well as socially she controls things."[16] She had married Nick after experiencing a "hysterical pregnancy," which we can rightly suspect, in light of George's discovery at the end of the second act that she has been aborting life without Nick's knowledge. Furthermore, like Martha, she has suffered at the hand of a loveless father, who was significantly a "man of the Lord." And for all their differences George and Nick are also closely related characters. Although George represents history, the record of man's choices, and Nick the genetic engineering which will annihilate history, they share a common guilt. In order to draw Nick's confession that he married Honey in part to acquire her father's wealth, George must similarly admit, "Look . . . Martha has money too. I mean, her father's been robbing this place blind for years" (p. 107). All four characters live in flawed relationships, afraid to accept the reality of their depraved state—the "unreality" of their illusory Edens.

Structurally, the play involves a series of ritual games. The first act, entitled "Fun and Games," contains several preliminary sparring matches in which the characters feel each other out. George half-playfully begins to penetrate Nick's mask of innocence; Martha begins recounting George's lost opportunities, as he in turn punctuates her commentary with well-aimed witticisms; Martha begins to play at seducing Nick; and Honey, in her drunken stupor, naively inches toward the margin of the arena. Primed and vulnerable, the characters then act out the perverse games of the *Walpürgisnacht*, the title of the second act: "Humiliate the Host," "Get the Guests," "Hump the Hostess." Finally, when each character's pretended innocence has been viciously shattered, comes the third act, "Exorcism," which like a fortunate fall promises the hope of salvation in the ruins of paradise. George calls the last game "Bringing Up Baby," an interesting reflection both of history (the "bringing up" of Martha's and George's illusory son) and the future (the potential child of Honey and Nick, the "wave-of-the-future" boy).

We get a brief glimpse of Martha and George before Nick and Honey arrive in the first act. George's feeble protest against Martha's father's "goddamn Saturday night orgies" and his easy capitulation to the coming of "guests" at 2:30 in the morning reveal his unwillingness to rebel openly against the tyrant god of New Carthage. Although Anita Stenz calls him a "man who would not violate his personal integrity,"[17] in truth he has done so. Ronald Hayman comments: George "calculates very carefully what gestures of protest he can afford. . . . His life has been a compromise."[18] And Martha, too, exposes a cowardly accommodation. An ironic Eve in the patriarchal Judeo-Christian tradition, she seeks to justify her existence by assuming the role of wife to a weak-willed Adam.

The childish banter about a Bette Davis movie, Martha's baby talk and her pseudo-seduction of George, George's bristling replies and his serious warning to Martha not to "start in on the bit" (i.e., mention their nonexistent child) depict a bizarre relationship poised to explode like a severely compressed spring. When Nick and Honey make their appearance, they seem totally opposite, apologetic, humble, and not a little embarrassed at Martha's unintended greeting—"SCREW YOU" (p. 19). The subsequent action shows that all four suffer a common guilt, however. Beginning almost immediately, they begin to rip away each other's defenses in the guise of playful humor, so by the time the first act ends they are all prepared to enter the dark *Walpürgisnacht* whose profound nihilism alone can lead to the Everlasting Yea.

George initiates the stripping action by mocking Nick's feigned cocktail chatter about an abstract painting on the wall:

NICK	It's got a . . . a . . . .
GEORGE	A quiet intensity?
NICK	Well, no . . . a . . . .
GEORGE	Oh. *(Pause)* Well, then a certain noisy relaxed quality, maybe?
NICK	*(Knows what GEORGE is doing, but stays grimly, coolly polite)* No. What I meant was . . . .
GEORGE	How about . . . uh . . . a quietly noisy relaxed intensity. (P. 22)

From this trivial beginning to the end of the act, George challenges Nick at every turn, baiting him with small talk, drawing him to the edge of anger and then quickly retreating. With disarming wit he attacks Nick's cool detachment and patronizing arrogance. In particular George assaults Nick as the young biologist, thereby establishing the basic conflict in the play, that between history and biology, life freely chosen with all its risks and life artificially designed to be without risks. As we shall see, history and biology embody the conflicting Dionysian and Apollonian forces that struggle toward reconciliation. As historian and biologist, George and Nick have both betrayed the life principle by compromising themselves in order to survive in New Carthage.

George stereotypes Nick as genetic engineer—"You people are rearranging my genes, so that everyone will be like everyone else" (p. 37). Couching condemnation in humor he strikes at the premises of Nick's scientific determinism. He tells Honey, "He's quite terrifying, with all his chromosomes, and all" (p. 62). And he envisions the technocratic achievements of a Urizenic universe in which "chromosomes can be altered" and "all imbalances will be corrected, sifted out . . . propensity for various diseases will be gone, longevity assured. We will have a race of men . . . test-tube bred . . . incubator born . . . superb and sublime" (p. 65). But, he goes on, "There will be a dark side to it, too. A certain amount of regulation will be necessary, . . . uh . . . for the experiment to succeed. A certain number of sperm tubes will have to be cut" (p. 66). Such a paradise "will not have much music, [or] much painting," it will require "a certain . . . loss of liberty," and history "will lose its glorious variety and unpredictability. I, and with me the . . . the surprise, the multiplexity, the sea-changing rhythm of . . . history, will be eliminated" (pp. 66–67).

Painting Nick as one of Blake's myopic Newtonian men, George rightly exposes Nick's fallen humanity. But George himself is revealed, and with unrelenting power. Martha shows us that if Nick's biology perverts the life force, so does George's history. With sadistic delight she tells how "the old bog in the History Department" flubbed the chance to take over as heir-apparent to Daddy's rule. Daddy had approved Martha's marriage to George because, as Martha remarks, he wanted someone "to take over the college," but "he watched for a couple of years and started thinking maybe it wasn't such a good idea after all . . . that maybe Georgie-boy didn't have the *stuff* . . . that he didn't have it in him!" (p. 84). Her accusation is not the most significant one, however; George himself admits to the greater offense of not standing up to Daddy—"Dashed hopes, and good intentions. Good, better, best, bested" (p. 32). History, he informs Nick, "is a great deal more . . . disappointing" than biology. He confesses to having given sufficient "loyalty and devotion" to "the old man" to remain in the idyllic realm of New Carthage. His denial of Nick's biology is therefore tempered by his own failed history.

Both George's cynical wit and her own crude behavior reveal Martha's depraved condition. Like George she has entropied in paradise because she lacks the courage to rebel against Daddy and the repressive system he represents. Rejected by her father and unreconciled to George's inadequacies, Martha takes out a Dionysian revenge in the form of a perverse "earth mother." When she returns from taking Honey to the bathroom, she has already changed into a seductive "Sunday chapel dress," as George sarcastically calls it. With numerous innuendoes, she openly entices Nick, who with feigned modesty confesses to having been a collegiate quarterback and champion boxer. When Martha tells him "you still got a pretty good body now," he remarks, encouraging her, "It's still pretty good. I work out" (p. 52). Martha exposes her demonic cruelty by recalling the time when her father wanted everyone to learn self-defense and George refused to put on boxing gloves to spar with Daddy. Martha had put on the gloves and accidentally knocked George into a huckleberry bush. "It was funny, but it was awful," she ruefully remarks. "I think it's colored our whole life. I really do! It's an excuse, anyway" (p. 57). The incident assumes the significance of a fall, David McDonald concludes, in that it symbolizes the destruction of their innocence.[19] At least it signaled George's defeat by the "satanic bitch" and initiated the humiliation he has long suffered for what Martha terms "the insulting mistake of loving me" (p. 191).

After George accuses Martha of arranging "blue games for the guests," he tells Nick that Martha eats chromosomes "for breakfast . . . she sprinkles them on her cereal" (p. 65). A deformed earth mother and "the only true pagan on the Eastern seaboard" (p. 73), Martha cannot bring life to birth in the sterile vacuity of New Carthage. She recalls how Daddy once annulled her marriage to a "gardener's boy" at "Miss Muff's Academy for Young Ladies" (p. 78). Martha claims that, forced into obedience by Daddy, she decided that she would marry into the college, "which," she goes on to say, "didn't seem to be quite as stupid as it turned out. I mean, Daddy had a sense of history . . . of continuation" (p. 79). Like a false god ruling over human destiny, Martha's father had set up his Eve and awaited his Adam, which George ironically turned out to be. Martha's and George's occasional babytalk implies that they are but grown-up children in Daddy's Eden.

As we watch the preliminary revelation of Nick's, George's and Martha's impotent lives, Honey appears on the margin of the action, rapidly falling into a drunken stupor and retching in the bathroom. If Martha is unable to give birth, Honey, we learn, is unwilling to. Like Martha the unloved daughter of a "man of the Lord," Honey also foreshadows the demonic games that occur in the *Walpürgisnacht*. At the end of the act when George starts singing "Who's afraid of Virginia Woolf?" to drown out Martha's humiliating portrayal of him as "someone without the guts to make anyone proud of him" (p. 85), Honey joins in—until she cries "I'm going to be sick . . . I'm going to be sick . . . I'm going to vomit" (p. 86). Predicting in her illness the Nietzschean "explicit nausea" about to be experienced by all the characters, Honey becomes a central figure in the "groaning toward creation" which compels the play forward.

Indeed, the integrating motif in the play is the labor to give birth, for all the characters in one way or other have aborted existence by not rebelling against a loveless god. Martha's and George's nonexistent son—"the apple of our eye . . . the sprout . . . the little bugger" (p. 83), and the younger couple's childless marriage, like Nick's scientific determinism and George's powerless history, portray an ontological crisis. When Martha breaks the rule about not mentioning the child, she introduces the elemental conflict between truth and illusion. Martha claims that the child, who is about to come of age, has "deep, pure green eyes" like hers and Daddy's, and indeed we realize that their fantasy offspring sunny-Jim figuratively is her father's child, the fruit of his ruthless domination of Martha's life. When George says, "Your father has tiny red eyes . . . like a white mouse. In fact, he *is* a white mouse" (p. 73), he claims his independence from Daddy. Ironically, Martha uses the child to justify her allegiance to Daddy: "Mommy died early, see, and I sort of grew up with Daddy. . . . I more or less grew up with him. Jesus, I admired the guy! I worshipped him. . . . I absolutely worshipped him. I still do" (p. 77). At his worst, sunny-Jim is for Martha a kind of incestuous child. For George the child has "blue eyes" like his own. He identifies with it in a futile attempt to battle the god who has usurped his role. When Martha mercilessly tells Honey and Nick that "deep down in the private-most pit of his gut, he's not completely sure it's his own kid," George can only rightly remark, "My God, you're a wicked woman" (p. 71).

The birth motif also appears when George repeatedly asks Nick if they have any children and Nick hedges in his response: "We want to wait . . . a little . . . until we're settled" (p. 40). But George pursues the subject. Noting that Honey is "slim-hipped," he keeps mentioning children, just as he does indirectly with all the talk about chromosomes and biology. His reference to the slicing of sperm tubes and annihilation of history by genetic engineering reiterates the theme. Throughout the act we see the mutual failure of the characters to "know" each other in the symbolic sense and their fraudulent attempts to give birth.

The first part of the second act completes the preparation for the forthcoming games of the *Walpürgisnacht.* Alone with his guest, George begins to probe Nick's vulnerability. Despite calling him "smug" and "self-righteous" and disdainfully mocking his "large, salty, unscientific tears," George draws the truth from the unsuspecting Nick. By acknowledging his own humiliation by Martha, "whatever-it-is . . . ridiculing me, tearing me down, in front of YOU" (p. 91), George leads the unsuspecting Nick to confess to marrying Honey because she was pregnant, although "she wasn't . . . really. It was a hysterical pregnancy. She blew up, and then she went down" (p. 94). Nick admits that there was no "particular *passion*" between them when they married because they grew up together and their families had "always taken it for granted" that they would marry. Armed with such knowledge, George penetrates to a further truth: "I'll bet she has money, too!" (p. 102). And indeed Nick acknowledges that his father-in-law died wealthy after spending "God's money" and presumably collecting fire insurance on two of the three churches he built. Having discovered the depraved relationship between Nick and Honey, George says with arresting directness: "You realize, of course, that I've been drawing you out on this stuff, not because I'm interested in your terrible lifehood, but only because you represent a direct and pertinent threat to my lifehood, and I want to get the goods on you" (p. 111). With utter naiveté, Nick "(*still amused*)" replies, "Sure . . . sure." He cannot "stand warned" because his very illusions about himself and George block the way to understanding.

But George can only get at the truth about Nick by admitting his own offense—"Accommodation, malleability, adjustment . . . those seem to be in the order of things, don't they?" (p. 102). He too married for money, position and security. When he accuses Daddy of having married Martha's stepmother, "a very old lady with warts who was very rich," for money, he partly admits his own guilt. He had accidentally shot his mother and later killed his father in an automobile wreck in which he drove "straight into a large tree" trying to avoid hitting a porcupine. Though George makes no personal references, it seems that he speaks of himself, as Martha insists later; for, like the boy in the story, he has been "in an asylum" for the past thirty years. At any rate, George's conversation with Nick directly and indirectly reveals his own spiritual illness.

As the scene ends, George entices Nick to join him in a game that prepares for the shattering ones that follow. He playfully encourages Nick to "start plowing pertinent wives" in order to achieve power in New Carthage, whereupon Nick, "*(still playing along)*," calls Martha "the biggest goose in the gaggle . . . Her father president and all," and threatens to "get her off in a corner and mount her like a goddamn dog" (p. 114). When George agrees, "You'd certainly better," Nick, "*his expression a little sick*," remarks, "You know, I almost think you're serious." George retorts, "No, baby . . . *you* almost think you're serious, and it scares the hell out of you" (p. 114). To this point Nick has claimed a haughty superiority over the decadent behavior of his hosts. Now George implies that Nick is equally depraved, and he offers him "a survival kit"—"There's quicksand here, and you'll be dragged down, just as . . ." (p. 115). But when Nick holds to his innocence and responds, "UP YOURS!!" George sees the unending cycle of history, the inevitability of the Fall in all human attempts to recover the Garden:

> You take the trouble to construct a civilization . . . to . . . to build a society, based on principles of . . . of principles; . . . you endeavor to make communicable sense out of natural order, morality out of the unnatural disorder of man's mind; . . . you make government and art, and realize that they are, must

> be, both the same; . . . you bring things to the saddest point . . . to the point where there *is* something to lose; . . . then all at once, through all the sensible sounds of men building, attempting, comes the *Dies Irae*. And what is it? What does the trumpet sound? Up yours. (P. 117)

In near-Freudian terms he prophesies the end of an already fallen Eden. In symbolic New Carthage the Apollonian and Dionysian principles have long since been perverted. Only by the obliteration of their false selves can the characters gain some hope—the *Walpürgisnacht* achieves that agonizing end.

Each game in the act is designed to strip bare a given character. In the first of them, Martha goes after George, ironically after he provokes her by charging her with molesting sunny-Jim—"He couldn't stand you fiddling at him all the time, with your liquor breath on him, and your hands all over his . . ." (p. 120). After hinting at the hidden truth about George when she tells him "You used to drink bergin, too" (p. 123), she gradually begins narrating how George "tried to publish a goddamn book, and Daddy wouldn't let him" (p. 124). And as she begins to dance seductively with Nick, she continues the story of the ill-fated "novel," which told the story of a "naughty boy-child who . . . uh . . . who killed his mother and his father dead" (p. 134). At first pleading, then quietly warning her to stop, George acts with increasing desperation. But Martha refuses to stop and informs Nick and Honey that "big brave Georgie" told Daddy, "*Sir*, it isn't a *novel* at all. . . . No, Sir, this isn't a novel at all . . . this is the truth . . . this really happened . . . TO ME!" (pp. 136–37). We discover, as Edward Rutenberg notes, that "the long silence retained by the psychotic boy in the asylum is in reality an allegory of his own silence as a writer, for which he has had to suffer a marital life of insanity."[20] When he was earlier humiliated by Martha's recounting of the boxing episode, he carried out a mock murder by "shooting" her with a fake gun that blossomed into a Chinese parasol. Now he acts out his threat in earnest. His protection gone, he cries "I'LL KILL YOU!" and grabs Martha by the throat. When Nick finally throws him to the floor, Albee notes in his stage directions that George "*is hurt, but it is more a profound humiliation than a physical injury*" (p. 138). Naked, he is the first to experience the full weight of the Fall.

Max Halperen contends that, having been the victim of the first game, "George rediscovers a demonic self he had long repressed, rediscovers it in the most extreme form—the urge to kill—and for the moment he emerges as a whole man."[21] Clearly things will never be the same again. Something inexorable has been set in motion, and we recognize that once one truth is out, others must follow. Self-knowledge comes with cataclysmic force to the other characters as George usurps control of the action. With unflinching purpose he now rips away their pretended virtue. Taking aim first at Nick's and Honey's counterfeit innocence, he introduces "Get the Guests."

He tells them about his "second novel," which he describes as "an allegory, really . . . a bucolic" about "a nice young couple who come out of the middle west" (p. 142). Using the truth Nick unwittingly revealed at the beginning of the act, George reiterates his guests' sordid love story. Just as George had done with Martha, Nick pleads with and then threatens his accuser. But with unabated cruelty George recounts the story of Nick "and his mouse . . . a wifey little type who gargles brandy all the time." Telling about "Mousie's pa" and his "Jesus money," he goes on to describe how "Blondie and his frau from out of the plain states came" to settle "in a town just like nouveau Carthage here." Directly stating that "Blondie was in disguise," George claims that "his baggage ticket had bigger things writ on it . . . H.I. HI! Historical inevitability," George's derisive term for the scientific determinism that would destroy history itself. Then referring to Nick's "baggage . . . of whom he was solicitous to a point that faileth human understanding," he finally provokes Honey's self-knowledge: "I know these people." George recalls how Nick and Honey married because "the Mouse got all puffed up one day." Honey completes the story with George:

HONEY . . . and so they were married. . . .
GEORGE . . . and so they were married. . . .
HONEY . . . and then. . . .
GEORGE . . . and then. . . .

But Honey's fear of the truth leads to hysteria, and George must complete the tale: "And then the puff went *away* . . . like magic . . . pouf!" (pp. 146–47). Again vomiting up the offense, Honey denounces Nick for having told George the truth and runs to the bathroom.

Remarkably, not even "Get the Guests" can sufficiently reveal Nick to himself. When George casually comments that Honey will recover from the damaging truth, Nick incredulously shouts, "DAMAGING!! TO ME!" (p. 149). Shocked by the amazing egocentricity of his guest, George warns Nick, "Rearrange your alliances boy. You just pick up the pieces where you can" (p. 149). In rich irony Nick threatens, "[I will] be what you say I am." To which George replies, "You are already; . . . you just don't know it" (p. 150). To "know it" Nick must endure further humiliation, and George realizes that only by descending "a rung or two on the old evolutionary ladder" can his rival experience much-needed contrition—in other words, only by playing "Hump the Hostess," mounting Martha "like a goddamn dog" so that he can no longer claim innocence. A crucial scene between Martha and George indicates that "Hump the Hostess" will also mark Martha's confrontation with herself, and so complete the series of self-revelations. By the end of the second act, each character has acted out the Fall and borne the consequences of self-knowledge.

In the exchange between George and Martha both realize that there is no turning back to an illusory garden. George tells her, "You've moved bag and baggage into your own fantasy world now, and you've started playing variations on your own distortions" (p. 155). Martha admits, "It's snapped, finally. Not me . . . *it*. The whole arrangement" (p. 156). She warns him, "Before I'm through with you you'll wish you'd died in that automobile, bastard" (p. 154); and George warns her, "Be careful, Martha . . . I'll rip you to pieces" (p. 158). At last unlocking all the pent-up frustrations of the years, they "both seem relieved" in declaring total war on each other. "Hump the Hostess" incorporates the four actors in a final act of humiliation and self-revelation. George *willingly* causes the degradation of Martha and Nick, and so degrades himself, even as Honey symbolically reenters the womb curled up like a fetus on the bathroom floor.

George's feigned nonchalance gives impetus to Martha's infidelity. Trying to generate a reaction from George, who is significantly reading Spengler's *Decline of the West,* Martha openly seduces Nick. George ignores her when she tells him she is necking with Nick. "You come off this kick you're on," she advises, "or I swear to God I'll do it." "*Softly, sadly,*" George replies, "have him . . . but do it honestly, will you? Don't cover it over with all this . . . all this . . . footwork" (p. 173). As Martha leaves, George quotes from Spengler: "And the west, encumbered by crippling alliances, and burdened with a morality too rigid to accommodate itself to the sway of events, must . . . eventually . . . fall" (p. 174).

When George cries in his despair and hurls the book at the doorbell chimes (perhaps an oblique reference to the Easter bells in *Faust*), Honey enters, suddenly awakened after passing out on the bathroom floor—curled up like a fetus and "sucking away." Foreshadowing a rebirth after experiencing the "explicit nausea" of the *Walpürgisnacht,* she takes on enormous significance in the resolution of the action. Honey and George, so opposite in their natures, become ironic partners in initiating a movement from death to resurrection.[22] What allows such a transfiguration is the crucial revelation that Honey has in her fear murdered her unborn children:

NO! . . . I DON'T WANT ANY. . . . I DON'T WANT THEM. . . . GO 'WAY. . . . (*Begins to cry*) I DON'T WANT . . . ANY . . . CHILDREN. . . . I . . . don't . . . want . . . any . . . children. I'm afraid! I don't want to be hurt. . . . PLEASE! (P. 176)

This essential confession of fear and George's subsequent assumption that Honey has been aborting life—"I should have known . . . the whole business . . . the headaches . . . the whining . . . the. . . . " (p. 176)—draw together the fallen characters in a moment of profound revelation.

George comments, "When people can't abide things as they are, when they can't abide the present . . . either they turn to a contemplation of the past, as I have done, or they set about to . . . alter the future" (p. 178). Symbolically escaping to the past in Martha's and George's "sunny-Jim" or to the future in Nick's and Honey's equally nonexistent children, the characters have all denied life to remain in an illusory garden. George now recognizes that such a place cannot be—all must confront their lost innocence. To achieve this end, the child who has camouflaged their true state must somehow be exorcised in order to bring to birth the child Honey symbolically carries in her womb. In rich irony, George initiates this in the game called "Bringing up Baby."

The significance of the "Exorcism," the title of the third act, is implied by Albee's original intent to call the whole play by that name. The exorcism is the culmination of the whole action. "The big problem" in producing the play, Alan Schneider remarked in an interview, was in deciding how to contain the third act in the first, that is, how to establish the inevitable progression of the action to its dramatic and thematic end.[23] The major concern of the act is not so much the revelation of the secret lie shared by Martha and George but the total integration of the characters in a communal psychological and religious ritual.

The first few moments complete the final humiliation and fall of Martha and Nick. In a somewhat sentimental soliloquy Martha shows her vulnerability for the first time, admitting that Daddy is in fact the red-eyed white mouse that George has made him, the image of an ineffectual god (like Honey's father, whom Nick calls a "church mouse"). Letting her mask slip, Martha laments to her absent Daddy, "I cry alllll the time; but deep inside, so no one can see me. I cry all the time. And Georgie cries all the time, too" (p. 185). Like a true repentant, she later tells Nick, "I disgust me" (p. 189). Denied escape and fully conscious of her fallen state, Martha is appropriately primed for George's grueling game.

Nick, too, can no longer elude his failure. Literally and symbolically impotent, he must suffer Martha's relentless abuse. Another "flop" among the "bunch of boozed-up . . . impotent lunk-heads" who cannot satisfy "the Earth Mother," Nick fails to realize the "dandy" life potential he represents. An impotent Apollo unable to channel the Dionysian power Martha desperately wills to release, Nick symbolizes the spiritual sterility of modern scientific and technological culture with its laboratory detachment from elemental life forces. "Poor babies," Martha says of Nick and the other "all-American" technocrats. They all "flop"—"that's how it is in a civilized society" (p. 189). Hereafter called a "stallion," "gelding," "poor little bastard," "houseboy," and "little boy," Nick proves no match for Martha's and George's overwhelming condemnation. Mockingly, Martha asks, "And you're going to take over the world, huh?" (p. 192). And she describes his spiritual blindness: "And you don't see anything, do you? You see everything but the goddamn mind; you see all the little specs and crap, but you don't see what goes on, do you?" (p. 192). Denying him any pretense of virtue, she challenges him: "You didn't chase me around the kitchen and up the goddamn stairs out of mad, driven passion, did you now? You were thinking a little bit about your career, weren't you? Well, you can just houseboy your way up the ladder for a while" (p. 194).

The sole character who can somehow lead the characters from the dark night of their buried selves is George, who, as we have noted, experiences a shock of recognition at the end of the second act. Martha amazes Nick by confessing to him that George "is the only one man in my life who has ever . . . made me happy" (p. 189), a further recognition she acquires in consequence of her fall. In fact, her admiration and even love for George can be traced to the first act, despite her sadistic treatment of him; but only after "Hump the Hostess" does she begin to acknowledge her deeply buried love. When George reappears at the front door, Martha naively greets him with delight and laughter, as Nick, not without meaning, simply says, "Christ."

In a very real sense George has usurped a deity, at least has rebelled like an Oedipal son against the oppressive god of New Carthage. He enters with "*flores para los muertos*" stolen from Daddy's greenhouse. In a brief debate about whether or not the moon was out,

George obliquely refers to his Promethean nature: "I have never robbed a hothouse without there is a light from heaven" (pp. 198–99). Though the argument about the moon being up or down carries sexual connotations, more is implied. Martha's father grows hothouse flowers; his is a spurious garden which George properly desecrates. When he further uses the stolen snapdragons as a weapon, he engages symbolically in a sexual act, the snapdragons, thrown stem first, serving as phallic images. Enacting what Lee Baxandall calls a "graceful symbolic revenge,"[24] George tells Martha it does not matter whether Nick is a "houseboy" or a "stud," whether it is "truth" or "illusion" that he succeeded in bed—"Either way . . . I've had it" (p. 204). Martha, sensing that the line has been crossed, asks, "(*a little afraid*) Truth or illusion, George. Doesn't it matter to you . . . at all?" (p. 204). When George without throwing anything pretends to do so and says "SNAP! . . . You got your answer, baby?" we too realize that there is no turning back.[25]

The last game involves the full community of four. George orders Nick to get the absent Honey: "Well, we can't play without everyone here. Now that's a fact. We gotta have your little wife" (p. 206). Though she does not know why, Martha fears the moment and pleads, "No more games . . . please" (p. 207). When she piteously moves to touch him, George slaps her hand away and commands her, "I want a little life in you, baby." The dialogue is punctuated with religious and mythic allusions ("Jesus God," "for God's sake," "a Easter pageant") as George begins a recitation about "bringing up sunny-Jim." He is about to "peel the label," as Honey unwittingly announces she has done, holding up her stripped brandy bottle. "We all peel labels, sweetie" (p. 212), George replies in reference to the stripping action all the characters have endured. Defining the ultimate end of the game, George concludes, "When you get down to the bone, you haven't got all the way, yet. There's something inside the bone . . . the marrow . . . and that's what you gotta get at" (p. 213). "Now, take our son," he goes on, until he compels Martha to recite *her* version of raising sunny-Jim, "born in a September night, a night not unlike today, though tomorrow, and twenty . . . one . . . years ago" (p. 217).

With lyric compassion, Martha, the unfulfilled earth mother, laments, "And I had wanted a child . . . oh, I had wanted a child." As she tells her made-up story of the "beautiful boy," George prods her, sometimes echoes her and at last breaks into the Latin requiem mass. Martha recalls once carrying "the poor lamb" across a great field after he broke his arm in a fall—"In Paradisum deducant te Angeli,"

George intones. The child's innocent world could not last, Martha goes on, changing from a lyrical to satiric tone: "Of course, this state, this perfection . . . couldn't last. Not with George . . . not with George around" (p. 223). A point-counterpoint develops as Martha and George offer conflicting accounts of sunny-Jim's growing up. Martha describes "a son who spends his summers away . . . because he can't stand the shadow of a man flickering around the edges of a house," and George a boy "who spends his summers away because there isn't room for him in a house full of empty bottles, lies, strange men, and a harridan who . . . " (p. 226). In a sweeping crescendo the two accusers finally speak together, Martha lamenting her vain attempt to save sunny-Jim from "this vile, crushing marriage" and George chanting, "*Libera me Domine de morte aeterna.*"

As George pronounces the Kyrie, Honey shouts, "JUST STOP IT!!" (p. 228). In fact, she alone knows the significance of the mass, for George had told her at the end of the second act, "Our son is dead, and Martha doesn't know." Ironically, Honey, who has long feared life, struggles vainly to preserve it by preventing George from telling Martha of sunny-Jim's death. And even in the midst of "Bringing up Baby" she had interrupted sunny-Jim's story to cry out three times, "I want a child. I want a baby" (pp. 222–23). Martha's desire for life has been transferred to Honey, and even now she wills it.

We see a death and resurrection, the death of the son who must be sacrificed to restore life and the resurrection of the children whom Honey has aborted. So too, Nick's "test-tube" baby, the symbol of his disinterested pragmatism, is replaced by his and Honey's potential child. Nick, the "wave-of-the future" boy, "tenderly" tells Martha that George cannot decide sunny-Jim's fate: "It's not his doing. He doesn't have the power. . . ." To which George aptly responds, "That's right, Martha; I'm not a God. I don't have the power over life and death, do I?" (p. 233).

The full light falls as George completes the story of receiving news of their son's death. Repeating his own story of a boy swerving to avoid a porcupine, George informs them of their son's smashing into a tree. He says of the telegram he received informing them of the accident, "I . . . ate . . . it" (p. 234), a reference to the Eucharist. When Martha catches on and spits in his face, George smilingly approves her realization that the "game" indeed has ended: "Good for you, Martha" (p. 234). The lie of sunny-Jim collapses at last. Like Christ, and like other deities, including Apollo, associated with the sun, sunny-Jim, the "poor lamb," must die to provide a means of salvation from the Fall.[26]

Sunny-Jim had experienced virgin birth, for as George tells Nick when the young scientist describes Honey's pregnancies, "Martha doesn't have hysterical pregnancies"—"Martha doesn't have pregnancies at all" (p. 97). Whereas Martha yearned to conceive but could not, Honey could conceive but feared doing so. Significantly, the first to understand the mystery of "Bringing up Baby," Honey is redeemed from her fallen state. She *wills* to give birth. Furthermore, her child can now be born of genuine love. Her humiliation, and Nick's, has at last disclosed the betrayal of love and has dissolved the gulf between them. Now realizing that sunny-Jim is an imaginary being, Nick too finally discovers the meaning of the requiem: "JESUS CHRIST I THINK I UNDERSTAND THIS!" (p. 236), he cries at last. "You couldn't have . . . any?" he now asks George. George answers, "*We* couldn't," implying that Nick and Honey can; and Martha mimics, "We couldn't" (p. 238), implying reunion with George. As George and Martha regain their love in communion, Nick now holds out his hand to Honey. As they leave hand in hand like Milton's Adam and Eve, it is symbolically near dawn—and it is "Sunday tomorrow; all day" (p. 239).

Although perhaps ambivalent, the play moves toward affirmation. As Thomas P. Adler puts it, "George and Martha have bared themselves so that Nick and Honey can be saved, and in the process they themselves are saved."[27] The striking tenderness of Martha's and George's last moments on the stage surely signals that, whatever the agony, something redemptive has occurred. There are risks aplenty, as George must admit:

GEORGE (*Long silence*) It will be better.
MARTHA (*Long silence*) I don't . . . know.
GEORGE It will be . . . maybe.
MARTHA I'm . . . not . . . sure.
GEORGE No.

With an ambiguous "Yes. No," Martha faces an uncertain future as George softly sings, "Who's Afraid of Virginia Woolf?" For us all, Martha concludes, "I . . . am . . . George. . . . I . . . am . . ." (p. 242). The allusion to Virginia Woolf reminds us just how real the risks *are* east of Eden, for she chose suicide as the alternative to a reality (or, as Martha would have it, an "unreality") too harsh to bear. But without such risk, Martha could not say, "I am"—and the true child of redemptive love would remain stillborn in the sterility of New Carthage.

Deliverance by James Dickey

Once I leapt out of the oldest dream of all—the oldest and the most dreamlike—the one about starting to fall. —Ed in James Dickey's *Deliverance*

Those familiar with James Dickey's verse will not be surprised to find that critics who admire *Deliverance* often refer to its mythic design. Scholars have found echoes of *The Odyssey*, *Moby-Dick*, the Leatherstocking tales, and *Tom Sawyer*; they have traced Dickey's ideas and patterns to Faulkner, Hemingway, Whitman, D. H. Lawrence, Theodore Roethke, Nietzsche, and especially to Wordsworth; they have related the narrative to the Bible, the Orpheus myth, the "night journey" and the quest of the "archetypal hero" in American literature. Richard E. Hughes concludes that *Deliverance* "is a wonderfully precise reenactment of the Orpheus myth, and a thoroughly perceptive dramatization of a psychoanalytic truth."[28] Barnett Guttenberg argues for a larger context and meaning. To him, Dickey as novelist assumes the role of Romantic poet-prophet and "recasts the Christian myth of fall and redemption."[29] But the elements and implications of the romantic version of the myth found in the novel merit further consideration than Guttenberg provides, for they not only help to explain the achievement of the novel but also reveal it as part of a continuum of vision in post-Enlightenment culture. Only by understanding the idea of a fortunate fall can we grasp the crucial distinction between "survival," what the macho hunter Lewis Medlock offers, and "deliverance," what the central character Ed Gentry finally achieves as a consequence of his personal fall.

We might recall that the romantic concept of a fortunate fall embraces but significantly modifies the traditional *felix culpa* expressed by St. Augustine. In the more orthodox version the Fall was fortunate largely because it led to the Incarnation and gave witness to God's love for humanity. The more essentially romantic idea, as we have seen, tends to emphasize individual freedom and the assertion of moral responsibility as the chief benefits of the Fall. Enlightenment thought had significantly "stripped the Bible of its allegorical garb," Murray Roston notes, and "preromantic poets were able to exploit the 'enlightened' unveiling of the scripture by finding within the biblical text a vivid and passionate literature."[30] Unrestrained by the severe orthodoxy of earlier periods, the romantic poets tended to merge a newfound humanism with Christian myth and to see Hebraic and Christian belief alongside Hellenic and pagan traditions.

Though Blake vigorously defended the Hebrew prophets and Old

Testament literature against Greek and Roman thought, his philosophy certainly was affected by gnostic and other "heretical" Eastern influences. And though Byron could never escape the Calvinism of his past, he freely used the biblical text to emulate personal freedom. As we have noted, in works like *Cain*, he shared Blake's rebellion against the constraints of a tyrannical god. The Fall in Byron's *Cain* marks his hero's individualism and courage against an unjust morality. Shelley's similar idea in *Prometheus Unbound* combines the fortunate fall and Greek myth. In other words, the interpretation of the Fall in many romantic works portrays the original sin as a testament of freedom. The Fall is therefore fortunate because it declares man's spiritual independence. Dickey's novel depicts the pattern of such a fortunate fall.

In this modern depiction of the myth, God has all but disappeared. The sterile garden Ed Gentry inhabits is of his own making. Like Blake's mythological figure Urizen, Ed at the beginning of the story has enclosed himself within the circumference of his own narrow vision. An already fallen man alienated from the energizing forces of the natural world, he has designed and regulates a miniature cosmos devoid of meaning and value. In the context of a fortunate fall, he must somehow escape his garden existence in order to release his spiritual powers from a bondage that Dickey describes succinctly in the section of the novel he calls "Before." To put it another way, to *sin* against the order he himself has concocted as would-be god is to acquire freedom from self-bondage, to be delivered.

The boundaries of Ed's garden are marked by his business and family, both of which he finds adequate but spiritually deficient. On one hand he seems to say of his world that "it is good." Looking over the "tasteful" advertising agency office he and his partner Thad Emerson have designed, he remarks, "I may not have had everything to do with this—with creating this . . . but I have had something to do with it. Never before had I had such a powerful sense of being in a place I had created."[31] His satisfaction impinges upon the same principle of adequacy that underlies the ad agency's work. The office was "no sweat shop," and it was "a pleasure to work at Emerson-Gentry." The pleasure was largely derived from the lack of challenge. "For we had grooved," Ed surmises; "I knew it and was glad of it; I had no wish to surpass our limitations" (p. 14). His workers "were competent," he observes, but "we demanded no very high standard from them" (p. 13). He and Thad even like working with agencies "which were most like us—that were not pressing. . . . We worked on small accounts. . . . We would ride with these" (p. 15). Even as a worker in his own garden, Ed carefully qualifies his success as artist and businessman: "I was better than adequate . . . as a graphics consultant and director" (p. 13).

His apparent content disguises a profound sense of despair: a growing "feeling of the inconsequence of whatever I would do, of anything I would pick up or think about or turn to see was at that moment being set in the very bone marrow. How does one get through this? I asked myself" (p. 18). Realizing that his workers "are in some way my captives" in this garden, Ed also recognizes that "I was not really thinking about them being my prisoners, but of being my own" (p. 17). In a sensitively developed passage he describes himself walking after lunch "under a heavy shade tree," burping beer "into my eyes." On this near autumn day "a leaf fell, touched with unusual color at the edges" as Ed "began to climb the last hill." Being struck by the fact that he was surrounded by women as he headed for his office, he was "filled . . . with desolation" watching the parade of stiff women with "their hair styles, piled and shellacked and swirled and horned." Futilely "looking for a decent ass," he stares vainly at a girl who shatters his illusion when she turns "her barren gum-chewing face . . . it was all over." The judgment falls more on him than on the women. His very act of "looking for a decent ass" exposes his own spiritual impotence. He concludes by acknowledging that he is no different from the secretaries with their trivial lives.

His quest for meaning is defined as well in his encounter with the Kitt'n Britches model who poses dressed only in panties for an ad. Offended by the "peculiar blue" light that "reminded [him] of prisons and interrogation" and by the pornographic quality of the ad itself, Ed notices a "tan slice" in the model's life eye, a "gold-glowing mote" that "was alive and it saw me" (p. 22). It signifies for him a promise, a promise of deliverance from his empty life. The model, illusory though she is, offers the hope of redemption. By contrast, she brings into focus Ed's relationship with Martha, his wife of fifteen years. Though he loves her, he sees her too as somehow only "adequate," an efficient lover, a nurse with "great hands" and a "practical approach to sex." As he makes love to Martha on the morning of his departure, he sees the model's golden eye shining on her back, "not with the practicality of sex, so necessary to its survival, but the promise of other things, another life, deliverance" (p. 28). By no means diminishing the need for survival, Ed seeks deliverance as well, deliverance from the "normalcy" that Martha represents. Dickey distinguishes here, and more importantly later, between the mere necessity for survival and the spiritual victory of deliverance. At this point Ed can survive *in* his restricted environment, but he cannot be delivered *from* it until he denies it values of security, "grooving," and minimal competence.

Having acknowledged a deeply buried dissatisfaction, Ed accepts Lewis Medlock's proposal that he, Drew Ballinger, and Bobby Tripe take a canoe trip down a wild North Georgia river about to be flooded by a dam. Ironically, Lewis functions as tempter and leads Ed into what Bobby aptly calls the "Kingdom of Snakes," another Eden altogether. In the natural world of the North Georgia mountains, Ed no longer functions as God but an unsuspecting Adam controlled by cosmic forces to which he must pay due respect. In the pattern of the Fall, Lewis presents the way to new knowledge, a knowledge that in the romantic sense is always self-knowledge. A necessary pole in the dialectic, like Mephistopheles in Goethe's *Faust* or Lucifer in Byron's *Cain*, he establishes the creative tension that paradoxically frees and threatens Ed.

A demonic figure who seemingly tells truth "to win us to our harm," Lewis accurately describes Ed's spiritual state in his city paradise. Denying Ed's concept of "sliding" ("living antifriction"), he claims that "survival" demands being "in touch" with the natural forces dulled or obscured in the urban-surburban environment. Those who would survive modern culture and, literally speaking, a nuclear war, he argues, will be those who can exist in the hills. Having built his own bomb shelter, he decided that it was not enough. He tells Ed, "I decided that survival was not in the rivets and the metal, not in the double-sealed doors and not in the marbles of Chinese checkers. It was in me. . . . The body is the one thing you can't fake; it's just got to be there" (p. 42). When Ed says he will "stay in the city," Lewis concludes, "The city's got you where you live" (p. 47). To be saved, Lewis seems to say, you must "break the pattern," your willingness to "groove," "ride" and "slide" through existence. You must risk confronting a world without anchors or guarantees—a "country of nine-fingered people." He tempts Ed in to a paradise of pastoral beauty and malevolent energy.

Nature is paradoxical in Dickey's view. He describes it in a Blakean sense as both fallen and regenerative, the symbol of man's fallen condition and the veiled image of spiritual power. It contains the most primitive Dionysian energy but carries as well a life-giving force. Obscuring and yet conveying the creative principle, it embodies the ambivalence of Blake's physical universe. It also suggests something of the nightmare world of Wonderland and *Heart of Darkness;* it threatens and restores, and images the underside of consciousness.

Ed drifts on the edge of consciousness as Lewis talks with him on the way to the river. "I was dead. . . . I heard Lewis saying something that strove in and out of consciousness" (p. 39). Like Blake's sleeping Albion, Ed gradually rouses from a dream-like state. Together with his aroused consciousness emerges the indelible mark of fallen man—duality. On one hand, Ed begins to see a self far different from the urban gardener tending to his closed little universe:

> I caught a glimpse of myself in the rear window. I was light green, a tall forest man, an explorer, guerrilla, hunter. I liked the idea and the image, I must say. Even if this was just a game, a charade, I had let myself in for it, and I was here in the woods, where such people as I had got myself up as were supposed to be. Something or other was being made good. (P. 69)

In the guise of hunter Ed closely parallels Lewis, whose image he struggles to emulate. Yet for all his sharply honed survival instincts, Lewis alone cannot *deliver* Ed. If he represents the hunter Ed would like to be, the artist Drew Ballinger represents the other needed pole in the dialectic.

Characterized most fully as a family man, civic leader and musician, Drew defends civilization against the warrior-hunter. Ed speaks of him as gentle and committed. In a moving scene Ed describes how Drew played guitar with a demented mountain boy on the way to the river. "I really began to listen deeply," Ed recalls, "moved as an unmusical person is moved when he sees that the music is meant" (p. 59). The "country kid" and the "the big faced decent city man, the minor civic leader and hedge clipper," tap a power, a harmony in existence that the solitary hunter Lewis cannot reach. If Drew cannot survive the brutality of the world he is about to confront, Lewis cannot tap the civilizing power of Drew's art-music. Ed, it seems, cannot gain totality of self without accommodating both. Neither the civilizing music of Drew nor the controlled physical strength of Lewis can rescue him. In a romantic sense, the consequence of the Fall is invariably estrangement from the self. As Dickey develops the narrative, Ed tastes a knowledge that makes him aware of his divided self. Naked, he must deal with his duality, must reconcile hunter and artist, Cain and Abel—Lewis and Drew. He must be both, and neither.

Significantly, just before the event that marks the beginning of the Fall in the internal narrative, Ed observes a snake slipping into the water, "a thing with a single spell, a single movement, and no barrier"

(p. 106). Coming to this moment Ed has rejoiced in the ironic Eden, ironic because its beauty conceals a devastating terror. "It's got me," he says of the snake-like river. "I wanted to let go of the river," he says at one point, but "the current entered my muscles and body as though I were carrying it; it came up through the paddle. . . . I felt marvelous" (p. 80). No paradise can last forever, though, and the snake signals a fall of horrifying consequences. Swept along by the rhythm and energizing force of river, the virtual "womb of being," the four men discover in true romantic fashion that terror and beauty always coexist. Fallen nature mirrors man's own divided being.

The sodomy endured by Bobby Tripe and nearly by Ed introduces the duality in Nature's deceptive Eden. It is no accident, of course, that Bobby is the victim of one of the two mountaineers who confront him and Ed. A bachelor, a "surface human being," he is the "fat ass" of the group, the one least suited to this paradoxical paradise. Ed and Lewis are invigorated by the potency and authority of the river. Drew shares in the music with the mountain boy, and satisfies a deeply buried longing—"I've always wanted to do this," he says as he tunes his guitar by the river, "only I didn't know it" (p. 85). Bobby, however, never quite belongs. An incompetent participant, he "had no coordination at all" when he tried to guide the canoe. When the others swim in the cold water, he sits alone on the bank. Significantly, he and Ed are together when the violation occurs, for in an ironic way Bobby represents the "fat ass" that Ed may well become if nothing changes his life. Bobby is Ed's potential self, the satisfied, devitalized urban business man cut off from the tap roots of the unconscious. He serves as a kind of surrogate for Ed. Violated in place of Ed, he provides a hideous knowledge that frees Ed from an incapacitating ignorance. Finding Bobby somehow "tainted," though "none of this was his fault," Ed cannot help but judge him for his feeble acquiescence— "The fact that he was not tied mattered in some way" (p. 113). In a sense the judgment is self-judgment. In rejecting Bobby, despite his sympathy for him, Ed rejects what his city-garden threatens to make of him.

The events in the novel from the point of the rape on have generated the critical debate about the moral implications of the work. It is therefore essential that we follow the events closely, for Dickey makes it apparent that, although Ed needs Lewis's knowledge to survive, he needs something more to be delivered. Survival implies just that—the ability and cunning to withstand any challenge from man or nature. It involves a "survival of the fittest" ethos. Deliverance, however, points to something more mythic than deterministic. The title gives a religious overtone to the novel, as does the biblical headnote from

Obadiah, for "deliverance" suggests that existence alone cannot satisfy Ed's deep spiritual hunger. Though he can be saved from his external enemy by his own survival instincts and Lewis's acquired knowledge, he cannot defeat the more essential enemy that haunts his unconscious—"the feeling of inconsequence of whatever I would do" that can only be relieved by a conscious act of will.

The "something more" requires of him a conscious fall, a willingness to kill that is conditioned by a knowledge Lewis cannot provide. Like the romantic hero, Ed must exist in "contraries," to use Blake's term, must confront his divided self by a profound act of self-knowledge. In a sense, then, there are two falls and two salvations. In the first case the Fall is imposed on Ed (and directly on his surrogate Bobby). He is saved initially not by his own efforts but by Lewis, whose knowledge allows Ed to "survive." In the second case the Fall is totally conscious—like Cain, Ed chooses to kill his "brother." Ed not only kills, he also accepts the moral consequences for his choice. In a romantic sense the difference between Lewis's disinterested act and Ed's agonizing choice depicts the progression from Adam's and Eve's all-but-innocent fall to Cain's definitive gesture of freedom.

What we might consider the first fall, the act of sodomy, is not really a personal fall for Ed. That is, he does not choose the threatened violation (and literally does not experience it) and does not rescue himself. Nonetheless, as with Adam and Eve, the act once and for all destroys the state of naive innocence that Ed brings to the encounter. Furthermore, the immediate consequences of the event demand choice and so drive him to experience.

Soon after the event, Ed realizes that he owes a frightening obligation to Lewis. As warrior-hunter Lewis acts not so much immorally as amorally when he kills one of the mountaineers. He faces Ed "smiling easily and with great friendliness" says to him, "Well now, how about this? Just . . . how *about* this?" (p. 119). Exulted by the kill itself, Lewis expresses no remorse—survival has demanded that he be the consummate hunter, that he use all his skill and savvy with complete detachment and competence. His knowledge as hunter saves Ed; but, to Ed, "The assurance with which he had killed a man was desperately frightening to me" (p. 128). Opposite Lewis stands Drew. When Lewis argues that they should bury the corpse and leave the death unacknowledged, Drew contends, "I can't go along with this. It's not a matter of guts; it's a matter of law" (p. 129). Fearfully, Ed sides with Lewis, not simply because Lewis provides the sole defense against the remaining mountaineer but also because he assumes the obligation Lewis has imposed on him by saving him ("I would have followed him anywhere, and I realized I was going to have to do just that," p. 128). But though Ed seems to choose Lewis, his choice reflects neither self-awareness nor courage. After all, his relationship with Lewis is parasitic—he hides under the wing of Lewis's wisdom and disinterested use of power. And even as the men journey into the dark woods to bury the body in "the center of the earth," Ed admits his wavering commitment: "I had a tremendous driving moment of wanting to dig him up again, of siding with Drew" (p. 136). The consequences of choice do not come home to him until the second mountaineer, the one most linked to him as a demonic shadow figure, compels him to stand independently of Lewis and to search out his undiscovered self.

Throughout the novel, dreams and death images abound. Clearly, Ed moves into a psychic twilight zone. As the mythic hero on the traditional "journey," he enters ever more deeply into the dark caverns of the self. As Hughes notes, Ed truly undergoes a night journey into the mysterious realm of the unconscious. The Fall motif here merges with classical myth, an integration apparent in romantic versions of the Fall such as Blake's and Shelley's use of the Prometheus myth and Nietzsche's later description of good and evil as manifestations of Apollonian and Dionysian principles. When the second mountaineer shoots Drew, he precipitates the confrontation with self that is the natural consequence of the Fall and drives Ed to the dark Erebus of his own soul. The end of the Fall is death, a death now made symbolically personal. Dead and buried, like the classical hero, Ed must be resurrected into a new being capable of spiritual independence and moral choice.

Critics often note that Drew's death implies that the civilized, gentle person cannot stand against terror and violence, that Dickey predicates a macho "nice-guys-finish-last" ethos. They ignore the importance of Lewis's broken leg. On the ride to the river, Lewis tells Ed about the time he broke his leg in the woods and had "to one leg through . . . woods. I was holding on to every tree like it was my brother" (p. 51). But communion with the woods proves deficient by itself. Dickey says very clearly that however capable and strong, Lewis cannot conquer the dark power of the woods, or, more importantly, the demonic potential unleashed by the mountaineer. Benjamin De Mott mistakenly claims that Ed resurrects Lewis by becoming "a new Mr. Vibrancy, a hunter, stalker, killer . . . a second Robin Hood, a king of energy."[32] In fact, to save himself both physically and ontologically, Ed must counterbalance the demands on self made both by Lewis and Drew while allowing neither to destroy its opposite. To do that he must know himself; he must be born into self-awareness.

Thrown into the water when the canoe capsizes, Ed experiences a death-rebirth. "I was dead," he remarks, and adds, almost paradoxically, "I got on my back and poured with the river, sliding over the stones like a creature I had always contained but never released" (p. 144). He calls the river an "immense dark bed," a womb-like image that Dickey repeats throughout the action until the survivors finally lunge "out over the top of the rock in one unstoppable motion," figuratively shot from the womb with a "bestial scream" (p. 225). Rising from the water after the shooting, Ed enters a new world "after the Fall," a world in which he must somehow act deliberately and consciously to save himself, Bobby, and Lewis. To succeed, Lewis insists, he must kill the enemy. "And don't have any mercy, Not any." "I won't if I can help it," Ed responds. "Help it," answers Lewis—" 'Kill him,' Lewis said with the river" (p. 160). Again, like the river, Lewis acts neither morally nor immorally. He is. To him, survival is the only issue: " 'This is what it comes to,' he said. 'I told you.' " (p. 160). But aware of "a deep feeling of nakedness," Ed must be in touch with himself as well as the natural forces. To confront the enemy he must, in true romantic fashion, confront the beast in himself.

The beast is most certainly reflected in the second mountaineer, a *Doppelgänger* or shadow figure who surfaces in an illicit nightmare of fantastic intensity. The relationship with "the other" is defined and heightened by the sexual allusions that run throughout the text. From the first reference to "looking for a decent ass" to the implied anal intercourse with Martha to the act of sodomy itself, sexual impotence or perversion illustrates the inability to be. Ironically, to defeat his enemy, Ed must be involved with the elemental libidinous forces that galvanize him into action.

The assault on the cliff that Ed must climb to seek out the mountaineer is described in obvious sexual terms. Watching "a long coiling image of light" beneath him, Ed keeps "inching up" the facing, "feeling it more gently than before." Almost falling he "burrowed in like an animal," hanging precariously over "the bright coiling of the pit." He experiences a pseudo-orgasm when "the urine in [his] bladder turned solid and painful, and then ran with a delicious sexual voiding like a wet dream" (p. 164). Finally, "fighting an immense rock" that "seemed to spring a crack under one finger of [his] right hand," he virtually achieves sexual union with the cliff. The description implies a form of sodomy: "The strength from the stone flowed

into me" (p. 165, emphasis added). The event provides a vision of what will follow as Ed stalks the nightmare image of himself.

The ascent up the cliff is merely the prelude to the real encounter. In existing in a libidinous wonderland, Ed participates in the indifferent power of the life force as he beholds the snake, "the river . . . in its far-below sound and indifference, in its large coil and tiny points and flashes of the moon, in its long sinuous form, in its incomprehending consequence" (p. 171). Feeling the pulsing in himself, he envisions "a layout for an ad, a sketch, an element of design" (p. 171). Projecting external reality upon the mysterious realm of the unconscious, he struggles to control it, as it were to *create* it like a wilful god. He dares consciously to impose order by accepting his essential role in a primeval drama. He acknowledges what he is in the dark ritual—"I was a killer." "I could be a snake" (p. 174), he adds later. To beat the shadow, he must be the opposite he seeks.

Once more Dickey employs sexual imagery to define how his protagonist must traffic with his illicit self. Placing himself above "the huge serpent-shape of light," Ed begins "to inch upwards again, moving with the most intimate motions of [his] body, motions [he] had never dared use with Martha, or with any other human woman. Fear and a kind of enormous moon-blazing sexuality lifted [him], millimeter by millimeter" (p. 176). Ed says of the object of that "lust," "I felt, in the moonlight, our minds fuse." He goes on, "If Lewis had not shot his companion, he and I would have made a kind of love, painful and terrifying to me, in some dreadful way pleasurable to him, but we would have been together in the flesh" (p. 180). To save himself, Ed engages in a form of psychological intercourse—"The minds would have to merge" (p. 185). Only by "knowing" him, can he gain a victory over the shadow figure that haunts his psyche.

Ed literally creates the other out of his unconscious. Whereas Lewis believed in archery that was "purely instinctive" and spurned the aid of a sight, Ed uses a sight. Looking out between the branches of the tree where he watches the enemy, he creates "a peculiar kind of intimacy," whereby the mountaineer "was shut within a frame within a frame, all of my making" (p. 141). Whereas Lewis denies communion with his human target and so kills a man without remorse as he would kill a deer, Ed commits a paradoxical act of murder-love.[33] He "falls" by choice; he kills his brother-lover, the deeply buried mirror-image of his undiscovered self.

Once he shoots the enemy, he seeks him out and finds him "holding onto one of the roots of the dead tree," like Blake's "The Poison Tree" another allusion to the Fall. He concludes, "Before there was everything to do there was nothing to do. His brain and mine unlocked and fell apart, and in a way I was sorry to see it go" (p. 199). After the Fall, Ed acts directly opposite Lewis. Rather than merely disposing of the body as incriminating evidence, he searches out his identity. Afraid he has killed the wrong man, given the fact that the dead man has teeth and the mountaineer who assaulted him did not, Ed pries "a partial upper plate" from the dead man's mouth. Still not certain, he must always question the legitimacy of his choice. He does just that—unlike the warrior-hunter Lewis.

Furthermore, Ed exists in total freedom to do whatever further mutilation he wishes. Like Marlow in *Heart of Darkness*, he realizes, "The mind of man is capable of anything." Like Bobby Tripe, he could vent his hate on the dead body, just as Bobby "kicked the body in the face, and again" (p. 124). He could cut off "the genitals he was going to use on me" or "cut off his head" or "eat him." But Ed steps back from the abyss, the libidinous savagery, and opts for civilization. He turns to Drew. Though "the ultimate horror circled me and played over the knife, I began to sing." He concludes with yet another implicit homosexual reference—"I finished and I was withdrawn from" (p. 200). With tremendous irony his lover-enemy has saved him, not unlike Leggatt's rescue of the captain in "The Secret Sharer"; and in gratitude and understanding he treats the body with respect—it is himself. Later carrying his other self, "nearly double [his] weight," he lowers the dead man by rope over the cliff. In his words, "Letting the man fall free . . . was shocking to me; I would not do that, no matter what" (p. 206).

For a fleeting moment the beast again arises in him. When Bobby and Lewis come into view early because Bobby "did everything wrong" by coming downstream before Ed told him to, Ed angrily sights Bobby down the barrel of the mountaineer's rifle. He temporarily becomes the enemy once more, assuming his very identity as the dead man says, "Do it; he's right there" (p. 202). Ed does not succumb to the demonic self, however, and lets the gun fall. Walking the thin line between the legitimate and the illegitimate use of power, he barely escapes the untamed savagery of a Kurtz.

The delicate balance of "good and evil" also appears when Ed "buries" both the enemy and Drew—"the best of us . . . the only decent one; the only sane one" (p. 186). Unwilling and unable to abide in the world of cruel madness, Drew earns Ed's love and respect: "I touched the callus on the middle finger of his left hand, and my eyes blinded with tears. . . . I could have cried as long as the river ran, but there was no time" (p. 220). Lewis's knowledge helped Ed survive; Drew's humanity has delivered him from a primordial savagery. In effect, Ed reenacts the Cain and Abel myth. The most essential version of the Fall to the romantics, the Cain and Abel story establishes the contrary principles of obedience and rebellion, "Civilization and Its Discontents." It relates to Neitzsche's Apollonian and Dionysian concepts, the conflicting claims of order and chaos which war "beyond good and evil" within the psyche. Ed achieves an equilibrium between the counterclaims of his Cain and Abel natures.[34]

In the romantic version of the fortunate fall, positive consequences coexist with the negative ones of nakedness, vulnerability, death, suffering and expulsion. The protagonist gains self-knowledge, a potentially saving awareness of good and evil, and freedom from the constraints of a stifling garden existence. He must play the creator and assume responsibility for his own life in a world now devoid of certainty and wholeness. Ed returns to his own degenerate garden with a limited victory over its spiritually debilitating power—no greater victory is possible. Having confronted his dual nature, he comes home to a world perhaps more frightening in its sinister force. If the ironic mountain Eden promises death by violence, the urban Eden promises death by stasis. Only by holding to the knowledge of that hidden realm can Ed hope "to be delivered" from the most dreaded of romantic ills—*ennui*.

From the point of view of several years later, Ed examines the three of them who took the ill-fated trip. Bobby Tripe has been too humiliated to reveal what happened—"He wouldn't want anybody to know that, no matter what" (p. 268). Like a Captain Archbold, unable to act, he drifts onto the bare margin of existence and finally goes to Hawaii. Lewis does change. Permanently maimed, he accepts his mortality, the immediate consequence of the Fall. "He can die now," Ed remarks; "he knows that dying is better than immortality" (p. 277). Ed's son, Dean, makes "something of an idol" of Lewis, and so reenacts something of Ed's past relationship with him. But Ed alone achieves a depth of understanding. He realizes that beauty and truth are somehow one, that the girl in the Kitt'n Britches ad promised something illusory, but necessary. Her mythical "gold-halved eye had lost its fascination," he remarks. "Its place was in the night river, in the land of impossibility" (p. 277). That nightmare land, so like Wonderland and the absurd "heart of darkness," is rife with paradox—beautiful but terrifying, freeing but destructive, real but "imaginary." Having journeyed into the dark interior, Ed resurfaces with a new awareness. The "golden eye" belongs to a forbidden realm that he has dared traverse, and he now comes back to the world in which he must live. Here the model loses her mythic power—"She is imaginary" (p. 277). Martha, however, marks Ed's return from the "night river"—"She was . . . what I had hoped for . . . what I had undervalued" (p. 270).

Having touched the elemental forces, Ed can hope to live meaningfully. The river, the Shelleyan preserver-destroyer, becomes part of him. "It pleases me in some curious way that the river does not exist, and that I have it. In me it still is, and will be until I die. . . . I had a friend there who in a way died for me, and my enemy was there" (p. 275).

One important testimony of Ed's possessing the river is his renewed friendship with a former employee, George Holley, "who has become [his] best friend, next to Lewis." When Holley first worked for Ed, he insisted to his employer, "I am with you but not of you" (p. 15). Passionately devoted to art, he wanted to apply "Braque's collage techniques to the layouts [they] were getting ready for fertilizer trade books and wood-pulp processing plants" (p. 14). A would-be artist who "hung Utrillo prints in his cubicle," Holley struggled against Ed's mechanical garden. Now Ed has rehired him, and they "do a lot of serious talking about art" (p. 276); he has begun to combat the pervasive *ennui* of the urban society. "The studio is still boring," he concludes, "but it is not as boring as it was" (p. 276).

Part of the integrity of Dickey's novel lies in his unwillingness to create a Pollyannish ending. Ed Gentry is not a "great American hero," his world changes little, and his end remains ambiguous at best. But having lived "the oldest dream of all"—that is, having run the risk, he challenges his sterile garden state, confronts his other self, paradoxically "sins" against himself, and suffers the consequences of the Fall. In so doing he joins the company of other post-Enlightenment heroes who undergo a fortunate fall, however qualified, in an age of spiritual despair.

And like Blake, Melville, Conrad, Faulkner, and others before him, Dickey seems to say that the Fall is an inevitable, indeed necessary, part of our humanity. "The Bible," he has written recently, "is buried and alive in us." For it portrays "the fabulous world we all have fallen from, and toward which we are always falling, not backward in time, but forward toward that moment when each story . . . will happen again."[35] *Deliverance* gives credibility to that claim.

‡ 8 ‡

Conclusion

> These are the people.
> This is the human dawn. As for me, I would rather
> Be a worm in a wild apple tree than a son of man.
> But we are what we are, and we might remember
> Not to hate any person, for all are vicious;
> And not to be astonished at any evil, all are deserved;
> And not to fear death; it is the only way to be cleansed.
>
> —Robinson Jeffers, "Original Sin"

It is the fulfillment of a prophecy commonly made by the romantics that religion in the modern age has become as much the province of the artist as of the priest. Often with more penetrating insight than accomplished theologians, even professedly agnostic writers have described with accuracy and compassion the spiritual plight of the twentieth century. We therefore do no violence to the Fall as religious statement to gather what perceptions we can from the humanistic authors who have employed it. The reverse is equally true: essentially nonreligious writers have found the mythic inheritance of the Fall an appropriate means of articulating their visions of alienated humanity. By no means can a narrowly orthodox concept of the Fall negate the validity of more essentially humanistic interpretations, nor can a secular reading of the myth permanently dislodge its theological significance. As Nathan Scott and others have noted, a Camus, a Beckett, a Faulkner belong on the theologian's bookshelf.

Frederick Dillistone concludes, "Theology and imaginative literature will always have this in common: each is concerned with the nature and experience and destiny of man." He illustrates his thesis by reference to the first great story of the human drama:

> From the psychological side the Fall has been seen to express a dimension of human existence which is powerfully present from the beginning to the end of life. The fear of falling is one of the earliest forms of anxiety in the human psyche, and it is never fully overcome. In a certain sense all life is falling—a falling before and away from one's aspirations, one's ideals, one's hopes, and one's intentions. Falling short is a reality even if the ideas of an aboriginal Fall and inherited guilt seem unimaginable and are virtually meaningless. From

> the side of social anthropology the Fall has been seen to express a crisis in social development which again constitutes part of the experience of any society wherever found; . . . modern artists have attempted to identify such crises in modern times—turning points in human affairs brought about by the onset of new knowledge bringing untold possibilities of good or evil. Even if the possibilities for good are kept in view, there cannot fail to be a sense of lost innocence, of a fall from a state which was easier to cope with and in which no such fearful possibilities threatened.[1]

Truly, the biblical truth lies buried somewhere in us all as individuals and as societies, whatever our theology—or lack of it, whatever our time, whatever our individual circumstances.

To reduce the magnitude of the Fall myth to a controllable focus and methodology, I have explored only a handful of representative subthemes and works. Though by no means arbitrary selections, the literature we have examined is varied and uneven—few would consider *2001: A Space Odyssey* the artistic equal of Conrad's *Heart of Darkness*. Nonetheless, the range of material studied provides a broad and, I trust, useful overview of the topic. We have seen the Fall on a desert island and in the midst of urban culture, in rural England and in pastoral Georgia, in outer space and in Wonderland. We have found it in the distant past, the present, and the future, in the processes of evolution and the simple act of growing up. Like all enduring and meaningful pieces of art, each of the works we have considered in one way or the other illuminates something of the vast residue of the unconscious which Jung locates in the deepest recesses of the self. As such, they share in common the substance of the myth and in diverse ways give it shape and meaning for our time.

To be sure, numerous other subtopics and works invite discussions of the Fall. Holocaust literature, for example, presents a tragically apt metaphor of the Fall of civilization. Any number of adolescent novels illustrate the Fall motif in the *Bildungsroman*, and a rich variety of postlapsarian protagonists haunt the pages of modern fiction and poetry. Science fiction provides yet another fertile field for exploration of the myth. My purpose here has been merely to approach a few literary works from the perspective of the Fall, to illuminate the pattern as it appears in each work and, in so doing, to suggest something of the prevalence, diversity and authority of the Fall motif in modern literature. For surely no paradigm has proven so lasting and accurate in describing the human condition. The Fall, as Paul Tillich reminds us, "is the original fact. . . . It is not an event of the past; for it ontologically precedes everything that happens in time and space. It sets the conditions of spatial and temporal existence. It is manifest in every individual person in the transition from dreaming innocence to actualization and guilt."[2] It marks the beginning of human history, the predicament of the present, and the promise of the future. As in all ages, much of the literature of our own time has redefined anew the primal story, with all its inherent multiplicity and ambiguity.

NOTES

INDEX

Notes

Chapter 1. Introduction

1. William Faulkner, *Requiem for a Nun* (New York: Random House, 1950), p. 247.

2. Arthur Miller, "With Respect for Her Agony—But With Love," *Life*, 7 Feb. 1964, p. 66.

3. For commentary on the text of Genesis, I am especially indebted to Gerhard von Rad, *Genesis, a Commentary*, trans. John H. Marks (Philadelphia: Westminster Press, 1961); J. M. Evans, *Paradise Lost and the Genesis Tradition* (London: Oxford University Press, 1968), ch. 1; E. A. Speiser, *Genesis: A New Translation with Introduction and Commentary* (New York: Anchor Bible, 1964).

4. See Joseph Anthony Mazzeo, "Fallen Man: Forbidden Knowledge, Forgotten Knowledge," *Notre Dame English Journal*, 11 (1968), 47–65. See also R. W. Hepburn, "Cosmic Fall," in *Dictionary of the History of Ideas: Studies of Selected Pivotal Ideas* (New York: Scribner's, 1973), vol. 1, pp. 504–13; Frederick W. Dillistone, "The Fall: Christian Truth and Literary Symbol," in *Comparative Literature: Matter and Method*, ed. A. Owen Aldridge (Urbana: University of Illinois Press, 1969), pp. 144–57.

5. Eric Smith, *Some Versions of the Fall: The Myth of the Fall of Man in English Literature* (Pittsburgh, Pa.: University of Pittsburgh Press, 1973), p. 10; see also ch. 5, "Romantic Attitudes," pp. 137–62.

Chapter 2. A Romantic Enlightenment

1. Mark Roberts, *The Tradition of English Morality* (New York: Barnes & Noble, 1973), p. 1.

2. Northrop Frye, *A Study of English Romanticism* (New York: Random House, 1968), p. 5.

3. Morse Peckham, *Beyond the Tragic Vision: The Quest for Identity in the Nineteenth Century* (New York: George Braziller, 1962), p. 49.

4. Ibid.

5. See Guyton B. Hammond, *Men in Estrangement: A Comparison of the Thought of Paul Tillich and Erich Fromm* (Nashville, Tenn.: Vanderbilt University Press, 1965).

6. J. Hillis Miller, *The Disappearance of God: Five Nineteenth-Century Writers* (Cambridge, Mass.: Harvard University Press, 1963), p. 12.

7. Robert Langbaum, *The Poetry of Experience: The Dramatic Monologue in Modern*

Literary Tradition (New York: Random House, 1957), p. 59. See also ch. 1 of Frye's *English Romanticism*.

8. Peter Conrad, "The Religion of Romanticism," *London Times Literary Supplement*, 23 May 1975, p. 551.

9. Rainer Maria Rilke, as translated from letter 74, *Briefe ans den Jahren 1907 bis 1914*, in Rollo May, *Love and Will* (New York: Norton, 1969), p. 122.

10. Gerhard von Rad, *Genesis, a Commentary*, trans. John H. Marks (Philadelphia: Westminster Press, 1961), pp. 85–87. Rollo May contends that "Satan, Lucifer, and the other daimonic figures . . . *had* to be invented, *had* to be created, in order to make human action and freedom possible" (*Love and Will*, p. 139).

11. Lucien Goldmann, *The Hidden God: A Study of Tragic Vision in the Pensées of Pascal and the Tragedies of Racine*, trans. Philip Thody (London: Routledge & Kegan Paul, 1964), p. 5.

12. M. H. Abrams, *Natural Supernaturalism: Tradition and Revolution in Romantic Literature* (New York: Norton, 1971), p. 255.

13. May, *Love and Will*, p. 165.

14. Ray Bradbury offered his definition in an interview on NBC's "The Today Show" on the morning of the first moon walk, 20 July 1969; Alan Watt, *Beyond Theology: The Art of Godmanship* (New York: Vintage Books, 1964), p. 79.

15. Søren Kierkegaard, *Journals*, trans. Alexander Dru (New York: Harper, 1959), p. 181. As Langbaum notes, "Subjectivity was not the program but the inescapable condition of the romantics" (*Poetry of Experience*, p. 28).

16. Mircea Eliade, *The Sacred & The Profane: The Nature of Religion*, trans. Willard R. Trask (New York: Harcourt Brace Jovanovich, 1959), p. 95.

17. Thomas Merton, "Blake and the New Theology," *Sewanee Review*, 76 (1968), 680.

18. J. G. Davies, *The Theology of Willliam Blake* (1948; rpt. Hamden, Conn.: Archon Books, 1966), p. 97; compare Thomas J. J. Althizer's *The New Apocalypse: The Radical Christian Vision of William Blake* (East Lansing: Michigan State University Press, 1967); and William Walling, "The Death of God: William Blake's Version," *Dalhousie Review*, 48 (1968), 237–50.

19. *Vala*, Night the First, 9–11, in *The Complete Writings of William Blake With Variant Readings*, ed. Geoffrey Keynes (London: Oxford University Press, 1966), p. 264. Subsequent references will be given in the text.

20. Northrop Frye, *Fearful Symmetry: A Study of William Blake* (Princeton, N.J.: Princeton University Press, 1947), p. 4.

21. Abrams, *Natural Supernaturalism*, p. 259.

22. See especially Kathleen Raine's *Blake and Tradition* (Princeton, N.J.: Princeton University Press, 1968) and "Berkeley, Blake and the New Age," *Thought*, 51 (1976), 356–77; see also George M. Harper, *The Neoplatonism of William Blake* (Chapel Hill: University of North Carolina Press, 1961); and Stuart Curran, "Blake and the Gnostic Hyle: A Double Negative," *Blake Studies*, 4 (1972), 117–33.

23. Eric Smith, *Some Versions of the Fall: The Myth of the Fall of Man in English Literature* (Pittsburgh, Pa.: University of Pittsburgh Press, 1973), p. 17.

24. Helmut Thielicke, *How the World Began: Man in the First Chapters of the Bible*, trans. John W. Doberstein (Philadelphia: Fortress Press, 1961), p. 146.

25. See especially Langbaum's characterization of the romantic hero in *The Poetry of Experience*, ch. 1, and Frye's examination of the relationship between the hero and the mythic tradition in *A Study of Romanticism*, ch. 1.

26. See Florence Sandler, "The Iconoclastic Enterprise: Blake's Critique of 'Milton's Religion,' " *Blake Studies*, 5, no. 1 (1972), 13–57.

27. David Eggenschwiler, "Byron's *Cain* and the Antimythological Myth," *Modern Language Review*, 37 (1976), 324–38.

28. In Truman Guy Steffan, ed., *Lord Byron's Cain: Twelve Essays and a Text with Variants and Annotations* (Austin: University of Texas Press, 1968). Subsequent references will be included in the text.

29. Rowland Prothero, ed., *The Works of Lord Byron. Letters and Journals*, rev. ed. (London: John Murray, 1902), vol. 5, p. 470.

30. Langbaum, *Poetry of Experience*, p. 63; see also Peter J. Manning's discussion of the relationship between Cain and Lucifer as Byron's expression of "the familiar central pattern of rebellion and stalemate, for the two seem successive stages of the same character" (*Byron and His Fictions* [Detroit: Wayne State University Press, 1978], p. 148).

31. Edward Bostetter, *The Romantic Ventriloquists: Wordsworth, Coleridge, Keats, Shelley, Byron* (Seattle: University of Washington Press, 1963), p. 286; Harold Bloom, *The Visionary Company: A Reading of English Romantic Poetry* (Garden City, N.Y.: Doubleday, 1961), p. 246.

32. Manning, *Byron and His Fictions*, p. 154.

33. William P. Fitzpatrick, "Byron's Mysteries: The Paradoxical Drive Toward Eden," *Studies in English Literature*, 15 (1975), 619–20.

34. Leonard Michaels, "Byron's *Cain*," *PMLA*, 84 (1969), 71.

35. Robert Gleckner, *Byron and the Ruins of Paradise* (Baltimore: Johns Hopkins Press, 1967), p. 324; Thomas A. Reisner, "Cain: Two Romantic Interpretations," *Culture*, 31 (1970), 124–43.

36. Recorded in Montague Summers, *The Vampire, His Kith and Kin* (London: K. Paul, Trench, Trubner, 1928), p. 281; and A. H. Nethercot, *The Road to Tyermaine* (Chicago: University of Chicago Press, 1939), pp. 12–20.

37. *Mary Shelley's Journal*, ed. F. L. Jones (Norman: University of Oklahoma Press, 1947), p. 61.

38. Mary refers specifically to Coleridge's play, *Remorse* (*Journal*, pp. 122–23).

39. Samuel T. Coleridge, "Christabel," in *Coleridge's Poems*, ed. E. H. Coleridge (London: Oxford University Press, 1962), vol. 1, pp. 213–36; Percy B. Shelley, *The Cenci*, in *The Complete Works of Shelley*, ed. Roger Ingpen and Walter E. Peck (New York: Gordian Press, 1965), vol. 2, pp. 77–155. Subsequent references will be included in the text.

40. Michael E. Holestein, "Coleridge's *Christabel* as Psychodrama; Five Perspectives on the Intruder," *Wordsworth Circle*, 7 (1976), 119–28. See also Robert H. Siegel, "The Serpent and the Dove: 'Christabel' and the Problem of Evil," in *Imagination and Spirit: Essays in Literature and the Christian Faith*, ed. Charles A. Huttar (Grand Rapids, Mich.: Eerdmans, 1971), pp. 159–86; and Jonas Spatz, "The Mystery of Eros: Sexual Initiation in Coleridge's 'Christabel,' " *PMLA*, 90 (1975), 107–16.

41. For discussions of Geraldine as a vampire or lamia, see especially Nethercot, *The Road to Tyermaine*; Werner W. Beyer, *The Enchanted Forest* (New York: Barnes & Noble, 1963), ch. 5; Elisabeth Schneider, "Notes on Christabel," *Philological Quarterly*, 32 (1953), 197–206.

42. Earl R. Wasserman, *Shelley: A Critical Reading* (Baltimore: Johns Hopkins Press, 1971), p. 89.

43. Richard H. Fogle, *The Idea of Coleridge's Criticism* (Berkeley and Los Angeles: University of California Press, 1962), p. 131.

44. Lawrence D. Berkoben, "*Christabel:* A Variety of Religious Experience," *Modern Language Quarterly*, 25 (1964), 404.

45. Carl Woodring, "Christabel of Cumberland," *Review of English Literature*, 7 (1966), 48–49.

46. Marshall Suther, *Visions of Xanadu* (New York: Columbia University Press, 1965), p. 101.

47. Siegel, " 'Christabel' and the Problem of Evil," p. 173.

48. See Stuart Curran, *Shelley's Cenci: Scorpions Ringed with Fire* (Princeton, NJ.: Princeton University Press, 1970); Milton Wilson, *Shelley's Later Poetry* (New York: Columbia University Press, 1959), pp. 78–92; and Wasserman, *Shelley*, pp. 84–128.

49. Coleridge says that in writing the second part of "Christabel" ("if, indeed . . . they did not suggest the whole poem") he was constantly thinking of Crashaw's lines on St. Theresa beginning, "Since 'tis not to be had at home, / She'd travel to a maryrdom" (*Conversations and Recollections of S. T. Coleridge*, ed. Thomas Allsop [London, 1936], vol. 1, pp. 194–96).

50. Lawrence Lockridge, *Coleridge the Moralist* (Ithaca, N.Y.: Cornell University Press, 1977), p. 75.

51. J. Robert Barth, *Coleridge and Christian Dogma* (Cambridge, Mass.: Harvard University Press, 1969), pp. 6–7.

52. C. S. Lewis, *Rehabilitations and Other Essays*, in *English Romantic Poets: Modern Essays in Criticism*, ed. M. H. Abrams (New York: Oxford University Press, 1960), p. 256; see also Joseph Anthony Wittreich, "The 'Satanism' of Blake and Shelley Reconsidered," *Studies in Philology*, 65 (1968), 816–33.

53. R. W. B. Lewis, *The American Adam* (Chicago: University of Chicago Press, 1955).

54. Frye, *A Study of English Romanticism*, p. 18.

55. Smith, *Some Versions of the Fall*, p. 14.

56. See David Thorburn, *Conrad's Romanticism* (New Haven, Conn.: Yale University Press, 1964).

57. Joseph Conrad, *Complete Works* (Garden City, N.Y.: Doubleday, Page, 1924), vol. 19, pp. 91–92. Subsequent references will be included in the text.

58. Thorburn, *Conrad's Romanticism*, p. 141.

59. Smith, *Some Versions of the Fall*, p. 17.

60. Langbaum, *Poetry of Experience*, p. 61.

61. Robert Stallman, "Conrad and 'The Secret Sharer,' " in *The Art of Joseph Conrad: A Critical Symposium* (East Lansing: Michigan State University Press, 1960), p. 281.

62. Porter Williams, Jr., "The Brand of Cain in 'The Secret Sharer,' " *Modern Fiction Studies*, 10 (1964), 28.

63. See J. D. O'Hara, "Unlearned Lessons in 'The Secret Sharer,' " *College English*, 26 (1965), 444; and Jocelyn Baines, *Joseph Conrad: A Critical Biography* (New York: McGraw-Hill, 1960), p. 357.

64. G. Jean-Aubrey, *Joseph Conrad: Life and Letters* (Garden City, N.Y.: Doubleday, Page, 1927), vol. 2, p. 143.

65. O'Hara, "Unlearned Lessons in 'The Secret Sharer,' " p. 444.

66. J. L. Simmons, "The Dual Morality in Conrad's 'The Secret Sharer,' " *Studies in Short Fiction*, 2 (1965), 213–14.

67. Conrad, *Complete Works*, vol. 16, p. 150.

68. O'Hara, "Unlearned Lessons in 'The Secret Sharer,' " p. 446.

69. Albert Guerard, *Conrad the Novelist* (Cambridge, Mass.: Harvard University Press, 1962), p. 26.

70. Williams, "The Brand of Cain in 'The Secret Sharer,' " p. 30.

Chapter 3. Childhood's End

1. James to F. W. H. Myers, 19 Dec. 1898, in *The Letters of Henry James*, ed. Percy Lubbock (New York: Scribner, 1920), vol. 1, p. 300.

2. Thomas M. Cranfill and Robert L. Clark, Jr., *An Anatomy of "The Turn of the Screw"* (Austin: University of Texas Press, 1965); preface to *The Aspern Papers*, reprinted in *The Art of the Novel: Critical Prefaces by Henry James*, intro. by Richard P. Blackmur (New York: Scribner, 1934), p. 172.

3. The tendency has been to lump together pro- and anti-"hallucination" studies. The extreme poles are represented on one side by Edmund Wilson ("The Ambiguity of Henry James," first published in *Hound and Horn*, 7 [1934], 385–406) and Harold C. Goddard, ("A Pre-Freudian Reading of *The Turn of the Screw*," *Nineteenth-Century Fiction*, 12 [1957], 1–37); and, on the other, by Robert Heilman ("*The Turn of the Screw* as Poem," *The University of Kansas City Review*, 14 [1945], 227–89) and Eli Siegel (*James and the Children: A Consideration of Henry James's A Turn of the Screw* [New York: Definition Press, 1968]).

4. Henry James, *The Turn of the Screw* (New York: Norton, 1960). Subsequent references will be cited in the text.

5. See Arthur Boardman, "Mrs. Grose's Reading of *The Turn of the Screw*," *Studies in English Literature*, 14 (1974), 619–35.

6. See Thomas J. Bontly, "Henry James's 'General Vision of Evil' in *The Turn of the Screw*," *Studies in English Literature*, 9 (1969), 721–35.

7. See Heilman, "*The Turn of the Screw* as Poem"; Eric Voegelin, "Postscript: On Paradise and Revolution," *Southern Review*, 7 (1971), 25–48; Howard Pearce, "Henry James's Pastoral Fallacy," *PMLA*, 90 (1975), 834–47.

8. Dorothea Krook notes that if the children were younger, they could not "show the effects of their corruption"; if older, they would be "too old to be properly innocent" (*The Ordeal of Consciousness in Henry James* [Cambridge: Cambridge University Press, 1962], pp. 110–11).

9. See Janet McMaster, " 'The Full Image of Repetition' in *The Turn of the Screw*," *Studies in Short Fiction*, 6 (1969), 377–82; Paul N. Siegel, " 'Miss Jessel': Mirror Image of the Governess," *Literature and Psychology*, 18 (1968), 30–38.

10. David Mogen, "Agonies of Innocence: The Governess and Maggie Verver," *American Literary Realism*, 9 (1976), 234.

11. Reinhold Niebuhr, *The Theology of Reinhold Niebuhr* (Grand Rapids, Mich.: Charles Eerdmans, 1951), p. 106.

12. Charles Samuels, *The Ambiguity of Henry James* (Urbana: University of Illinois Press, 1971), p. 20; and Joseph J. Firebaugh, "Inadequacy in Eden: Knowledge in *The Turn of the Screw*," *Modern Fiction Studies*, 3 (1957), 57.

13. Oscar Cargill, "Henry James as Freudian Pioneer," *Chicago Review*, 10 (1956), 13–29.

14. Voegelin, "Postscript: On Paradise and Revolution," p. 48; Samuels, *The Ambiguity of Henry James*, p. 22.

15. William Golding, "The Meaning of It All," interview with Frank Kermode, in *Lord of the Flies*, ed. James R. Baker and Arthur P. Ziegler, Jr. (New York: G. P. Putnam, 1954), p. 127. Subsequent references will be given in the text. See also Bernard S. Oldsey and Stanley Weintraub, "*Lord of the Flies*: Beelzebub Revisited," *College English*, 25 (1963), 90–99; Margaret Walters, "Two Fabulists: Golding and Camus," *Melbourne Critical Review*, 4 (1961), 18–29; John Peters, "The Fables of William Golding," *Kenyon Review*, 19 (1957), 577–92.

16. Samuel Hynes, *William Golding* (New York: Columbia University Press, 1964), p.

6. See J. Dierickx's thesis that Golding's novels constitute "*une variation nouvelle et originale sur le thème très ancien de la Chute*." "*La Thème de la Chute dans romans de W. Golding*," *Etudes Anglaises*, 16 (1963), 230–42.

17. David Henderson, "Is Golding's Theology Christian?" in *William Golding: Some Critical Considerations*, ed. Jack I. Biles and Robert O. Evans (Lexington: University of Kentucky Press, 1978), p. 19. E. C. Bufkin extensively treats what he calls the "Christian myth of the Fall of Man" in *Lord of the Flies*, relating it in particular to *Paradise Lost*. My commentary parallels some of his conclusions but is less concerned with the possible derivation of Golding's imagery and themes ("Lord of the Flies: An Analysis," *Georgia Review*, 19 [1965], 40–57).

18. Peter Green, "The World of William Golding," in *Lord of the Flies*, ed. Baker and Ziegler, p. 173.

19. Gerhard von Rad, *Genesis, a Commentary*, trans. John H. Marks (Philadelphia: Westminster Press, 1961), p. 87.

20. Erich Fromm, *You Shall Be As Gods: A Radical Interpretation of the Old Testament and Its Traditions* (Greenwich, Conn.: Fawcett, 1966), p. 70.

21. James Keating, "Interview with William Golding," in *Lord of the Flies*, ed. Baker and Ziegler, p. 190.

22. Samuel Hynes, "William Golding," in *Six Comtemporary British Novelists*, ed. George Stade (New York: Columbia University Press, 1976), p. 179.

23. Mark Kinkead-Weekes and Ian Gregor, *William Golding: A Critical Study* (London: Faber and Faber, 1976), p. 21.

24,.Claire Rosenfield, " 'Men of a Smaller Growth': A Psychological Analysis of William Golding's *Lord of the Flies*," *Literature and Psychology*, 11 (1961), 271; see also Howard S. Babb's discussion in *The Novels of William Golding* (Columbus: Ohio State University Press, 1970), pp. 24–28.

25. Golding, "The Meaning of It all," p. 201.

26. Carl Niemeyer, "The Coral Island Revisited," *College English*, 22 (1961), 223. To James Ginden the ending is "a 'gimmick,' a trick, a means of cutting down or softening the implications built up with the structure of the boys' society on the island" (*Postwar British Fiction* [Berkeley: University of California Press, 1962], p. 197). E. C. Bufkin calls the ending the act of a "cosmic ironist," "merely another beginning to this mythic story" of the Fall, for he perceives in himself "a boy, decorated with his official insignias just like the children are depicted with clay and charcoal" ("Lord of the Flies: An Analysis," p. 57).

27. Henri Talon, "Irony in *Lord of the Flies*," *Essays in Criticism*, 18 (1968), 309.

28. Baker, "Decline of *Lord of the Flies*," p. 460. In reference to all Golding's novels, J. Dierickx finds "*une sorte de compassion et même d'admiration*" (p. 241).

29. William Mueller, "An Old Story Well Told," *Christian Century*, 2 Oct. 1963, p. 1205.

30. William Golding, *Free Fall* (1959; New York: Harcourt, Brace & World, 1962), p. 47. At the end of the book, Golding once remarked, we discover that man is free—"free" in Milton's classic sense, "to fall." Jack I. Biles, Talk: *Conversation With William Golding* (New York: Harcourt Brace Jovanovich, 1970), p. 76.

Chapter 4. Civilization and Its Discontents

1. The My Lai massacre occurred 16 March 1968 when American soldiers in Vietnam killed and raped villagers in the small hamlet of My Lai. The Republic of Biafra suffered mass starvation and political abuse after claiming independence from Nigeria in 1967.

Idi Amin ruled Uganda with extreme brutality and political torture between 1971 and 1979.

2. Meg Greenfield, "Heart of Darkness," *Newsweek*, 4 Dec. 1978, p. 132. Some nine hundred racially mixed followers of the Rev. Jim Jones committed mass suicide and murder in Jonestown, Guyana, in November 1978.

3. Albert Guerard, *Conrad the Novelist* (Cambridge, Mass.: Harvard University Press, 1962), p. 36. Indispensable is Bruce E. Teets and Helmut E. Gerber, *Joseph Conrad: An Annotated Bibliography of Writings About Him* (DeKalb: Northern Illinois University Press, 1971).

4. Joseph Conrad, "Geography and Some Explorers," in *Last Essays*, ed. Richard Curle (London: J. M. Dent, 1926), p. 17.

5. Walter J. Ong, "Truth in Conrad's Darkness," *Mosaic*, 11 (1977), 155, 152.

6. Joseph Conrad, *Complete Works* (Garden City, N.Y.: Doubleday & Page, 1924), vol. 16, pp. 45–162. Hereafter page references will be given in the text.

7. Bernard Mayer relates both Kurtz and Marlow to Conrad's own divided nature in *Joseph Conrad: A Psychoanalytic Biography* (Princeton, N.J.: Princeton University Press, 1967), p. 346.

8. Guerard, *Conrad the Novelist*, p. 36. See Marion B. Brady, "Conrad's Whited Sepulcher," *College English*, 24 (1962), 24–29.

9. John Vernon, *The Garden and the Map: Schizophrenia in Twentieth-Century Literature and Culture* (Urbana: University of Illinois Press, 1973), p. 86. I shall discuss Vernon's study in more detail in chapter 5.

10. Lawrence Graver, *Conrad's Shorter Fiction* (Berkeley and Los Angeles: University of California Press, 1969), p. 85.

11. Frances B. Singh, "The Colonial Bias of *Heart of Darkness*," *Conradiana*, 10 (1978), 41–54. Michael J. C. Echeruo argues that Conrad does not use the figure of the black prejudicially but artistically or symbolically (*The Conditioned Imagination from Shakespeare to Conrad* [New York: Holmes & Meier, 1978], pp. 93–112).

12. Gerhard von Rad, *Genesis, a Commentary*, trans. John H. Marks (Philadelphia: Westminster Press, 1961), pp. 79–80.

13. Stanley Tick, "Conrad's *Heart of Darkness*," *Explicator*, 21 (1963), Item 67.

14. See Robert F. Haugh in *Joseph Conrad: Discovery in Design* (Norman: University of Oklahoma Press, 1957), pp. 38–39; William F. Zak in "Conrad, F. R. Lewis, and Whitehead: *Heart of Darkness* and Organic Holism," *Conradiana*, 4 (1972), 14.

15. Bruce Johnson, " 'Heart of Darkness' and the Problem of Emptiness," *Studies in Short Fiction*, 9 (1962), 399. See also Peter Glassman, *Language and Being: Joseph Conrad and the Literature of Personality* (New York: Columbia University Press, 1976), pp. 227–49; Jerome Thrale, "Marlow's Quest," *University of Toronto Quarterly*, 24 (1955), 356.

16. Jocelyn Baines, *Joseph Conrad: A Critical Biography* (New York: McGraw-Hill, 1960), p. 229.

17. Bruce Stark, "Kurtz's Intended: The Heart of *Heart of Darkness*," *Texas Studies in Literature and Language*, 16 (1974), 540. Lillian Feder calls her "a shade in Hell . . . because of her unwillingness to face life" ("Marlow's Descent into Hell," *Nineteenth-Century Fiction*, 9 [1955], 292). Thomas Moser goes so far as saying that "she does not deserve to hear the truth" (*Joseph Conrad: Achievement and Decline* [Cambridge, Mass.: Harvard University Press, 1957], p. 81).

18. Stewart Wilcox, "Conrad's 'Complicated Presentations' of Symbolic Imagery," *Philological Quarterly*, 39 (1960), 16; see also C. B. Cox, *Joseph Conrad: The Modern Imagination* (London: J. M. Dent, 1974), p. 47.

19. Lee M. Whitehead, "The Active Voice and the Passive Eye: *Heart of Darkness* and Nietzsche's *The Birth of Tragedy*," *Conradiana*, 7 (1975), 132.

20. Ralph Maud, "The Plain Truth of *Heart of Darkness*," *Humanities Association Bulletin*, 17 (1965), 13–17. David J. McConnell calls Marlow "the earthly vicar of Kurtz" who, "like Kurtz, cannot express . . . truth. And the reader . . . can only ask with Eliot 'after such knowledge what forgiveness?' " (" 'The Heart of Darkness' in T. S. Eliot's *The Hollow Men*," *Texas Studies in Literature and Language*, 4 [1964], 152).

21. Eloise Hay, *The Political Novels of Joseph Conrad: A Critical Study* (Chicago: University of Chicago Press, 1963), pp. 128–53.

22. Ford Madox Ford, *Portraits from Life* (Boston: Houghton Mifflin, 1936), pp. 61–63.

23. William Bysshe Stein, "The Lotus Posture and *Heart of Darkness*," *Modern Fiction Studies*, 2 (1956–1957), 237.

24. Bruce Harkness, in *Conrad's Heart of Darkness and the Critics*, ed. Bruce Harkness (San Francisco: Wadsworth, 1960), p. 113.

25. Jeffrey Berman, *Joseph Conrad: Writing as Rescue* (New York: Astra Books, 1977), p. 66.

26. Theodore Ziolkowski, *The Novels of Hermann Hesse: A Study in Theme and Structure* (Princeton, N.J.: Princeton University Press, 1965), p. 107.

27. Anna Otten, *Hesse Companion* (Albuquerque: University of New Mexico Press, 1977), p. 17.

28. Rudolf Koester, "Self-Realization: Hesse's Reflection on Youth," *Monatshefte*, 57 (1965), 183.

29. Otten, *Hesse Companion*, p. 28.

30. For the influence of Freud on Hesse, see A. W. Brink, "Hermann Hesse and the Oedipal Quest," *Literature and Psychology*, 24 (1974), 66–79; George Wallis Field gives more emphasis to Jung's influence in his *Hermann Hesse* (New York: Twayne, 1970), pp. 46–56. Joseph Mileck discusses both influences in *Hermann Hesse: Life and Art* (Berkeley and Los Angeles: University of California Press, 1978), pp. 100–05.

31. Ziolkowski, *Novels of Hermann Hesse*, p. 144.

32. Hermann Hesse, *Demian: The True Story of Emil Sinclair*, trans. Michael Roloff and Michael Lebeck (New York: Bantam, 1966), p. 4. Subsequent references will be included in the text (based on the text in *Gesammelte Schriften* [Suhrkamp Verlag, 1957]).

33. Henry Crabb Robinson, *Blake, Coleridge, Wordsworth, Lamb, Etc.: Being Selections from the Remains of Henry Crabb Robinson*, ed. Edith J. Morley (London: Longmans, Green, 1922), p. 3.

34. Ziolkowski, *Novels of Hermann Hesse*, p. 120.

35. Ernst Rose, *Faith from the Abyss: Hermann Hesse's Way from Romanticism to Modernity* (New York: New York University Press, 1965), p. 52.

36. Mileck, *Hermann Hesse: Life and Art*, p. 94.

37. Hans Luthi, *Hermann Hesse: Natur und Geist* (Stuttgart, Berlin, Köhn, Mainz: Verlag W. Kohlhammer, 1970), p. 39.

38. Kurt Fickert, *Hermann Hesse's Quest: The Evolution of the DICHTER Figure in His Novels* (Fredericton, N. B., Canada: York Press, 1978), p. 66; elsewhere Fickert says that Sinclair is an artist "*in ovo*—devoted not to a craft, but to a way of life" (p. 68).

39. Ziolkowski, *Novels of Hermann Hesse*, p. 116; see also Otten, *Hesse Companion*, p. 31.

40. Mark Boulby, *Hermann Hesse: His Mind and Art* (Ithaca, N. Y.: Cornell University Press, 1967), p. 114; Ziolkowski, *Novels of Hermann Hesse*, p. 108.

41. Martin Buber, "Hermann Hesse in the Service of the Spirit," trans. Theodore Ziolkowski, in *Hesse: A Collection of Critical Essays*, ed. Theodore Ziolkowski (Englewood Cliffs, N.J.: Prentice-Hall, 1963), p. 27.

42. Irina Kirk, "Hermann Hesse's *Demian*: Paradise Lost and Regained," in *Texte und Kontexte: Studien zur Deutschen und Vergleichenden Literaturwissenschaft. Festshrift für Norbert Fuerst zum 65. Geburstag*, eds. Manfred Durzak, Eberhard Reichmann and Ulrich Weisstein (Burn und München: Francke Verlag, 1973), p. 111.

43. Ralph Freedman, *The Lyrical Novel: Studies in Hermann Hesse, André Gide, and Virginia Woolf* (Princeton, N. J.: Princeton University Press, 1963), p. 61.

44. Ziolkowski, *Novels of Hermann Hesse*, p. 58.

Chapter 5. The Fall and After

1. Allen J. Koppenhaver, "*The Fall* and After: Albert Camus and Arthur Miller," *Modern Drama*, 9 (1966), 206–09.

2. Albert Camus, *Notebooks 1942–1951*, trans. Justin O'Brien (New York: Alfred A. Knopf, 1965), p. 209.

3. Thomas Hanna, *The Thought and Art of Albert Camus* (Chicago: Henry Regnery, 1958), p. 230. To many, *La Chute* is a response to Francis Jeanson's and Sartre's critical review of *L'Homme révolté* in *Les Temps modernes* in August 1952. See Herbert R. Lottman's recent biography *Albert Camus* (Garden City, N.Y.: Doubleday, 1979), pp. 561–64, and Marthe La Vallée-Williams, "Biblical Allusions in *La Chute*," *Agora*, 2, no. 2 (1973), 13–31.

4. Roger Quilliot, *The Sea and Prisons: A Commentary on the Life and Thought of Albert Camus*, trans. Emmett Parker (University: University of Alabama Press, 1970), p. 250; see also Donald Lazere, *The Unique Creation of Albert Camus* (New Haven, Conn.: Yale University Press, 1973), pp. 183–86.

5. Albert Camus, *The Fall*, trans. Justin O'Brien (New York: Alfred A. Knopf, 1956), pp. 32, 36. Subsequent references will be included in the text.

6. Lazere, *Unique Creation of Albert Camus*, p. 187.

7. Geoffrey Hartman, "Camus and Malraux: The Common Ground," *Yale French Studies*, 25 (Spring 1960), 106.

8. Camus, *Notebooks* p. 119.

9. R.W.B. Lewis, *The Picaresque Saint: Representative Figures in Contemporary Fiction* (Philadelphia: J.B. Lippincott, 1959), p. 105.

10. William Mueller, *The Prophetic Voice in Modern Fiction* (New York: Association Press, 1959), p. 74.

11. David Madden, "Ambiguity in Albert Camus' *The Fall*," *Modern Fiction Studies*, 12 (1966), 464–65.

12. Albert Chesneau, "Un Modèle possible du héros de *La Chute*," *French Review*, 40 (1967), 467.

13. Phillip Rhein, *Albert Camus* (New York: Twayne, 1969), p. 108.

14. Camus, *Notebooks*, pp. 221–22.

15. Dominique Aury, "Talk with Albert Camus," *New York Times Book Review*, 24 Feb. 1957, p. 36.

16. Albert Maquet, *Albert Camus: The Invincible Summer*, trans. Herma Briffault (New York: Braziller, 1958), p. 156.

17. Irina Kirk, "Dramatization of Consciousness in Camus and Dostoevsky," *Bucknell Review*, 16 (1968), 104.

18. Ralph Berets, "Van Eyck's 'The Last Judges' in Camus' *The Fall*," *Research*

Studies, 42 (1974), 114; see also Jeffrey Meyers, "Camus' *The Fall* and Van Eyck's *The Adoration of the Lamb*," *Mosaic*, 7, no. 3 (1974), 43–51.

19. Sara Toenes, "Public Confession in *La Chute*," *Contemporary Literature*, 4 (1963), 317.

20. Lottman, *Albert Camus*, p. 563.

21. Mildred Hartsock, "Camus' *The Fall*: Dialogue of One," *Modern Fiction Studies*, 7 (1961–62), 362.

22. Rhein, *Albert Camus*, p. 108.

23. Hartman, "Camus and Malraux," p. 107.

24. Conor Cruise O'Brien, *Albert Camus of Europe and Africa* (New York: Viking, 1970), p. 100. Hanna argues that Clamence himself is a Christ figure (pp. 234–35).

25. Lewis, *Picaresque Saint*, p. 107. In "Biblical Allusions in *La Chute*," La Vallée-Williams argues that Camus uses the Bible as "a mythic document exploring the contradictory and unreconciled statements on the human dilemma." His rejection of resurrection "is a modern refusal to make too easy a jump between human and divine" (p. 25).

26. Frederick W. Dillistone, "The Fall: Christian Truth and Literary Symbol," in *Comparative Literature: Matter and Form*, ed. A. Owen Aldridge (Urbana: University of Illinois Press), p. 155. See also John Cruickshank, *Albert Camus and the Literature of Revolt* (New York: Oxford University Press, 1959), pp. 187–88. Phan Thi Ngoc-Main and Pierre Nguyen Van-Huy write that the sin is an instant, but the Fall is a long history. *"La Chute" de Camus: le dernier testament* (Neuchâtel: Editions de lay Bonçonnière, 1974), p. 194.

27. Leonard Moss, "Biography and Literary Allusion in *After the Fall*," *Education Theatre Journal*, 18 (1966), 40. In *Arthur Miller*, Moss insists that "Miller reinterprets Old and New Testament ethical concepts in a wholly secular manner" (New York: Twayne, 1967), p. 94. Raymond H. Reno agrees: "From *All My Sons* to *After the Fall*, Miller has been dismantling the Christian myth. However, to accomplish this he has had to use myth, and so has been caught in a rhetorical trap. His symbolic figures . . . have forced on him questions he was perhaps not prepared to answer" ("Arthur Miller and the Death of God," *Texas Studies in Literature and Language*, 11 [1964], 1084).

28. Phillip Gelb, "Morality and Modern Drama," *Education Theatre Journal*, 10 (1958), 22. Interview with Arthur Miller.

29. Arthur Miller, *After the Fall* (New York: Viking, 1964), p. 1. Subsequent references will be given in the text.

30. Arthur Miller, foreword to *After the Fall*, *Saturday Evening Post*, 1 Feb. 1964, p. 32. The foreword, not contained in the book edition, was published with the first printing of the play in the *Saturday Evening Post*.

31. *New York Times Magazine*, 3 Jan. 1965, p. 48.

32. Interview with Richard I. Evans, *Psychology and Arthur Miller* (New York: E. P. Dutton, 1969), p. 74.

33. Edward Murray, *Arthur Miller, Dramatist* (New York: Frederick Ungar, 1967), p. 138.

34. Tom Prideaux, "A desperate search by a troubled hero," *Life*, 7 Feb. 1964, p. 64C. See also C.W.E. Bigsby's thesis that "the man who strikes his chest in confession may derive his satisfaction not so much from his admission of guilt as from the exquisite nature of the blow" ("The Fall and After—Arthur Miller's Confession," *Modern Drama*, 10 [1967], 134).

35. Murray, *Arthur Miller, Dramatist*, pp. 148–49.

36. According to Benjamin Nelson, Maggie senses "that the Savior is also the Destroyer" (*Arthur Miller: Portrait of a Playwright* [New York: David McKay, 1970], p. 266).

37. Arthur Ganz, "Arthur Miller: After the Silence," *Drama Survey*, 3 (1964), 526.

38. Robert Corrigan, introduction to *Arthur Miller: A Collection of Critical Essays*, ed. Robert W. Corrigan (Englewood Cliffs, N.J.: Prentice-Hall, 1969), p. 11.

39. Robert Hogan, *Arthur Miller* (Minneapolis: University of Minnesota Press, 1964), p. 43; Nelson, *Portrait of a Playwright*, p. 253.

Chapter 6. The Fall in Fantasy

1. Donald Rackin, "Alice's Long Journey to the End of Night," *PMLA*, 81 (1966), 314.

2. Robert Pattison, *The Child Figure in English Literature* (Athens: University of Georgia Press, 1978), pp. 159, 156.

3. Peter Coveney, *Poor Monkey: The Child in Literature* (London: Rockliff, 1957), p. 195; see to the contrary Nina Auerbach, "Alice and Wonderland: A Curious Child," *Victorian Studies*, 17 (1973), 46.

4. James Kincaid, "Alice's Invasion of Wonderland," *PMLA*, 88 (1975), 92–99.

5. Lewis Carroll, *Alice in Wonderland: Authoritative Texts of Alice's Adventures in Wonderland, Through the Looking-Glass, The Hunting of the Snark. Backgrounds. Essays in Criticism*, ed. Donald J. Gray (New York: Norton, 1971), pp. 15–16. Subsequent references will be given in the text.

6. Claire Rosenfield, " 'Men of Smaller Growth': A Psychological Analysis of William Golding's *Lord of the Flies*," *Literature and Psychology*, 11 (1961), 100.

7. Auerbach, "Alice and Wonderland," p. 43.

8. Kincaid, "Alice's Invasion," p. 92.

9. Roger Sale, *Fairy Tales and After: From Snow White to E. B. White* (Cambridge, Mass.: Harvard University Press, 1978), p. 115.

10. Rackin, "Alice's Long Journey," p. 320.

11. Lionel Morton, "Memory in the Alice Books," *Nineteenth-Century Fiction*, 33 (1978), pp. 304–05. Roger B. Henkle writes that "the Knave's trial draws on the idea that there is something that one is guilty of but cannot remember—which may, in fact, be a primordial sin lying deep in one's consciousness" (*Comedy and Culture: England 1820–1900* [Princeton, N.J.: Princeton University Press, 1980], p. 213).

12. Coveney, *Poor Monkey*, pp. 197–98.

13. Morton, "Memory in the Alice Books," p. 305.

14. William Empson, "The Child as Swain," *Some Versions of the Pastoral* (1935; rpt. Norfolk, Conn.: New Directions, 1950), p. 257.

15. Morton, "Memory in the Alice Books," p. 306.

16. John Vernon, *The Garden and the Map: Schizophrenia in Twentieth Century Literature and Culture* (Urbana: University of Illinois Press, 1973), p. xiii.

17. Richard Kelly, *Lewis Carroll* (Boston: Twayne, 1977), p. 105.

18. Martin Gardner, *The Annotated Alice: Alice's Adventures in Wonderland & Through the Looking-Glass* (New York: Bramhall, 1960), p. 87.

19. Kincaid, "Alice's Invasion," p. 99.

20. Pattison, *Child Figure in English Literature*, p. 158. To Donald Rackin, "Alice's quest for reasonable experience whisks her back to her only possible, albeit artificial world, where the ultimately irrational makes life sane" ("Alice's Long Journey," p. 325).

21. Morton, "Memory in the Alice Books," p. 306.
22. Kincaid, "Alice's Invasion," p. 95.
23. Elizabeth Sewell, "The Nonsense System in Lewis Carroll's Work and in Today's World," in *Lewis Carroll Observed: A Collection of Unpublished Photographs, Drawings, Poetry and New Essays*, ed. Edward Guiliano (New York: Clarkson N. Potter, 1976), p. 66.
24. Harry Levin, "Wonderland Revisited," *Kenyon Review*, 27 (1965), 605.
25. Alan Brody, "*2001* and the Paradox of the Fortunate Fall," *Hartford Studies in Literature*, 1 (1969), 7–19.
26. James Agel, ed., *The Making of Kubrick's 2001* (New York: New American Library, 1968), p. 10; "Playboy Interview," *Playboy*, Sept. 1968, p. 94.
27. M. H. Abrams, *Natural Supernaturalism: Tradition and Revolution in Romantic Literature* (New York: Norton, 1971), p. 217.
28. Arthur C. Clarke, *2001: A Space Odyssey* (New York: New American Library, 1968), p. 14. Subsequent references will be given in text.
29. Brody, "*2001* and the Paradox of the Fortunate Fall," p. 10.
30. Ibid., p. 12.
31. Don Daniels, "*2001:* A New Myth," *Film Heritage*, 3, no. 4 (1968), 2, 4.
32. Ibid., p. 5.
33. Gerhard von Rad, *Genesis, a Commentary*, trans. John H. Marks (Philadelphia: Westminster Press, 1961), p. 79.
34. Eric Smith, *Some Versions of the Fall: The Myth of the Fall of Man in English Literature* (Pittsburgh: University of Pittsburgh Press, 1973), p. 17.
35. Tim Hunter, with Stephen Kaplan and Peter Jaszi, "*2001: A Space Odyssey*," *Film Heritage*, 3, no. 4 (1968), 18.
36. Erich Fromm, *The Heart of Man: Its Genius for Good and Evil* (New York: Harper and Row, 1964), p. 20.
37. Brody, "*2001* and the Paradox of the Fortunate Fall," p. 11.
38. Teilhard de Chardin, *The Phenomenon of Man*, trans. Bernard Wall (New York: Harper and Row, 1959), p. 165.

Chapter 7. Running the Risk

1. Alfred Chester, "Edward Albee: Red Herrings & White Whales," *Commentary*, 35 (1963), 301; says Chester, "We are being dumped into the graveyard" (p. 299).
2. Tom Driver, "What's the Matter with Edward Albee?" *Reporter*, 2 Jan. 1964, p. 244.
3. Richard Schechner, "Who's Afraid of Edward Albee?" *Tulane Drama Review*, 7 (Spring 1963), 8. Diana Trilling, though acknowledging Albee's "message" as a "terrible" truth, claims that the playwright reverts to "comfort" rather than the true "terror" of truth as it appears in O'Neill's *Long Day's Journey Into Night* (*Claremont Essays* [New York: Harcourt, Brace & World, 1964], p. 214).
4. C. W. E. Bigsby, *Confrontation and Commitment: A Study of Contemporary American Drama 1959–66* (Columbia: University of Missouri Press, 1967), p. 84.
5. Arthur Evans, "Love, History and Edward Albee," *Renascence*, 19 (1967), 115.
6. David McDonald, "Truth and Illusion in *Who's Afraid of Virginia Woolf?*" *Renascence*, 17 (1964), 68.
7. Edward Albee, *Writers at Work: The Paris Review Interviews*, 3rd ser. (New York: Viking, 1967), p. 337.
8. Alan Schneider, "Reality Is Not Enough," *Tulane Drama Review*, 9 (Spring 1965), 183. Interview with Richard Schechner.

9. Richard Kostelanetz, "The New American Theatre," in *The New American Arts*, ed. Richard Kostelanetz (New York: Horizon, 1965), p. 89.

10. Emil Roy, "*Who's Afraid of Virginia Woolf?* and the Tradition," *Bucknell Review*, 13 (1965), 36.

11. Lee Baxandall, "The Theatre of Edward Albee," *Tulane Drama Review*, 9 (Summer 1965), 30.

12. Edward Albee, *Who's Afraid of Virginia Woolf?* (New York: Atheneum, 1964), p. 40. Subsequent references will be given in the text.

13. Rictor Norton, "Folklore and Myth in *Who's Afraid of Virginia Woolf?*" *Renascence*, 23 (1971), 163.

14. Baxandall, "Theater of Edward Albee," pp. 20–21. James P. Quinn calls him a "sterile king" figure in "an ironic parody of romance" ("Myth and Romance in Albee's *Who's Afraid of Virginia Woolf?*" *Arizona Quarterly*, 30 [1964], 199). Thomas E. Porter also discusses the play as a satire of romance in *Myth and Modern Drama* (Detroit: Wayne State University Press, 1969), pp. 225–47.

15. Schneider, "Reality Is Not Enough," p. 146.

16. Anita Stenz, *Edward Albee: The Poet of Loss* (The Hague: Mouton, 1978), p. 52.

17. Ibid., p. 54.

18. Ronald Hayman, *Edward Albee* (New York: Frederick Ungar, 1973), p. 42.

19. McDonald, "Truth and Illusion," pp. 68–69.

20. Edward Rutenberg, *Edward Albee: Playwright in Protest* (New York: D.B.S. Publishers, 1969), p. 110.

21. Max Halperen, "What Happens in Who's Afraid . . .?" in *Modern American Drama: Essays in Criticism*, ed. William E. Taylor (Deland, Fla.: Everett/Edwards, 1968), p. 133.

22. See Anne Paolucci, *From the Tension to Tonic: The Plays of Edward Albee* (Carbondale: Southern Illinois University Press, 1972), p. 56.

23. Schneider, "Reality Is Not Enough," p. 148.

24. Baxandall, "Theater of Edward Albee," p. 32.

25. Baxandall comments, "The truth for Martha is in the act. For George, intention is the truth" ("Theater of Edward Albee," p. 33). See Ruby Cohn's discussion of "snap" as a sound metaphor (*Dialogue in American Drama* [Bloomington: Indiana University Press, 1971], p. 21).

26. Bigsby also sees George as a Christ figure in that he "is fully responsible for the destruction of illusion." He annihilates Martha's illusions, he notes, just as Quentin shatters Maggie's in *After the Fall* (Bigsby, *Confrontation and Commitment*, p. 85).

27. Thomas P. Adler, "Albee's *Who's Afraid of Virginia Woolf?*: A Long Night's Journey into Day," *Educational Theatre Journal*, 25 (1973), 70.

28. Richard E. Hughes, *The Lively Image: 4 Myths in Literature* (Cambridge, Mass.: Winthrop, 1975), p. 135.

29. Barnett Guttenberg, "The Pattern of Redemption in Dickey's *Deliverance*," *Critique*, 18, no. 3 (1977), 90.

30. Murray Roston, *Prophet and Poet: The Bible and the Growth of Romanticism* (Evanston, Ill.: Northwestern University Press, 1965), p. 59.

31. James Dickey, *Deliverance* (New York: Houghton Mifflin, 1970), p. 17. Subsequent references will be given in the text.

32. Benjamin De Mott, "The 'More Life' School and James Dickey," *Saturday Review*, 28 Mar. 1970, p. 38.

33. See Paul Italia, "Love and Lust in James Dickey's *Deliverance*," *Modern Fiction Studies*, 21 (1975), 203–13.

34. Barnett Guttenberg refers to "a Jungian reintegration of the divided psyche" ("The Pattern of Redemption in *Deliverance*," p. 91).

35. James Dickey, introduction to *God's Images. The Bible: A New Vision* (Birmingham, Ala.: Oxmoor House, 1977).

Chapter 8. Conclusion

1. Frederick W. Dillistone, "The Fall: Christian Truth and Literary Symbol," in *Comparative Literature: Matter and Method*, ed. A. Owen Aldridge (Urbana: University of Illinois Press, 1969), pp. 156–57.

2. Paul Tillich, *Systematic Theology* (Chicago: University of Chicago Press, 1957), vol. 2, p. 36.

Index